COASTAL ZONE MANAGEMENT

COASTAL ZONE MANAGEMENT

A Study of the Political Economy of Sustainable Development

(Volume 2)

Dr. Ramakrishana Korakandy

Publications

KALPAZ PUBLICATIONS

DELHI - 110052

Coastal Zone Management

A Study of the Political Economy of Sustainable Development

Rs. 1800 (Set)

ISBN : 81-7835-302-4 (Set)
ISBN : 81-7835-304-0 (Vol. 2)

Published in 2005 in India by
Kalpaz Publication,
C-30, Satyawati Nagar,
Delhi-110 052
Email : kalpaz@hotmail.com

Lasertype Setting by: Tact Computer Graphics, Delhi
Printed at: Mehra Offset Press, Delhi

Contents

List of Tables

List of Appendix

7

Coastal Zone Management in Kerala—Coastal Issues

7.1. Introduction

The key to coastal zone management in Kerala is an understanding of the coastal issues. This chapter is devoted to an understanding of the major coastal issues confronting the state. The coastal issues facing Kerala may be broadly categorised as (a) ecological, (b) economic and (c) socio-cultural.

An attempt is made in the following sections to discuss these issues at some length.

7.2. Ecological issues

Some of the ecological issues identified by Clark in the global context included (a) pollution, (b) threat to bio-diversity and (c) natural hazards. Non-sustainable development was also noted as a critical problem. The specific ecological resources threatened and the environmental concerns of the coast as reported by Healy and Zinn and quoted by Clark (1992) have been noted in table 4.11 in chapter four.

The critical environmental concerns noted in table 4.11 related to (a) coastal resources, (b) wetlands, (c) fish/fisheries, (d) public access, (e) critical areas, (f) vegetation, (g) marine biology, (h) wild life, (i) water quality, (j) beaches/dunes, (k) water resources, (l) estuaries, (m) aesthetics, (n) resource protection, (o) living marine resources, (p) cultural/historical resources, (q) ground water, (r) barrier islands, (s) open space, (t) preservation, (u) coral reefs, and (v) air resources. It may be noted here that Healy and Zinn (1985) had also reported 24 developmental concerns and eight environment/ development interaction concerns which were quoted by Clark (1992) and reproduced in table 4.11 earlier in chapter four. The developmental concerns are again being raised in the next section. It may not be out of place to note here that almost every one of the environmental, developmental and interaction concerns noted by Healy and Zinn and quoted by Clark as reproduced in table 4.11 has its manifestations in the Kerala coast. It would, however, appear that empirical presentation of these concerns may be practically difficult for want of specific studies and their ubiquitous nature. The attempt, therefore, in these sections is to present a general picture of some of the outstanding ecological/environmental issues affecting coastal resource use and their sustainability. For convenience in presentation, the ecological issues are discussed in four groups, viz. (1) coastal pollution, (2) over-exploitation of natural resources, (3) habitat destruction and bio-diversity loss, and (4) natural hazards.

7.2.1. Coastal pollution

Coastal pollution is one of the very severe problems affecting the coastal community. Quoting a United Nations report of 1990 Clark reports that the 'major causes of immediate concern' in the global marine environment upon entering the decade of the 1990s were 'coastal development and the attendant destruction of habitat, eutrophication, rnicrobial contamination of seafood and beaches, fouling of the seas by plastic litter, progressive buiid up of chlorinated hydrocarbons, especially in the tropics and subtropics, and accumulation of tar on beaches' (Clark, 1998, p.385). This writer further observes that being at 'sea level elevation, the coast is the eventual receiving basin for all land run off water and the wastes it carries. Coastally discharging rivers gather and carry large amounts of pollutants to the coast with their rampaging flood waters ... Consequently, a large share of the world's pollution ends up in coastal lagoons, estuaries, wetlands, submerged grass beds, and coral reefs ... contaminants are transported from land to sea by rivers, direct runoff, or point discharges. They are partly retained in the water and sediments of estuaries, bays, beaches or open coastal waters, and partly transported through these boundary areas to the open ocean. The disposal of domestic sewage and industrial effluents from population and industrial centres located along the coastlines extends coastal pollution beyond the estuaries. Moreover, coastal waters are not only, more polluted than the open ocean, they also offer significantly more opportunities for exposure through contamination of the world's most important fisheries and recreation areas ...' (ibid, p. 383).

Writing on the state of the coastal environment in Kerala in 1985, the Expert Committee on Marine Fisheries in Kerala noted that 'with increasing industrialisation, urbanisation and exploitation of natural resources, there is not only increasing deterioration of environmental quality and depletion of exploitable resources, but also human health hazards through consumption of contaminated food. Environmental pollution or alterations in Kerala that affect harvestible fisheries resources from the sea, rivers and estuaries including the backwaters and lagoons owe largely to industrial effluents, domestic sewage, pesticides and also land reclamation' (Expert Committee, 1985, p. 340).

The Committee also observes that 'in Kerala there are about 175 large and medium scale industries discharging such effluents. There are also more than 8000 small scale industrial units out of which at least 2000 contribute to the pollution load. It is estimated that 6.5 lakh m^3 of trade effluents are being dumped into the rivers and tidal waters every day. Of this, 45 per cent of the wastes are from chemical industries containing chemical pollutants and another 45 per cent from industries with organic pollutants. The balance represents wastes from engineering industries and other categories' (ibid, p. 340). The quantity and mode of effluents discharged by major industries operating in Kerala are given in table 7.1.

Table 7.1

Quantity and mode of effluent discharge by major industries in Kerala

S.No.	*Name of industries/enterprises*	*Waste water disposed (Litres/day)*	*Mode of disposal*
I. Non-ferrous metalurgical industries			
1.	Indian Aluminium Co., Alwaye	13,700,000	into Periyar river
II. Ore processing industries			
1.	Cominco Binani Zinc Ltd., Binanipuram	23,150,000	into Periyar river
2.	Indian Rare Earths Ltd., Chavara	2,299,000	into Ashtamudi lake
3.	Indian Rare Earths, Udyogamandal	4,586,400	into Periyar river
III. Petroleum industries			
1.	Cochin Refineries, Ambalamugal	8,250,000	into Chitrapuzha river

(Contd.)

(Table 7.1 contd.)

S.No.	Name of industries/enterprises	Waste water disposed (Litres/day)	Mode of disposal
IV. Chemical industry			
1.	Titanium Products, Trivandrum	1,000,000	into Arabian sea
2.	T.C. Chemicals, Trivandrum	77,000	disposal in land
3.	Travancore Electro Chemicals Ltd., Chingavanam, Kottayam	40,000	in Mulakanchira canal leading to Vembanad lake
4.	Premier Tyres Ltd. Kalamassery	600,000	disposal in land
5.	Travancore Cochin Chemical Ltd., Udyogamandal	10,200,000	into Periyar river
6.	Hindustan Insecticides Ltd., Udyogamandal	325,000	into Periyar river
7.	Periyar Chemicals, Binanipuram	120,000	into Periyar river
8.	Apollo Tyres, Chalakaudy	1,138,000	into irrigation canals and land
9.	Gwalior Rayons, Mavoor	51,110,000	into Chaliyar river
V. Textile industry			
1.	Madura Coats, Koratty, Trichur	2,500,000	into Chalakudy river
2.	Sitaram Textiles, Trichur	720,000	into Karimpuzha thodu
3.	Travancore Rayons, Perumbavoor	73,000,000	into Periyar river
VI. Paper industry			
1.	Punalur Paper Mills, Punalur, Quilon	8,900,000	into Kallada river
2.	Hindustan Paper Corporation, Velloor	33,000,000	Into Muvattupuzha river
VII. Fertilizer industry			
1.	FACT, Cochin Division Phase I	12,000,000	into Chitrapuzha river
2.	FACT, Cochin Division Phase II	40,000,000	into Chitrapuzha river
3.	FACT, Udyogamandal	61,000,000	into Periyar river
VIII. Processing of animal or vegetable products			
1.	Lakshmi Starch, Kundara	1,150,000	into Ashtamudi lake
2.	Padinjarekkara Agencies, Kottayam	92,000	disposal in land
3.	Travancore Sugars and Chemicals	45,815,000	into Pamba river
4.	Tata Oil Mills	12,700,000	into Vembanad lake
5.	Milk Project, Edappally, Ernakulam	90,000	into Pathadipalam canal
6.	Kerala Chemicals and Proteins Ltd., Koratti	2,400,000	into Chalakudy river
7.	Western India Plywood Ltd., Baliapattom, Cannanore	50,000	into Valapattanam river
8.	Vanchinadu Leather, Kuttipuram	120,000	into Bharathapuzha river

Source: Expert Committee, 1985, pp.340-342.

Referring to the state of water pollution in the state, the Expert Committee noted that 'there are 44 rivers in the state of which 41 are west flowing and three east flowing. Out of the 41 west flowing rivers, 10 are major ones. These are Chandragiri, Valapattanam, Chaliyar, Chalakudy, Bharathapuzha, Periyar, Pamba, Achancoil, Muvattupuzha and Kallada. These 10 rivers carry nearly 45,100 M.m^3 (million cubic metres) of water per year. The other 31 west flowing rivers carry only 91,200 M.m^3 water per year. About 71.5 per cent of the utilizable yield is contributed by these 10 major rivers. The stretches of five out of the ten major rivers, namely, Chaliyar, Chalakudy, Periyar, Pamba and Kallada and certain portions of the backwaters like Vembanad and Ashtamudi are subjected to pollution due to waste discharges. Lower reaches of all these rivers are tidal and tidal reaches receive most of the chemical wastes of the state. Similarly, the freshwater stretches of these major rivers are contaminated by organic effluents.

The river Periyar receives the maximum quantity of effluents, of which a major portion is from the chemical industry. A cluster of chemical and metallurgical industries, which is about 25 per cent of the industries of the state, is located within a short stretch of one km on the banks of this river in the Udyogamandal area. This lower reach of Periyar below Udyogamandal is heavily polluted. The discharge of wastes containing mercury from the major Chlor-Alkali industry, viz., M/s. Travancore-Cochin Chemicals, the likely presence of radioactive materials from the discharges of M/s Indian Rare Earths Ltd., and the D.D.T. and other insecticides from the Hindustan Insecticides Ltd., combined with polluting chemicals from the industries make the pollution problem in this river serious, which warrants urgent control measures and strict enforcement of the standards. The water in the Chaliyar river downstream of the two factories of the Gwalior Rayons at Mavoor is polluted heavily due to their effluent discharges. Stretches of river Chalakudy are polluted due to the discharges from industrial establishments like M/s Madura Coats, Polson's Distillery, Tapioca Starch Products and Kerala Chemicals and Proteins Limited.

River Pamba receives waste discharge from M/s Travancore Sugars and Chemicals and stretches of river Kallada are heavily polluted due to the discharge from the Punalur Paper Mills. Bharathapuzha river is under the risk of pollution hazards due to discharges from Vanjinad Leathers' (ibid, pp.343-344).

Since 1980s the Kerala State Pollution Control Board has been in the forefront of combating water pollution in the state but water pollution and fish killing in the state have been continuing unabated.

Highlighting the extent of pollution in the backwaters, the Committee reports that 'a comparative study between six polluted (sewage and particulate matter) stations and one unpolluted or clean station in the Cochin backwaters between Aroor and the barmouth revealed high biological oxygen demand of upto 420.6 ppm, low and fluctuating dissolved oxygen values from less than 0.05 to 3.81 ml per litre, and total sulphide upto 4.92 ppm ... the extent of occurrence of pathogenic bacteriae like *Escherina Coli* and *Salmonella faecelis* in the Cochin backwaters warrants thorough bacteriological quality control of the seafoods marketed ... The main source of faecal pollution in the Cochin backwaters is the latrines from about one million households which opens directly into the backwaters while the remaining four million households have latrines opening into septic tanks ... Retting of coconut husk is another cause for water quality deterioration in Kerala backwaters ... Environmental degradation in the Cochin backwaters has evidently been so high that out of the 22 species of bryozoans that flourished here during 1963-67 only four species which are the hardiest remained in 1983-84. Extensive infestation of Kerala backwaters by the water hyacinth locally known as the African *payal* (*Salvinia moleste*) has reduced the biological productivity potential of this otherwise high productive ecosystem considerably. Decaying water hyacinth contributes extensively to the biological pollution of Cochin backwaters ...' (ibid, p. 351).

Speaking about the marine (near shore) pollution, the Committee noted that 'a decrease in inter-tidal and sub-tidal sea life in the polluted near shore environment of Travancore Titanium Plant, Trivandrum has been reported ... Every day, this plant discharges about 4000 m^3 of effluents, characterised by very high temperature (at discharge point) of 45°C to 50°C, sulphuric acid content of 3 per cent and ferrous sulphate of content of 10-40 g/litre ... However, except for aesthetic degradation of nearshore regions, gross ecological variations have not taken place and the marginal changes that occur in the environment can considerably be reduced by controlling the source of pollution ...' (ibid, p. 351).

Baba, *et al.* noted that 'the water bodies in the coastal zone are susceptible to pollution mainly due to effluents discharged from industries, domestic and community sewage. Drainage from agricultural lands (containing fertilisers, pesticides, fungicides, etc.), coconut husk retting areas and spillage of oil and kerosene in the vicinity of major commercial fishing harbours also contribute to pollution of water bodies. Some of the major industries that discharge waste materials into the coastal zone are Western India Plywood, Mavoor Rayons, FACT, Cochin Refineries, Lakshmi Starch Factory, Hindustan Insecticides, Indian Rare Earth and TTP. Long-term monitoring of the pollution of the coastal waters is being carried out under COMAP Projects in which Kerala coastal zone is studied by CESS and NIO. This study indicates that the threshold values exceeded nowhere in Kerala. However, if precautions are not taken, pollution can reach dangerous levels at several locations' (Baba, *et.al.* 1995, p. 20).

Writing on coastal zone governance and the issue of pollution in Cochin, Devaraj , *et.al.* observed that 'the industrial effluents (ammonia, ammoniac nitrogen, fluorides, mercury, DDT, acidic chemicals and suspended solids) discharged from the Eloor-Edayar industrial belt into the Periyar river (which joins the Cochin backwaters) is estimated to be over 200 million litres/day' (Devaraj, *et.al.*1999, p.12). These writers also noted that 'a recent report on the status of pollution in the Periyar river has quantified the annual load of mercury (2000 kg), zinc (10,095 kg), copper (327 kg), fluorides (250 t) and iron (30 t) dumped into this river ...' (ibid, p.12). They further pointed out that 'mass mortality of fish due to industrial pollution has been reported from the upper reaches of Cochin backwaters at Chitrapuzha and Champakara. Ammonia load of 432 to 560 ppm alongwith acids and the suspended solids has been found to be deleterious to fish in this backwater lake. Mercury concentration ranged from 0.15 to 1.10 ppm in the monsoon season in the sediment while at the effluent discharge point, it recorded 5.5 to 11.5 ppm. Indiscriminate application of about 10 types of pesticides to the tune of 480 t/year in the Periyar catchment area has led to the occurrence of DDT in clams and organochlorine in the black clams and fishes in the Cochin backwaters. High concentration of coliform bacteria has been detected in fish and bivalves from Cochin backwaters. About 40 ha of saline mud flat within the Cochin backwaters is being used for coconut husk retting. This has resulted in anoxic conditions and hydrogen sulphide accumulations rendering the area unsuitable for almost any type of life. An EIA study conducted in the Cochin backwaters during 1994-95 has revealed low benthic population in the Udyogamandal canal and a general decline in fish production[1] (ibid, p.12).

The severity of the pollution problem has been highlighted by the Expert Committee for Fisheries Management Studies, Kerala in 2000. It noted that the inland water bodies of Kerala are subjected to various types of pollution hazards mainly from industrial effluents, pesticides, chemical fertilizers and sewage' (Expert Committee, 2000, p.51). Giving the details of this problem, it stated that 'there are over 200 medium scale industries and about 2000 small scale industries discharging effluents into the inland water bodies. Discharge of heavy metals such as copper, mercury, zinc and cadmium above the permitted levels lead to serious pollution problems. High concentrations of zinc, copper, iron, manganese and mercury were observed in the water, sediments and sedentary populations inhabiting the Cochin backwaters. Frequent incidence of mass mortality of fishes is a usual affair in the major rivers such as the Periyar (Chitrapuzha), Chaliyar, Kallada, and the lakes, viz. Vembanad, Ashtamudi, etc.

The fishes inhabiting these water bodies are facing reproductive hazards, growth retardation and morphological abnormalities, apart from total destruction of eggs and larvae. Fish mortality due to industrial effluents carrying heavy load of ammonia at the rate of 432-560 ppm pouring into the area together with many pollutants such as acids, suspended solids, alkalies, fluorides, radio active materials, etc. could change the water quality to extreme toxic conditions and result in heavy fish mortality. Fish shoals entering the polluted zone could not tolerate the cumulative effects of pollution and results in their sudden mortality. The Eloor-Varapuzha regions of the Cochin backwaters are getting transformed into barren contaminated cesspools.

Indiscriminate application of pesticides has been noticed in the paddy fields of Kuttanad which eventually get washed off and reach the down stream region. According to the data compiled by the KWBSP, 10 types of pesticides with a total quantity of 490 tonnes, are used in Kuttanad annually of which 370 tonnes are applied for *Punja* and 120 tonnes for *Viruppu*. High levels of DDT have been detected in water, sediment and clams collected from lower Kuttanad region in April. Similarly, significant concentration of organochloride pesticides are also detected in the samples of black clam arid fishes analysed from this part of the lake.

In the absence of adequate facilities for the disposal of sewage and sullage from human settlements, they are directly discharged into the inland waterbodies. Hung latrines visible all along the backwaters are the major source of faecal contamination. Sewage discharge cause detrimental environment to fish life. In the canals of Alappuzha, the cell number of *E. Coli* varied from 500-5000, while in the stagnant channels it reached upto 13000 faecal coli per 100 ml sample. High concentrations of coli form bacteria were detected in fishes collected from the Cochin backwater. Very high concentrations of pathogenic bacteria *Vibrio parahaemolyticus* from the shell fishes of Cochin backwaters have also been recorded.

The backwaters of Kerala are also used for the retting of coconut husk. Fishes used to desert such areas due to the presence of noxious gases such as H_2S_1 , methane and high BOD, turbidity, etc. In the Vembanad lake alone around 245 ha. are used for husk retting[1] (Expert Committee, 2000, pp. 51-52).

Two other industries which pollute the coastal waters on a large scale are aquaculture and fish processing. The former, apart from polluting the water bodies lead to the destruction of mangroves, wetlands and biodiversity. The last issue is discussed elsewhere.

Highlighting the scale of aquatic pollution caused by aquaculture, Shiva and Karir note that 'the large scale pumping of seawater into the shrimp farms is one of the most serious environmental impacts of shrimp farming. The massive extraction of freshwater from underground aquifers for salinity control in the ponds poses a serious threat to the salinity control of the coastal ecosystem' (Shiva and Karir, 1999, p.39). They further noted that 'prawn culture activity requires the pumping of sea water into ponds, since the majority are marine prawn species which require a salinity between 25-30 parts per trillion (ppt). The growing period for prawn is between 120-150 days, meaning water is also on the land for this period of time which is sufficient to allow salt water to seep into the neighbouring agricultural farm areas and as well into the water table.

Destruction of mangrove forests also leads to increased salinity as there is an increase in flood area thereby allowing further intrusion of salt water on to land. The massive extraction of freshwater from underground aquifers for salinity control in the ponds also intensifies the problem of salinity. Estimates show that roughly 6600 m^3 of freshwater are needed to dilute full seawater on a one hectare pond at one metre water depth over a cropping period of four months.

Emptied aquifers are subject to saltwater intrusion. Seepage from the tanks also increases salinisation of ground water' (ibid, pp. 39-40).

The potential for aquaculture to pollute the water base is further indicated by these authors. They point out that 'shrimp farms flush their effluents and waters directly into the sea and neighbouring mangrove and agricultural lands. The water quality of prawn farms is maintained by the regular refilling of ponds with 'fresh' seawater. The out-flowing pond water contaminated with heavy concentrations of pesticides and antibiotics, is discharged either back to the sea or to rivers and canals. Further pollution occurs, as a result of the use of organic waste and commercially produced food pellets, instead of natural feed. The use of various chemicals in the feed, some 32 ingredients, accumulate at the 'surface bottom' of the pond causing deposits of algae and bacteria which affect the oxygen balance of the water ... The prawn industry utilises feed and fertilizers to help maintain the production of the shrimp. A fair amount of the fertilizers and feed gets collected at the bottom of the pond ... intensive shrimp farming is based on dense stocking rate and over-crowding, which induces stress problems and increases susceptibility to diseases. Over-crowding leads to poor water quality due to increased oxygen level, high accumulated metabolic products and excreta, rapid growth of and transmission of noxious parasites, micro-organisms and pathogens' (ibid, pp.41-43).

Another major source of aquatic pollution in the coastal regions alongwith agriculture, aquaculture and other industries is the fish processing industry. Indeed, this industry has been included in the list of prohibited activities in the 'coastal zone[1] as per the CRZ notification of the Government of India in 1991. The concentration of a large number of fish processing plants in the coastal/backwater stretches of Ernakulam, Alappuzha and Kollam districts is believed to be causing large scale aquatic pollution in the vicinity of those plants. A comparative picture of pollution caused by fish processing plants can be obtained from table 7.2.

It appears from table 7.2 that fish processing plants are releasing more effluents than do all other sources noted above. Some of the hot spots of industries/enterprises causing water pollution in the coastal areas of Kerala as reported by the Department of Fisheries in 2001 are presented in appendix 7.1.

Table 7.2
Comparative levels of pollution caused by fish processing plants, shrimp farms and domestic sources

S. No.	Parameter (mg/l)	Effluent Form					Fish processing plants
		Shrimp farm	Harvest effluent	Domestic water			
				Untreated	Primary	Biological	
1.	BOD	4.0–10.2		300	200	30	10,000–18,000
2.	Total nitrogen	0.03–1.24	5.25–14.8	75	60	40	700–4,530
3.	Total phosphorus	0.001–2.02	0.03–0.08	20	15	12	120–298
4	Suspended solids	119–225	60–243	500	—	15	1,880–7,475

Source : Raghu, K.V., 2002, p.226.

Table 7.3
Newspaper reports relating to water pollution in Kerala from February 1997 to August 2002

S.No.	Name of newspaper	Place of report	Date	News heading
1.	Indian Express	Kozhikode	6.2.1997	Use of copper sulphate polluting Chaliyar
2.	do	Cochin	6.8.1999	Toxic algae spotted in coastal area
3.	do	Kozhikode	9.8.1999	Alleged rights violation by Grasim-NHRC sends notices to State, Central PCBS
4.	do	Thiruvananthapuram	24.8.1999	Green Peace asks Government, Grasim to take corrective steps
5.	do	Cochin	18.9.1999	CRL plant must not use Periyar water
6.	do	Cochin	8.10.1999	Corporation passes resolution to ban use of plastics
7.	do	Aluva	28.10.1999	Action Plan to save Periyar in the offing
8.	do	Sabarimala	19.11.1999	PCB closes eight hotels in Pamba
9.	do	Thiruvanathapuram	23.11.1999	Steep rise in faecal coliform in Alappuzha
10.	do	Cochin	27.11.1999	Waste management: onus to be on municipal bodies
11.	do	Pathanamthitta	4.12.1999	Pollution of river Pamba goes unchecked
12.	do	Pathanamthitta	11.12.1999	Concern over pollution of Pamba
13.	do	Cochin	16.12.1999	Meet on management of urban waste
14.	do	Aluva	23.12.1999	Rights Panel to take evidence on pollution
15.	do	Cochin	23.12.1999	Eloor belt declared 'global toxic hot spot'—Green Peace board near FACT creates tension
16.	do	Cochin	19.2.2000	Toilets : HC calls for statements
17.	do	Cochin	25.2.2000	Mass dharna against polluting canal
18.	do	Aluva	27.3.2000	Concern at dumping pollutants into Periyar
19.	do	Aluva	28.3.2000	Plan for waste water treatment plant at Aluva
20.	do	Cochin	30.3.2000	HC order on discharge of waste into river
21.	do	Aluva	4.4.2000	Opposition to regulator bridge near Pathalam
22.	do	Cochin	5.5.2000	Petronet awaits enviromental clearance for Kochi LNG project

(Contd.)

(Table 7.3 contd.)

S.No.	Name of newspaper	Place of report	Date	News heading
23.	do	Kasargode	3.6.2000	Mylatti diesel plant work to resume today
24.	do	Aluva	5.6.2000	Toxic wastes killing fish in Periyar
25.	do	Cochin	10.6.2000	H.C. issues notice on pollution
26.	do	Cochin	20.6.2000	Eloor eco-campaign to have wider impact
27.	do	Kasargode	20.6.2000	Stir against diesel plant: Two held for stoning security guards
28.	do	Cochin	22.6.2000	Periyar : Pollution Board promises monitoring cell
29.	do	Pathanamthitta	13.7.2000	Alleged pollution by factory in Mankoottam : Action Council's hunger stir on
30.	do	Kozhikode	24.8.2000	Mavoor residents observe black day
31.	do	Cochin	1.9.2000	H.C. notice on Mavoor pollution
32.	do	Thiruvanathapuram	30.10.2000	TTP effluent issue: Minister cancels talk
33.	do	Cochin	2.11.2000	Implement H.C. Verdict on waste disposal
34.	do	Cochin	13.11.2000	Reduce pollution with people's help
35.	do	Cochin	19.11.2000	Industrial effluents wreck Periyar's ecosystem
36.	do	Aluva	22.11.2000	Reports on Periyar pollution to be submitted within three months
37.	do	Thiruvanathapuram	25.11.2000	Government, agitators agree to help reopen TTP
38.	do	Thiruvananthapuram	29.11.2000	TTP reopening stalled
39.	do	Kozhikode	4.1.2001	Draft policy on environmental protection—State Government yet to initiate public debate
40.	do	Kozhikode	11.1.2001	Compensation case filed against Grasim industries
41.	The New Indian Express	Cochin	13.1.2001	Garbage dumping posing health hazards
42.	do	Thruvanathapuram	18.1.2001	Hospitals fail to keep PCB deadline
43.	do	Aluva	25.2.2001	Establish a movement for river protection : Rawat

(Contd.)

(Table 7.3 contd.)

S.No.	Name of newspaper	Place of report	Date	News heading
44.	The New Indian Express	Kozhikode	9.4.2001	Western coast under 'laughing gas'
45.	do	Thiruvananthapuram	26.6.2001	Green flay authorities for not punishing guilty
46.	do	Cochin	30.6.2201	Waste disposal plan: threat, set back for Cochin Corporation
47.	do	Pathanamthitta	9.7.2001	Workshop on Pamba Action Plan on July 15
48.	do	Cochin	21.7.2001	Disband KPCB
49.	do	Aluva	27.7.2001	AIYF threatens to launch stir
50.	do	Cochin	31.7.2001	Threat due to ballast water highlighted
51.	do	Cochin	3.8.2001	Comprehensive plan for solid waste management
52.	do	Cochin	17.8.2001	Disposal of bio-medical waste–H.C. admit plea
53.	do	Cochin	25.9.2001	Ernakulam tops in chemical mishap threats
54.	do	Alappuzha	12.11.2001	Stir against pollution–row over Dheevara Sabha announcement
55.	do	Thiruvanathapuram	25.11.2001	Country bombs hurled at garbage disposal van
56.	do	Aluva	4.12.2001	Greens demand Compliance
57.	do	Cochin	11.12.2001	Saline Periyar stiffing Eloor belt
58.	do	Thripunithura	19.12.2001	A funeral protest against pollution
59.	do	Cochin	20.1.2002	Canal pollution fires a revolt at the grass roots
60.	do	Aluva	23.1.2002	HRC step in to save the Periyar
61.	do	Cochin	10.2.2002	*Malineekarana Vimuktha Samithi dharna*
62.	do	Eloor	27.3.2002	Alarming radiation from toxic deposits of Rare Earths
63.	do	Cochin	1.4.2002	Merchem gets time for appeal
64.	do	Cochin	18.5.2002	Disiltation of canal on a war footing
65.	do	Eloor	20.5.2002	Pathalam bund bursts-Residents allege sabotage
66.	do	Cochin	24.5.2002	Projects for desilting Vypeen canals a non-starter

(Contd.)

(Table 7.3 contd.)

S.No.	Name of newspaper	Place of report	Date	News heading
67.	do	Aluva	25.5.2002	Pond polluted
68.	do	Cochin	10.6.2002	25 city based eco-activists arrested
69.	do	Aluva	11.6.2002	Government urged to form river protection force
70.	do	Thiruvanathapuram	3.7.2002	Action plan to protect Periyar soon
71.	do	Cochin	3.8.2002	Disaster lurks over water: barges wait for their turn
72.	do	Cochin	10.8.2002	Improper management of municipal waste: HC admits writ plea
73.	do	Thiruvananthapuram	25.8.2002	TTP, Government flayed for pollution
74.	do	Cochin	27.9.2002	Death by polluted water for 15 buffaloes-farmers point an accusing finger at FACT, Cochin Division.

Source : The Indian Express/The New Indian Express, Cochin, 1997-2002.

The continuing crises of water pollution in the Kerala coast is also reflected in the frequency of newspaper reports relating to it as they appeared in recent times. Table 7.3 notes some of the newspaper reports relating to water pollution in Kerala as reported in the *Indian Express/New Indian Express* daily from February 1997 to September 2002.

What is appearing from table 7.2 and appendix 7.1 is that water pollution in the state, especially in the coastal belt, has become a devastating issue, which only an ICM approach can ameliorate.

7.2.2. Overexploitation of natural resources

A major ecological problem facing the coastal zone of Kerala is the over exploitation of the natural resources, both living and non-living. The living resources of the coast, especially the fish stock, both in the marine and the inland (land side) environments are subject to over exploitation. Other living resources like mangroves, seagrass and other vegetation are also subject to heavy exploitation or destruction in recent years. This issue is further discussed in the section on habitat destruction.

Non-living resources like river sand, mineral sand, lime shell, etc. are also heavily exploited, making the industries depending on them unsustainable.

A closer look at the recent trends in marine fish production in Kerala reveals the possibility of over-exploitation of certain species of fish. Table 7.4 shows the trend in the production of major species of marine fish in Kerala during 1983-87, 1988-92 and 1992-97.

It is apparent from table 7.4 that there was a clear decrease in the average output of elasmobranchs, catfishes, oil sardine, anchoviella, whitebaits, seerfish, tunnies and penaeid prawns during 1992-97 as compared to the previous period. This seems to be indicative of the over-exploitation problem, especially with regard to the preferred commercial varieties of fishes. Sustaining the catches of these varieties is a crucial issue for fisheries management in Kerala.

Over exploitation of the stock seems to be a problem in inland fisheries as well. Table 7.5 depicts the trend in the landings of major species of inland fishes in Kerala from 1994-95 to 1999-00.

Table 7.4
Trend in the production of major species of marine fish in Kerala during 1983-87, 1988-92 and 1992-97

(Quantity in tonnes)

S. No.	Species	1983-87	Average of 1988-92	1992-97
1.	Elasmobranchs.	6531	5035	4533
2.	Catfishes	9068	3914	397
3.	Oil sardine	93315	117009	37760
4.	Lesser sardines	6288	16010	21548
5.	Anchoviella	35306	42301	37378
6.	Perches	28717	47985	60107
7.	Sciaenids	9070	11032	13808
8.	Ribbon fish	11979	6842	13645
9.	Carancgids	27479	660041	69374
10.	White baits	5773	5633	4794
11.	Lactarius	1168	1156	1320
12.	Pomfrets	1696	1957	2803
13.	Mackerel	14894	59887	92081
14.	Seerfish	6334	7379	5448
15.	Tunnies	9433	19429	14514
16.	Soles	12296	17695	17900
17.	Penaeid prawns	36404	55537	53071
18.	Cephalopods	7711	22588	35676
19.	Others	34718	73396	78070
	Total	**358180**	**580825**	**564250**

Source: Expert Committee for Fisheries Management Studies, 2000, p.14.

Table 7.5, while showing an increasing trend in total inland fish production in the state (which is largely due to the expansion in aquaculture) also reveals an unsteady or even declining trend in the production of certain species like etroplus, murrels, mullets, catfishes, jewfish and tilapia. The stocks of these species are feared to be under stress of over exploitation and environmental degradation. The Expert Committee for Fisheries Management Studies, Kerala notes in this regard thus: 'based on the qualitative and quantitative changes noted in the exploited stock of fin fishes and shell fishes from the inland water bodies of Kerala, a steady decline in the commercially important food fishes, could be descernible. In contrast, it has not been duely compensated by the increase of biomass of desirable species. For instance, in the estuaries and backwater, species such as *Muqil cephalus, Lates calcarifer, Chanos chanos*, etc. have almost disappeared and the niches of them are found occupied by forage fishes like Ambassis, catfishes, etc. Similarly, in some part of the lake *Oreochromls mossambicus* has emerged as the principal species against *Etroplus suratensis.* On

Table 7.5
Trend in the landings of major species of inland fishes in Kerala from 1994-95 to 1999-00

(Quantity in tonnes)

S.No.	*Species*	*1994-95*	*1995-96*	*1996-97*	*1997-98*	*1998-99*	*1999-00*
1.	Prawns	12265	11984	12531	13010	14346	16459
2.	Etroplus	4468	4640	4883	4964	4756	4860
3.	Murrels	4179	4386	4616	4568	4369	4596
4.	Catfish	4546	4682	4928	5239	4420	4816
5.	Mullets	3943	4075	4289	4634	4532	4607
6.	Jewfish	2566	2652	2791	3181	3012	3054
7.	Tilapia	6836	7347	7732	8532	7219	8510
8.	Labeo rohita	572	710	747	1508	3656	4167
9.	Labeo fimbriatus	598	642	676	986	2718	3055
10.	Barbus	507	465	489	509	498	518
11.	Mrigal	546	598	629	1400	3205	3605
12.	Crabs	638	686	722	712	697	719
13.	Common crabs	981	1056	1111	2082	4686	5620
14.	Catla	612	734	773	1583	3824	4250
15.	Chanos	364	385	405	447	434	445
16.	Eels	45	47	50	54	53	55
17.	Miscellaneous	4526	4497	4733	4806	3427	4794
	Total	**48192**	**49586**	**52105**	**58215**	**65855**	**74130**

Source: Directorate of Economics and Statistics, 2001, p.163.

the contrary, the rivers of Kerala were once dominated by *Labeo dussummieri, Wallaqo attu, Puntius curmuka, P. Sarina*, etc. In recent years the above mentioned species are mostly replaced by lesser barbs, *Ambly pharyngodon mola, Aplocheilus,* etc. This shows the prevalence of 'eco-system over fishing' in the inland water bodies of Kerala ...' (Expert Committee for Fisheries Management Studies, 2000, p. 53).

Some of the reasons pointed out by the Committee for this over-exploitation (over fishing) in the inland fisheries of the state are, (1) increased fishing pressure, (2) destructive method of fishing and (3) wanton destruction of spawner population. Writing about the first, it notes that 'inland water bodies, especially the backwaters of Kerala are subjected to high fishing pressure exerted by the unusual increase in the number of fixed and wandering (floating) gears. Based on the survey conducted by the Fisheries Department, there are 12,900 stakenets, 5000 Chinese dip nets and more than 20,000 wandering gears which are in operation. Of the total 12,900 stake nets, 30 per cent are illegally operated without any valid license and the highest number is recorded in Ernakulam district. In the Vembanad lake, the number of stake nets put into operation is around 3862 of which 30 per cent are unauthorised; 90 per cent of the stake nets have a cod end mesh size of less than 13 mm, while in 47 per cent the cod end mesh size is less than 8 mm. It is estimated that on an average annual basis about 7000 tonnes of juveniles of the penaeid prawns are indiscriminately filtered from the Vembanad lake ... Stake nets are also operated during high tide period which is locally known as *Ettamettal* or *Tharachukettal* and the exact number in operation is unknown. Among the 4823 Chinese dip nets operated in the backwater of the five southern districts, 1692 are listed as unauthorised. Indiscriminate intervention through this fishing pressure on the estuarine environment is disturbing the migration of juvenile prawn and also hampering the eco-balance of the natural resources' (ibid, p. 52).

Referring to the destructive fishing methods, it states that 'a diversified type of destructive fishing activities are also being practised in the inland water bodies of Kerala, such as poisoning, dynamitising, electric fishing, *padal kolli*, which also have resulted in the devastation of inland fishery resources' (ibid, p. 52). Highlighting the wanton destruction of spawner population, it notes that 'intensification of fishing activities with the onset of the monsoon in the rivers and backwaters of Kerala is a common practice. The spawning stock of fishes used to migrate against the incoming swiftly flowing turbid water, locally known as *Oothayirayil,* which is taking place with the onset of the first rain when wanton destruction of the spawning stock with the help of *madavala, ottal,* gill net, dynamiting, poisoning, etc. is practised. These types of destructive activities will adversely affect the spawning and recruitment of the stock' (ibid, p.53).

As observed earlier, the exploitation of the non-living resources of the coast, like river-sand, mineral sand, lime shells and clay has increased significantly leading to nun-sustainable or declining levels of production. Table 7.6 presents the trend in the production of major minerals (other than mineral sand) in Kerala from 1994-95 to 1998-99.

Table 7.6
Trend in the production (raw) of major minerals (other than mineral sand) in Kerala from 1994-95 to 1998-99

(in tonnes)

S. No.	*Name of mineral*	*1994-95*	*1995-96*	*1996-97*	*1997-98*	*1998-99*
1.	China clay	223842	247211	-	118180	230210
2.	Limestone	423675	893769	-	336217	350000
3.	Silica sand	62753	124827	-	196770	174365
4.	Limeshell	146800	145775	-	73823	106878
5.	Quartz	5213	4962	-	230	800
6.	Bauxite	-	-	-	9597	27479
7.	Magnesite	65	Nil	-	-	-
8.	Graphite	100	500	-	-	-

Source: State Planning Board, Economic Review, 1996, 1998 and 1999.

Table 7.6 shows notable decreases in the production of most of the minerals. This, apart from being in response to the fluctuating market conditions for the resource, must be considered as conditioned by the economic constraints of exploiting a finite natural resource of varying qualities. Table 7.7 shows the trend in the production of mineral sand in Kerala from 1994-95 to 1999-00.

Table 7.7
Trend in the production of mineral sand in Kerala from 1994-95 to 1999-00

(in tonnes)

S. No.	Name of mineral sand	1994-95	1995-96	1996-97	1997-98	1998-99	1999-00
1.	Ilmenite	157646	126152	-	150115	125751	136909
2.	Rutile	9197	7304	-	8821	8443	9201
3.	Zircon	15856	13539	-	12639	16027	14037
4.	Silimenite	8291	6745	-	9323	7227	9595
5.	Lencorene	-	-	-	648	470	745
6.	Zirflor	-	-	-	-	-	4920
7.	Microzir twin	-	-	-	-	-	106

– *Figure not available.*

Source: State Planning Board, Economic Review, 1996, 1998, 1999 and 2000.

Table 7.7 indicates that as in the case of major minerals, the production of mineral sand in the state is subjected to notable fluctuations indicating the unsustainability of the activity.

The crises in the mineral sand mining sector has been reported in the last chapter and their sustainability issue noted therein. The piquant situation in the river sand mining sector is worth noting here. River sand mining in the state has become the most complex issue with ecological, economic and socio-cultural values at stake. Sand mining in the rivers has severely affected the river ecology, leading to bank subsidence, soil erosion, lowering the water table, droughts, loss of vegetation, etc. This problem was reported as most acute in the Periyar, Pamba, Chalakudi, Bharathapuzha, Chaliyar, etc. Justifiably, this has led to the formation of several voluntary organisations to protect the rivers of the state from the dangers of sand mining and pollution. Some of the notable institutions are the 'Save Periyar' Action Group, Pamba Action Council, All Kerala River Protection Council, etc. formed in the recent past. These institutions have succeeded in mobilising support for introducing a seasonal ban on sand mining in the state during the monsoon period. Not surprisingly, this has also led to counter moves by the building/ construction sector to resist the controls on sand mining introduced in the past couple of years. The volatile situation in the river zone of Kerala is reflected in the recurring reports of violation of sand mining rules and the resulting conflicts.

Table 7.8 presents a documentation of newspaper reports relating to river sand mining issue in Kerala between September 1996 and September 2002.

Table 7.8

Documentation of newspaper reports relating to sand mining in Kerala from September 1996 to September 2002

S. No.	Name of newspaper	Place of report	Date	News heading
1.	Indian Express	Aluva	11.09.1996	Dredging of limeshell stayed
2.	do	Pattambi	14.02.1997	Call to check sand mining in Bharathapuzha
3.	do	Cochin	19.03.1997	H.C. asked CESS to submit report on dredging
4.	do	Thirunavaya	25.03.1997	Action plan mooted to save Bharathapuzha
5.	do	Cochin	23.09.1997	H.C. notice on extraction of lime shell
6.	do	Thiruvananthapuram	09.07.1999	Sand mining permit to CM,s Kin : Jacob alleges flouting of rules
7.	do	Thiruvananthapuram	16.07.1999	Sand mining : CM dares opposition to produce evidence
8.	do	Pathanmmthitta	09.08.1999	Illegal sand mining racket thriving in Pathanamthitta
9.	do	Aluva	10.08.1999	Sand seized
10.	do	Thiruvananthapuram	04.10.1999	Government under pressure to relax rules on sand mining
11.	The New Indian Express	Aluva	12.03.2000	Sand shutters reopen in Vazhakulam and Perumbavoor
12.	do	Aluva	16.03.2000	Sand mining using banned polescoop
13.	do	Perumbavoor	18.03.2000	Three sand miners held
14.	do	Cochin	23.03.2000	Water, soil being grossly exploited in Kerala
15.	do	Aluva	08.06.2000	Sand shutters closed to prevent smuggling
16.	do	Kollam	11.07.2000	Sand mining takes a heavy toll in West Kallada
17.	do	Cochin	10.10.2000	H.C. orders decision on Manalpuram protection scheme
18.	do	Aluva	18.12.2000	11 arrested for stealing boat with sand
19.	do	Cochin	10.01.2001	18 panchayats yet to contribute to river fund
20.	do	Cochiin	17.02.2001	H.C. direction on sand mining
21.	do	Cochin	08.06.2001	One arrested for sand mining
22.	do	Thiruvananthapuram	07.07.2001	Sand mining regulated

(Contd.)

(Table 7.8 contd.)

S. No.	Name of newspaper	Place of report	Date	News heading
23.	The New Indian Express	Thiruvananthapuram	9.08.2001	Protest march planned
24.	do	Cochin	15.08.2001	Acute shortage of river sand Construction sector experimenting with crusher sand
25.	do	Cochin	21.08.2001	Government to introduce bill on sand mining
26.	do	Cochin	24.08.2001	Sand mining–H.C. dismisses Government petition
27.	do	Kozhikode	26.08.2001	Laws to regulated sand mining soon
28.	do	Cochin	04.09.2001	Division Bench directive on sand collection
29.	do	Cochin	12.09.2001	Massive rally held against ban on sand mining
30.	do	Cochin	12.09.2001	Sand mining permit to individual stayed
31.	do	Thiruvananthapuram	29.10.2001	CITU plea on sand mining
32.	do	Alappuzha	6.11.2001	Sand mining and reclamation of paddy fields drain water source: Experts
33.	do	Kozhikode	10.11.2001	Policy laxity alleged on curbing sand mining.
34.	do	Thiruvananthapuram	29.11.2001	Government proposed to regulate sand mining through expert panels
35.	The Hindu	Thiruvananthapuram	29.11.2001	Speaker warns against too many curbs on sand mining
36.	The New Indian Express	Malappuram	11.02.2002	Sand mining lobby turns river banks into battle fields
37.	do	Cochin	06.04.2002	H.C. orders probe into illegal sand mining in Eloor
38.	do	Cochin	11.06.2002	Ban on sand mining from July 1
39.	do	Cochin	14.08.2002	Sand Mining holiday : High Court admits writ petition
40.	do	Cochin	17.09.2002	Sand mining : Crucial decision taken

Source: The Indian Express/The New Indian Express/The Hindu Daily, Cochin 1996-2002.

What is emerging from table 7.8 is the growing concern for regulating sand mining in the state and the wide public interest in the sustained use of the natural resource. River sand mining, in spite of it being an upland activity affects the coast directly by its impact on water quality and sedimentation. Soil erosion upstreams and siltation downstreams and in the port area are all accentuated by sand mining. An ICM approach to these issues become apparent when the inter-industry interactions and externalities are considered. An attempt is made in the later sections to further highlight these issues.

7.2.3. Habitat destruction and biodiversity loss

Yet another major ecological problem affecting the coast of the state is habitat destruction and the resulting loss of biodiversity. Habitat destruction is considered as one of the major causes of biodiversity loss. Three other well known reasons for biodiversity loss are over exploitation of the stock, purposeful or accidental introductions of exotic species and diseases (Swanson, 1995, p.129). The problem of over exploitation of the fish stock has already been noted. The issue of biodiversity loss, however, needs to be examined in some detail, notwithstanding the paucity of data.

The two elements of aquatic bio-diversity of the coast are aquatic plants and aquatic animals, predominantly, fishes. Referring to the destruction of mangroves in the state, the Expert Committee for Fisheries Management Studies, Kerala, states that 'in Kerala, a century ago there were about 70,000 ha. of mangroves. However, in recent years it has been reduced to isolated patches less than 70 ha. Available reports suggest that penaeid prawns and fishes such as pearlspot, mullets, sea bass, etc. used to take shelter in these mangrove sanctuaries and the destruction of these vegetation occurring in the fringes of backwaters might have adversely affected the fisheries resources of the State' (Expert Committee for Fisheries Management Studies, Kerala, 2000, p. 51). The latest estimate of mangrove areas in Kerala by the Department of Fisheries puts it at 1924 ha. (Department of Fisheries, 2002, p.viii).

A newspaper report by Karunakaran from Cochin in 2001 states that 'Kerala's mangrove eco-systems which once dotted the entire coast line, withstanding ravages of severe storms and changing tides for many millinia have been disappearing at an accelerating rate with little public empathy, remorse on the part of authorities, or even the environmentalists ...' (Karunakaran, 2001).

An earlier newspaper report from Kannur in 1997 by Mohammed Nazeer states that 'the process of destruction of mangroves continues in the district despite protests from environmentalists. In a latest instance of reclaiming the wetland for construction in the mangrove rich areas in the district, hundreds of natural mangroves on a plot adjoining the Valapattanam river at Pappinisseri near here were destroyed allegedly by the land owner ...' (Nazeer, 1997). Nazeer also notes that 'a state convention on protection of wetlands held here recently had highlighted the large-scale destruction of mangroves in Kannur which has 755 hectares of mangrove forests, the largest in the state, scattered in Payyannur, Thalassery and Pappinisseri. Conversion of vast areas of wetland into aquaculture ponds has caused irreparable damage to mangroves, which constitute a rich eco-system ...' (ibid.).

As already noted, habitat destruction is considered as one of the major reasons for the loss of biodiversity in the coastal waters of the state. Writing about the habitat destruction in the inland water areas of the state, the Expert Committee for Fisheries Management Studies, Kerala, noted 'the inland waterbodies are prone to various types of man-made stresses which have eventually resulted in the loss or impairment of the natural habitat of many fishes and shell fishes' (Expert Committee for Fisheries Management Studies, Kerala, 2000, p.40). Some of the factors pointed out by the Committee which ultimately led to the loss of habitat and the resulting fall in the fish catch and bio-diversity are, (a) construction of bunds, barriers, anicuts, weirs, dams, etc., (b) shrinkage in the extent of inland water bodies, (c) fall in the depth of inland water bodies and (d) deforestation of mangroves.

Referring to the impact of these and other factors on the freshwater fish biodiversity of the region, the Committee noted: 'over exploitation of the fish resources coupled with habitat destruction result in the shrinkage of fish populations. Due to these factors a number of fishes in some conventional fishing grounds are declining rapidly and some have become endangered. Recently in the CAMP workshop held at the National Bureau of Fish Genetic Research (NBFGR), Lucknow, the status of some 90 species of freshwater fishes of Kerala were assessed as per IUCN red list criteria. Of these, 18 species were listed as critically endangered, of which 12 are facing serious risks of extinction in the wild in the near future due to alarming population decline, habitat destruction and deterioration. Among them, 13 are endemic to Kerala. Thirty one species have the status of endangered species which are also facing high risk of extinction in the world in the near future of which 12 are also endemic to Kerala. Under vulnerable category there are 18 species which are also facing high risk of extinction in the near future. Among them two are endemic to Kerala waters. Under threatened species of lower risk, there are 13 species, while there are five species under lower risk of least concern category. The status of five species could not be ascertained due to insufficient data base' (ibid, pp. 53-54).

The other factors which affect the biodiversity of the resource base, also have their impacts felt in Kerala. The clandestine introduction of exotic species and fish diseases have created havoc in the inland fisheries of the state. The Committee notes that 'the exotic varieties of fishes such as *Oreochromis mossambicus*, *Cyprinus carpio*, silver carp, grass carp, *Gambusia* and the African catfish *Clarius qariepinus* are likely to have interaction with indigenous fish species. Instances of extermination of indigenous species by the exotic species have already been reported in different parts of the country.

Likewise, *Oreochromis mossambicus* has established itself in the backwaters of Kerala and has resulted in the partial replacement of the native species such as *Etroplus suratensis* and *E, maculatus.* The indigenous fishes are under threat due to the clandestine introduction of the predatory and carnivorous African catfish *Clarius qariepinus* which is being bred in controlled systems in Kerala. Though the Union Agriculture Ministry ... ordered ... to destroy the existing stock, it is understood that ... this species is still available in some of the hatcheries of Kerala and growouts in Alappuzha, Kottayam, Thrissur and Ernakulam' (ibid, p. 54).

The impact of fish diseases has also been noted by the Committee. It states that among the various diseases caused by bacteria, fungi, viruses, etc. the most virulent and menacingly threatening many species is the Epizootic Ulceration Syndrome (EUS). The outbreak of EUS was first noticed in Kuttanad in Kerala in June 1991 and its recurrence in varied intensities could be registered in the past several years in different parts of the state. The species mainly affected by EUS are muliets, *thooli,* barbs, pearlspot, etc. As a result of the outbreak of this disease, the economy of the state has been adversely affected and has thrown around 25000 full time and 7000 other persons engaged in fishery related activities out of employment' (ibid, p. 54).

Reporting on the biodiversity loss of the fish fauna of the Muriyad Wetlands of Thrissur *Kole* lands, recently, Subash Babu *et. al.* noted that 'one significant feature observed in the present study is that there is the absence of *Wallago attu* and *Heteropenustus fossilis* in the present collections ... it is said that Wallago of about six feet in length was not rare from certain parts (Kokrachal area) of the wetland. A sudden decline in the availability of two economically important species required detailed investigation and urgent attention ... It is relevant to note that both these species are bottom feeders and hence accumulation of aquatic pollutants like pesticides in the bottom sediments affecting the normal physiology of the fish species cannot be ruled out ...' (Subash Babu, *et. al.* 2002, p. 62).

A corresponding picture of the loss of biodiversity in agriculture, especially in the cultivation of paddy in the state is discernible from the dismal state of this activity which is almost on the verge of extinction. This situation may be compared with the number and variety of paddy strains cultivated in Travancore in the early part of the last century. Velu Pillai reported in 1940 that 83 varieties of paddy were cultivated in Nanjinad, of South Travancore, 26 varieties in Onattukara, in the Quilon-Alleppey belt and 20 varieties in the Kuttanad region of North Travancore (Velu Pillai, 1940, Reprint 1996, pp. 303-315).

The transition that has taken place in the coastal environment affecting its biodiversity is further reflected in the wetland reclamation that has been going on for more than a century. The earlier efforts at reclamation of wetland for paddy cultivation was noted in chapter six. Referring to the state of land reclamation in the coastal zone of Kerala in the early eightees of the last century the Expert Committee on Marine Fisheries in Kerala noted in 1985 that 'high demographic pressures and intensive land-use practices, especially in the coastal zone, have given rise to extensive land reclamation along the estuaries and backwaters of Kerala. According to one estimate, the total reclamation of land in Kerala is over 120,700 hectares ... Reclamation is done by constructing bunds and dewatering from low lying lands along the waterways. Changes in geomorphology, due to reclamation, drastically changes the sediment transport pattern, give rise to siltation and erosion and also adversely affect the nursery grounds of prawns and fish in the backwaters and estuaries. It has also resulted in the upstream incursion of saline waters in the rivers. Similarly, the bunds put up in the backwaters affected the circulation of water and transport of young prawn especially in the traditional *Pokkali* (paddy-cum-prawn cultivation) fisheries (Expert Committee, 1985, p.351).

The recent trend in land reclamation has been noted by the Expert Committee for Fisheries Management Studies, Kerala. It observes that 'in recent years a substantial reduction in the total extent of water bodies could be discernible due to indiscriminate reclamation being carried out, especially in the backwaters of Kerala for the purpose of agriculture, urbanisation, housing, aquaculture, etc. The reclamation is done either as part of various developmental scheme of the central or state governments or undertaken by private parties illegally. These activities could result in the reduction of the nursery ground of shrimps, besides also considerably altering the physical features of the estuary such as the tidal flow, water circulation, current flow, etc., which together adversely affect the fishery wealth. The available reports suggest that the total area of the Vembanad lake which was 44,000 ha. in the beginning of the 19th century has now been reduced to 21,000 ha. as a result of reclamation for the purpose of agriculture, prawn farming, urbanisation, housing, harbour development, etc.' (Expert Committee for Fisheries Management Studies, Kerala, 2000, p.50).

The latest instance of large scale land reclamation from the backwaters is the one carried out by the Goshree Island Development Authority at Cochin. The island development project with its main component of the Ernakulam-Vypeen bridge to be built in three segments of Ernakulam-Bolgatti (339.4 m), Bolgatti-Vallarpadom (595 m) and Vallarpadom-Vypeen (435 m) will be reclaiming a total of 25 hectares of backwaters for the purpose. Of the total area reclaimed, 40 per cent is said to be utilised for common service facilities like roads and public places and the rest sold for funding the project. The bridge, while expecting to boost the developmental prospects of Vypeen, even while evicting 30 families, is feared to cause havoc to the local eco-system including 7000 hectares of shrimp farms/*pokkali fields* (*The Hindu,* 13.2.1997 and *Indian Express,* 29.12.2000).

The threat to the coastal eco system posed by the proposed project for inter-linking of rivers is considered to be great. The project to inter-link Pamba and Achankovil with the Vaipar river in Tamil

Nadu is believed to spell disaster to the Vembanad lake. The lake will soon become a marsh and then a 'biological desert' loosing its biodiversity (Thomas, 2002).

It is apparent from the above that habitat destruction and biodiversity loss are crucial issues of the coast having their impacts on the economy and culture of the coastal community. Sustainable development of the coast demands minimising the damage to the coastal eco-system and harmonising the multiple uses of the environment. The need for an ICM approach to coastal development is obvious here as well.

7.2.4. Natural hazards

Natural hazards such as floods, typhoons, or tsunamis are not characteristic of the state's coast. The major natural hazard affecting large parts of the state's coast is beach erosion, particularly during the monsoons. This has been well documented.

The Kerala State Gazetteer notes that '... the problem is of serious magnitude along the Kerala coast line. Kerala with an area of 38863 sq.km. has a coast line of about 590 km. Of this, about 320 km. is subject to erosion, especially during the monsoon. Annually about two to five meters width of land is lost on an average. In one place near Cochin about two km width of land has been eroded since 1850.

Besides permanent loss of valuable land, erosion also poses a serious threat to the communication system. The national highway and the railway line are quite vulnerable at some points along the coast ... During the south west monsoon from June to September waves measuring about four metres in height poured the coast from the south-west direction and erosion is very severe during this time' (Kerala Gazetteers Department, 1989, pp.322-323).

The Expert Committee on Marine Fisheries in Kerala noted that 'a characteristic of the 590 km long coast line of Kerala is that almost 25 per cent of it is subjected to varying degrees of erosion, especially during the monsoon season. The shoreline between Trivandrum and Alleppey, a track of several kilometres north and south of Cochin, the shoreline between Calicut and Cannanore and in the coastal area of Manassery, Thottapally and Purakkad, are prone to severe sea erosions. Though no direct correlation between erosion and fisheries is on record, the socio-economic impact of this environmental phenomenon on the fishermen community through considerable reduction in the traditional shore landing facilities is quite alarming' (Expert Committee, 1985, pp. 351-352).

The problem of coastal erosion has been further highlighted by Baba, *et. al.*, in 1995. They noted that 'coastal erosion is a major problem confronting Kerala. Erosion occurs along this coast either as a long-term shore line retreat or as a short-term cyclic shoreline oscillation, involving alternating erosion and accretion. In most of the cases short-term cyclic erosion is superimposed on long-term changes. Kerala's coastal zone being a very thickly populated region, even short-term shore line oscillations with no net erosion can be detrimental. It is equally important to note that there are areas of continuous accretion along the coast also' (Baba, *et. al.* 1995, p.15). These writers also report that the 'PWD has earlier estimated that 320 km of Kerala's coastline is undergoing erosion. A later assessment of PWD indicated that 470 km area are vulnerable to erosion. A recent CESS study has shown that only 150 km are undergoing severe erosion (including those protected by sea walls) and about 110 km are consistently accreting ...' (ibid, p.16).

A further understanding of the coastal hazards problem in Kerala can be had from the regularity of newspaper reports relating to this issue. Table 7.9 gives the list of newspaper reports relating to coastal hazards between June 2000 and June 2002.

The listing in table 7.9 indicates only sporadic cases of sea erosion or coastal floods reported in the local newspaper. There is, however, a regularity and pattern in the areas and timing of the hazards. They are closely coinciding with the monsoons and are frequent to the coasts of Alappuzha, Ernakulam, Kozhikode, Kannur and Kasargode districts. The emerging conclusion from these is the need to integrate the natural hazard phenomenon by adopting the 'nature synchronous' or 'design-with-nature' approach to development (Clark, 1996, p. 364). ICM programmes in Kerala will have to take note of this factor.

7.3. Economic issues

The coastal zones of Kerala while being the theatre of many economic activities are also the seat of many economic problems. Some of the most outstanding economic problems of the region are: (1) population growth and unemployment, (2) low income, (3) intra-use and inter-use conflicts and (4) stagnation (unsustainable development). A brief description of these problems is given in the following sections.

7.3.1. Population growth and unemployment

The fact that coastal areas witness high population growth and attract people from other areas leading to high density of oopulation

Table 7.9
Newspaper reports relating to coastal hazards in Kerala between June 2000 and June 2002

S.No.	*Name of newspaper*	*Place of report*	*Date*	*News heading*
1.	Indian Express	Cochin	8.6.2000	Sea erosion : Hundreds of houses destroyed in west Kochi
2.	do	New Delhi	23.8.2000	MPs demand steps to check sea erosion
3.	The New Indian Express	Alappuzha	9.5.2001	Proposals submitted for sea wall work
4.	do	Delhi	19.5.2001	Melting of ice in Antartica–parts of Kerala may be inundated in future
5.	do	Kasargode	12.6.2001	Coastal area under threat of sea erosion
6.	do	Cochin	14.6.2001	Collector convenes meet to tone up relief work : sea erosion
7.	do	Cochin	23.7.2001	50 houses damaged in sea erosion
8.	do	Kannur	24.7.2001	Waves destroy 12 houses in Kannur : 55 families rehabilitated
9.	do	Cochin	9.9.2001	Defend state from Arabian Sea
10.	do	Cochin	10.6.2002	Sea erosion threatens Fort Kochi beach
11.	do	Alappuza	17.6.2002	Coastal areas under threat of sea erosion
12.	do	Kozhikode	18.6.2002	Sea threat : 10 families shifted to safer places
13.	do	Kozhikode	20.6.2002	Sea erosion : Rs. 50 lakh sought
14.	do	Chellanam	24.6.2002	Use Science, not sand bags to check sea erosion
15.	do	Chellanam	25.6.2002	Chellanam witnesses waves of protest.
16.	do	Kozhikode	2.9.2002	Project to save coastal belt urged.

Source: The Indian Express/The New Indian Express/The New Indian Express, Cochin 2000-2002.

Table 7.10
Population, non-working population and those seeking employment in the age group of 15-59 in the different districts of Kerala in 1991

S. No.	District	Population*	Non-Working Population	Non-Working seeking employment	Non-working as per cent of population	Non-working seeking employment as per cent of population**
1.	Kasargode	619043	286102	58322	46.21	9.42 (2.06)
2.	Kannur	1351465	746994	213899	55.27	15.82 (7.59)
3.	Wayanad	407815	162684	39406	39.89	9.66 (1.39)
4.	Kozhikode	1600172	954575	283130	59.65	17.69 (10.03)
5.	Malappuram	1680384	979145	240930	58.26	14.33 (8.53)
6.	Palakkad	1398097	623447	159470	44.59	11.40 (5.65)
7.	Thrissur	1701522	898575	253010	52.81	14.86 (8.96)
8.	Ernakulam	1824011	952620	283571	52.22	15.54 (10.04)

(Contd.)

(Table 7.10 contd.)

S. No.	District	Population*	Non-Working Population	Non-Working seeking employment	Non-working as per cent of population	Non-working seeking employment as per cent of population**
9.	Idukki	692387	290722	85630	41.98	12.36 (3.03)
10.	Kottayam	1168661	649878	199448	55.60	17.06 (7.06)
11.	Alappuzha	1256302	639319	226592	50.88	18.03 (8.02)
12.	Pathanamthitta	730588	418892	135715	57.33	18.57 (4.80)
13.	Kollam	1510089	801372	332953	53.06	22.04 (11.79)
14.	Thiruvananthapuram	1872411	982722	310260	52.48	16.57 (10.92)
	Total	**17812947**	**9387047**	**2822336**	**52.69**	**15.84 (100)**

* Population in the 15-59 age group alone is shown.

** Figure in parenthesis are percentage of state total.

Source: Directorate of Census Operations, Kerala, 1999 pp.76-119.

has been noted in chapter five. The density of population in most coastal panchayats, and municipalities/corporations was found to be significantly higher than the state's over all density in 1991. This tendency is expected to prevail even now.

With no significant development in the coast's economy and with limited potential for emigration, the natural outcome is likely to be an increase in the rate of unemployment. Table 7.10 shows the population, non-working population and those seeking employment in the age group of 15-59 in the different districts of Kerala during 1991.

Table 7.10 makes it clear that nearly 53 per cent of the population of the state in the age group of 15-59 in 1991 was non-working. This percentage, however, varied between the districts. It was found to be the highest in Kozhikode district, followed by Malappuram, Pathanamthitta, Kottayam, Kannur, Kollam, Thrissur, Thiruvananthapuram, Alappuzha, Kasargode, Palakkad, Idukki and Wayanad, in that order. The percentage of non-workers was the lowest in Wayanad district (39.89 per cent). In absolute terms, Kollam had the highest number of non-working population (3,32,953) in the age group of 15-59. It is followed by Thiruvananthapuram, Ernakulam, Kozhikode, Thrissur, Malappuram, Alappuzha, Kannur, Kottayam, Palakkad, Pathanamthitta, Idukki, Kasargode and Wayanad in the same order.

A better picture of the unemployment situation in the districts can be obtained by looking at the population in the 15-59 age group seeking employment (involuntary unemployment). Table 7.10 also shows that about 28,22,336 persons constituting 15.84 per cent of the population in the 15-59 age group were seeking employment in the state in 1991. Of these, about 75 per cent were from the districts of Thiruvananthapuram, Kollam, Alappuzha, Ernakulam, Thrissur, Malappuram, Kozhikode and Kannur. Thiruvananthapuram and Kollam each had more than three lakh persons seeking employment in 1991. Kannur, Kozhikode, Malappuram, Thrissur, Ernakulam and Alappuzha had more than two lakh persons seeking employment in each during this period. What is apparent from the above is the high concentration of population in the coastal districts and the high proportion of (unemployed) population seeking employment in these districts. Table 7.11 gives details of work seekers in Kerala during the period from 1990 to 2000.

Table 7.11
No. of work seekers in Kerala from 1990 to 2000

Year	General work seekers	Professional/ technical work seekers	Total work seekers
1990	33,04,003	1,16,032	33,20,035
1991	35,29,781	1,09,023	36,38,804
1992	37,18,926	1,28,137	38,47,063
1993	40,20,822	1,36,070	41,56,892
1994	40,39,063	1,29,606	41,68,669
1995	31,06,892	1,19,413	32,26,305
1996	31,58,515	1,28,959	32,87,474
1997	34,12,211	1,38,597	35,50,808
1998	36,29,499	1,54,750	37,84,249
1999	37,48,493	1,52,148	39,00,641
2000	40,19,811	1,66,060	41,85,871

Source: State Planning Board, 2001, p.S.14.

It appears from table 7.11 that the number of work seekers have increased from 33.20 lakhs in 1990 to 41.85 lakhs in 2000. The majority (96 per cent) of the work seekers were general work seekers.

The district-wise distribution of work seekers in Kerala in 2000 is given in table 7.12.

Table 7.12
District-wise distribution of work seekers in Kerala during 2000

S. No.	District	General work seekers	Professional/ technical work seekers	Total	Per cent of state total
1.	Thriuvananathapuram	5,81,605	37,863	6,19,468	14.79
2.	Kollam	4,80,878	17,686	4,98,564	11.91
3.	Alappuzha	3,63,263	14,068	3,77,331	8.22
4.	Pathanamthitta	1,50,818	6,758	1,57,576	3.76
5.	Kottayam	2,72,471	10,809	2,83,280	6.76
6.	Idukki	1,29,049	4,136	1,33,185	3.18
7.	Ernakulam	3,95,947	29,249	4,25,196	10.15
8.	Thrissur	3,33,807	15,079	3,48,886	8.33
9.	Palakkad	2,80,796	4,554	2,85,350	6.81
10.	Malappuram	2,39,125	5,963	2,45,088	5.85
11.	Kozhikode	3,65,299	8,198	3,73,497	8.92
12.	Wayanad	83,931	1,649	85,580	2.04
13.	Kannur	2,47,835	8,451	2,56,286	6.12
14.	Kasargode	94,987	1,597	96,584	2.30
	Total	**40,19,811**	**1,66,060**	**41,85,871**	**100.00**

Source: State Planning Board, 2001, p. S.15.

Table 7.12 shows that about 62 per cent of the work seekers are concentrated in the districts of Thiruvananthapuram, Kollam,

Alappuzha, Ernakulam, Thrissur and Kozhikode. Thiruvananthapuram had the highest number of work seekers both in the general as well as professional/technical categories.

The extent of the unemployment problem in the coastal zone can be further understood from the distribution of population, non-working population and those seeking employment in the age group of 15-59 in the principal coastal towns/cities of Kerala in 1991 as shown in table 7.13.

Table 7.13

Population, non-working population and those seeking employment in the age group of 15-59 in the principal coastal towns/cities of Kerala in 1991

S. No.	*Town/ city*	*Population*	*Non-working population*	*Non-working seeking employment*	*Non-working as per cent of population*	*Non-working seeking employment as per cent of population*
1.	Kanhangad	70,977	35,312	11,559	49.75	16.28
2.	Kannur	2,91,933	1,76,785	59,602	60.55	20.41
3.	Vadakara	62,346	37,626	10,630	60.35	17.05
4.	Kozhikode	5,07,823	3,10,314	1,02,500	61.10	20.18
5.	Malappuram	80,251	48,401	13,450	60.31	16.75
6.	Palakkad*	1,12,721	59,235	14,371	52.55	12.74
7.	Guruvayur*	70,388	42,588	8,570	60.50	12.17
8.	Thrissur*	1,78,184	96,420	28,540	54.12	16.01
9.	Cochin	7,50,697	4,10,703	1,21,570	54.70	16.19
10.	Kottayam *	1,08,185	60,775	20,655	56.17	19.09
11.	Cherthala	86,337	36,732	14,810	42.54	17.15
12.	Alappuzha	1,68,804	88,851	36,060	52.63	21.36
13.	Kollam	2,31,468	1,29,679	54,402	56.02	23.50
14.	Thiruvana-nthapuram	5,39,821	2,98,933	1,01,298	55.37	18.76

* *Non-coastal.*

Source: Directorate of Census Operations, Kerala, 1999, pp.124-137.

Table 7.13 reveals that the number of persons in the age group of 15-59 who remain unemployed was maximum in Cochin with 4.10 lakh persons and it is followed by Kozhikode, Thiruvananthapuram, Kannur, Kollam, Thrissur, Alappuzha, Kottayam, Palakkad, Malappuram, Guruvayoor, Vadakara, Cherthala and Kanhangad in that order.

The component of the population in the 15-59 age group seeking employment was also found to be the maximum in Cochin with

1,21,570 persons, followed by Kozhikode with 1,02,500 persons. Thiruvananthapuram came next with 1,01,298 persons. Kannur and Kollam also had significant number of persons in this age group seeking employment. Within this age group, the percentage of population seeking employment was found to be more in Kollam, Kozhikode, Kannur, Alappuzha, Kottayam and Thiruvananthapuram. It is also worth noting here that the percentage of the population in this age group seeking employment in these towns/cities is found to be higher than the corresponding percentages at the district and state levels shown in table 7.10. It is apparently indicative of the higher level of unemployment prevailing in the coastal zones, particularly, the coastal towns/cities of the state.

A partial but closer picture of the unemployment problem in the coastal zones can be obtained from the non-working component of the fishermen population who constitute the bulk of the 'coastal' population of the state as shown in table 7.14.

Table 7.14
Non-working fishermen (marine) in the coastal districts of Kerala in 1999-2000

S. No.	*Districts*	*Fishermen population*	*Active fishermen*	*Non-Active fisher men*	*Non-active as per cent of total*	*Non-Active excluding <15 and >60 age group**
1.	Thiruvana-nthapuram	1,70,135	51,488	1,18,647	69.73	30.95
2.	Kollam	95,752	20,531	75,221	78.55	39.77
3.	Alappuzha	1,13,647	30,435	83,212	73.21	34.43
4.	Ernakulam	73,981	15,157	58,824	79.51	40.73
5.	Thrissur	71,183	9,694	61,489	86.38	47.60
6.	Malappuram	81,641	23,131	58,510	71.66	32.88
7.	Kozhikode	1,00,754	18,312	82,442	81.82	43.04
8.	Kannur	56,909	5,404	51,505	90.50	51.72
9.	Kasargode	44,636	10,697	33,939	76.03	37.25
	Total	**8,08,638**	**1,84,849**	**6,23,789**	**77.14**	**38.36**

* The <15 and >60 age group constituted 38.78 per cent of the population of the state. This percentage is deducted from the figures of the previous column to give an estimate of the workable unemployed.

Source: Department of Fisheries, 2000 a, p.7. Non-active-extrapolated from the original.

Table 7.14 shows that out of the total fishermen population of 8.08 lakhs in 1999-00, only 1.84 lakhs were active leaving 6.23 lakhs as non-active (non-working). The non-working population constituted 77.14 per cent of the population. Excluding the normal non-working population in the age-group of below 15 and above 60 (38.78 per cent for total population of the state), the percentage of the non-working population among fishermen can be estimated at 38.36 per cent which is still quite significant. At the district level, this percentage is found to vary between 30.95 per cent in Thiruvananthapuram and 51.72 per cent in Kannur indicating high levels of unemployment among the coastal marine fishermen of the state. A similar picture of unemployment among inland fishermen can also be visualised as shown in table 7.15

Table 7.15

Non-working fishermen (inland) in Kerala in 1999-00

S. No.	*Districts*	*Fishermen population*	*Active fishermen*	*Non-Active fisher men*	*Non-active as per cent of total*	*Non-Active excluding <15 and >60 age group**
1.	Thiruvananthapuram	1,357	350	1,001	74.09	35.31
2.	Kollam	34,323	8,080	26,243	76.45	37.67
3.	Pathanamthitta	1,450	466	984	67.86	28.78
4.	Alappuzha	62,388	10,140	52,248	83.74	44.96
5.	Kottayam	24,985	6,664	18,321	73.32	34.54
6.	Idukki	52	30	22	42.30	3.52
7.	Ernakulam	64,482	16,118	48,362	75.00	36.22
8.	Thrissur	19,947	4,832	15,115	75.77	36.99
9.	Palakkad	1,041	495	546	52.44	13.66
10.	Malappuram	4,387	1,227	3,160	72.03	33.25
11.	Kozhikode	12,124	2,814	9,310	76.78	38.00
12.	Wayanad	1,039	254	785	75.55	36.77
13.	Kannur	1,548	920	628	40.56	1.78
14.	Kasargode	953	285	668	70.09	31.31
	Total	**2,30,070**	**52,675**	**1,77,395**	**77.10**	**38.32**

* The <15 and >60 age group constituted 38.78 per cent of the population of the state. This percentage is deducted from the figures of the previous column to give an estimate of the workable unemployed.

Source: Department of Fisheries, 2000 b, p.6. Non-active extrapolated from the original.

Table 7.15 shows that out of a total inland fishermen population of 2,30,070, only 52,675 were working, leaving 1,77,395 as non-working. The non-working group constituted 77.10 per cent of the inland fishermen population. Excluding the below 15 and above 60 age group, the non-working population formed 38.32 per cent of the population, again marking a large contingent of unemployed (non-working) persons. This percentage is high in almost all districts, with only three exceptions of Kannur, Palakkad and Idukki. The non-working component was more in Alappuzha, Ernakulam, Kollam, Kottayam and Thrissur districts where the inland fishermen population is found concentrated.

An adverse situation developing in Kannur district as a result of modern shrimp farming leading to the displacement of labour has been reported by Nandakumar and Muraleekrishna in 1998. They noted that 'on an average, labour displacement takes place at 1:5 ratio, i.e., a modern shrimp farm employs one person whereas traditional systems would have five workers ... In a state like Kerala, where the population is high and more so in poverty ridden primary sector, this labour displacement has far reaching consequences. This labour displacement weighed against mere foreign exchange earning for a few, the social costs created exerts an imbalance, accentuating social inequality' (Nandakumar and Muraleekrishna, 1998, pp. 64-65). It is perhaps such inequality that lead to social tensions between communities as seen at Marad in Kozhikode district or at Poovar and Vizhinjam in Thiruvananthapuram district.

The extent of unemployment in other sectors/ sections of the coast could not be considered for want of relevant statistics. It, however, appears from the general statistics of the non-working population reported in the 1991 census tables in the earlier sections and from the low participation rates found in both the coastal (marine) and inland fishing community of the state, that unemployment is a major economic problem of the coast. The likelihood of a higher level of unemployment would become apparent if the disguised unemployment prevailing in the cashew, coir, fishing, fish processing, mining and agricultural sectors of the economy are also taken into account.

The conclusion emerging from this section is that unemployment is a critical economic problem in coastal Kerala for which an ICM strategy would be needed to find any solution.

7.3.2. Low incomes

With the predominance of the primary sector related activities like fishing, agriculture, aquaculture, coir, cashew, etc. and the prevailing high density of population and unemployment in the coastal region, the per capita income of the population is presumed to be generally very low. However, in the absence of any concrete sectoral income data relating to coastal communities, an attempt is made here to look at the per capita income of the coastal districts of Kerala to draw some general conclusions about its trend and pattern.

Table 7.16 presents the details of per capita income in the coastal and other districts of Kerala from 1997-98 to 1999-00.

Table 7.16

Per capita income in the coastal and other districts of Kerala from 1997-98 to 1999-00

(Rs at current prices)

S. No.	*District*	*1997-98*	*1998-99*	*1999-00*	*Increase/ decrease in 1999-00 over 1997-98*
1.	Thiruvananthapuram	15005	17260	20484	36.50
2.	Kollam	14971	17148	18426	23.07
3.	Pathanamthitta	14170	16191	17980	26.88
4.	Alappuzha	14061	16137	21916	55.86
5.	Kottayam	15793	18205	21871	38.48
6.	Idukki	16062	18256	21297	32.59
7.	Ernakulam	18305	21035	23020	25.75
8.	Thrissur	15216	17470	21362	40.39
9.	Palakkad	12483	14316	18031	44.44
10.	Malappuram	10590	12185	13782	30.14
11.	Kozhikode	14752	16990	18105	22.72
12.	Wayanad	14477	16555	34123	135.70
13.	Kannur	14830	17046	17260	16.38
14.	Kasargode	15956	18283	16121	1.03
	State	**14642**	**16811**	**19461**	**32.91**

Source: State Planning Board, 2001, pp.S.9, S.11 and S.13.

Table 7.16 makes it clear that the per capita income of the state which stood at Rs 14642 (at current prices) in 1997-98 increased to Rs 19461 in 1999-00, showing an increase of 32.91 per cent during two years. Higher per capita incomes and higher growth rates were observed in some districts. The per capita income was found to be higher than the state average in the districts of Tiruvananthapurarn, Alappuzha, Kottayam, Idukki, Ernakulam, Thrissur and Wayanad. The growth rates were also considerably higher in these districts, with Wayanad showing a phenomenal growth rate of 135.70 per cent.

The per capita income and growth rates were, however, found to be lower than the state average in the districts of Kasargod, Kannur, Kozhikode, Malappuram, Pathanamthitta and Kollam. In Palakkad, the growth rate was found to be higher, although the per capita income was lower than the state average. It appears that the per capita income of the northern districts with the exception of Wayanad was generally lower than the state average. In the south, Kollam and Pathanamthitta also stood behind the other districts. The relatively low per capita income of the northern districts along with Kollam and Pathanamthitta in the south is indicative of the limited options available to the local community and the unsustainability of development in the state. Promoting sustainable development with intra-generational equity must be a concern for ICM in Kerala.

7.3.3. Intra-use and inter-use conflicts

These are undoubtedly very critical issues facing the coast and they are likely to tear off the socio-economic fabric of the coastal society. Intra-use conflict and inter-use conflict, in varying degrees, have been in operation in the coast for several years. Now with growing population and increased focus on urban, commercial/ industrial development;these conflicts have become very intense and focused. Most of these conflicts are for the use of the limited coastal natural resource base for 'exclusive' use by a 'few' users within a 'single' industry or by a number of users in a large number of industries/activities. The coastal zones being the theatre of many activities,intense conflicts over the resource use have now become a regular feature of the coast. Some of the marked intra-use conflicts and inter-use conflicts are explained below.

7.3.3.1. Intra-use conflicts

These refer to conflicts prevailing within a single industry, but between different users of the same resource base. This occurs when many individual units simultaneously try to use the resource base. The most well known instance of such intra-use conflicts existing in the coastal zones of Kerala is the conflict between the so called 'traditional' fishermen and the users of mechanised fishing boats.

The conflicts between the traditional fishermen and the mechanised boat operators had its beginning in the early eighties of the last century when the traditional fishermen suffered heavy loss of fish catch and income in the face of growing competition from the mechanised boat operators in the inshore sectors of the Kerala coast. The conflicts manifested itself initially in the form of burning of mechanised boats by traditional fishermen at several places in Cochin and Quilon and in the confiscation of the catch of the nechanised boats by the traditional fishermen. The main complaints of the traditional fishermen were: (1) the mechanised boats destroyed their gear while passing through the fishing ground where they operated, (2) destroyed the juveniles, larvae and egg of the fishes they catch by using indiscriminate fishing techniques and (3) the mechanised boat operators virtually ousted them in the fishing ground and in the market place. The traditional fishermen felt that their very survival was at stake.

It may be noted in retrospective here that the traditional, fishermen responded to this crisis by following a two pronged strategy of (I) organising large-scale protests, including burnings of mechanised boats and demanding controls on mechanised fishing and (2) improving their technology to compete with the mechanised sectcr. With the help of the former, the group has succeeded in getting the Government of Kerala implement the provisions of the Kerala Marine Fishing Regulation Act of 1980 and implement the ban on monsoon trawling in Kerala since 1988, which have helped the traditional fishermen in establishing their sovereignty over their lost fishing grounds. With the help of the second strategy, the traditional fishermen have been able to conquer new territories and enhance their share of economic value (output) produced by the fishing industry. This has, however, led to further intensification of conflicts with the mechanised sector and the mechanised boat operators' lobby pleading for the scrapping of the ban on monsoon trawling, which is believed to have affected their catches and their economy and the seafood processing and export sector supporting their cause. A new dimension to this conflict has also come to the fore with the so called 'traditional' fishermen now using very powerful fishing boats which are as destructive as the mechanised fishing units. The conflict is further aggravated with the 'pure' traditional fishermen using the indigenous crafts without outboard engines finding the competition for resources very tough and finding themselves loosing in the game.

The intra-use conflict in the industry is reflected in the diverse trends in the output of the different segments of the marine fishing industry of the state. Table 7.17 shows the trend in the output of the main segments of the marine fishing industry of Kerala for the period from 1982 to 1997.

It appears from table 7.17 that out of the nine segments (craft-gear combinations) of the marine fishing industry of the state, only five segments were able to increase their output during the period from 1982 to 1997. These consisted of the mechanised trawlers, mechanised hook and line operators, motorised ring seines, motorised drift/gillnets and motorised other gear operators. The output of these

Table 7.17
Trend in the output of main segments of the marine fishing industry of Kerala for the period from 1982 to 1997

(in tonnes)

Year	Mechanised trawl net	Mechanised drift/gill net	Mechanised purseseine	Mechanised hook and line	Motorised boat seine	Motorised ring seine	Motorised drift/gill net	Motorised other nets	Non-motorised other nets
1982	64493	18065	11176	293	65534	-	4478	2520	177269
1983	59876	21614	14744	259	76014	-	17137	5407	175617
1984	90862	13738	7820	251	103000	-	37783	14660	108516
1985	98425	15981	10230	110	56629	-	21645	50686	83372
1986	118020	8888	4517	462	113100	23998	30869	11961	88464
1987	144018	5373	904	978	48409	30390	21662	11187	40180
Average	**95949**	**13943**	**8232**	**392**	**77114**	**27194**	**22262**	**16070**	**107236**
1988	202433	8456	1171	730	91103	88074	34607	33747	32942
1989	200627	5319	8786	813	48068	270820	32647	30489	34768
1990	225239	3803	4426	8355	42555	263718	51295	9798	43802
1991	214270	1814	4124	438	24600	220753	56395	33371	40067
1992	251319	1825	6273	785	18878	193522	35481	18634	28222
1993	299147	1559	6839	617	13075	156562	27633	28625	36559
1994	315550	991	5903	755	13745	156241	33995	21938	19958
1995	206833	1453	4988	1008	13951	215341	33449	17755	20141
1996	261599	1553	10223	1430	9624	185305	52380	37183	22071
1997	267561	1835	2853	2320	19282	157290	• 47340	40060	20059
Average	**244458**	**2861**	**5559**	**1725**	**29488**	**190763**	**41023**	**27160**	**29859**

Source: Expert Committee for Fisheries Management Studies, Kerala, 2000, pp.108-111.

sectors have shown remarkable improvement as reflected in the average output for the periods 1982-87 and 1988-97. It may be noted here that these periods in fact represent the period prior to and coinciding with the period of the introduction seasonal ban on monsoon trawling in Kerala, along with the upgradation of technology (motorisation of country crafts) by the so called traditional fishermen in the state.

Paradoxically, table 7.16 also shows that the output of four segments of the marine fishing industry of the state has been declining over the years. Declining output was noted in mechanised drift/gill net, purseine, motorised boatseine, and the non-motorised traditional sectors. The decline in the output of the mechanised drift/ gill netters, motorised boat seines and non-motorised traditional crafts was significant.

Part of this decline in the output of these sectors must be due to the shift in the operation by some vessels or their switch over to other fishery (gear) as an optimisation measure. Notwithstanding this possibility, the sharp fall in the output of these sectors, especially of the non-motorised sector, poses questions of their survival and sustainability in the wake of globalisation and high-tech fishing. Fisheries management in Kerala seems to be aware of this issue. It, however, needs to be incorporated into the ICM framework for their sustainability.

Among the other intra-use conflicts prevailing in the coastal zones may be noted the conflicts between full-time fishermen and part-time fishermen or commercial fishermen and recreational fishermen. Conflicts between small scale operators and large scale (industrial/ commercial) operators in the agricultural, mining, coir, cashew and other sectors are also likely to prevail. There may also be instances of conflicts between private sector and public sector uses of the same resource base in an industry. It appears that the private/public sector use conflicts are going to be acute in the future when the coastal 'common property resources are being privatised in the wake of globalisation of the state's economy. The role of ICM as a 'peace keeping mission' in Kerala is obvious.

7.3.3.2. Inter-use conflicts

These are conflicts over the use of the same resource base simultaneously by many industries. In fact, the crux of ICM is inter-use conflicts. It is actually the multiple uses of the coastal resources and the resulting conflict of interests that led to the evolution of the concept and practice of ICM world wide. It is no wonder that the need for ICM in Kerala is also resting on this argument. It may perhaps have a facilitating role to play, i.e., to promote multiple uses, or more profitable uses in the future, especially in the wake of liberalisation, privatisation and globalisation of the state's economy. Notwithstanding this intent of ICM as a global business strategy, and the liberal 'peace keeping' role it has to play in coastal environments, the nature of inter-use conflicts prevailing in the state may be noted briefly.

As a matter of fact, inter-use conflicts are rampant in the coastal zones of Kerala. They are prevalent both on the 'land side' and on the 'water side'. There are conflicts between economic uses and non-economic uses as well. Some of these conflicts are quite manifest, while others are not. In fact, on the land side, these conflicts are manifest between agriculture and fisheries (aquaculture), agriculture and mining (clay), fisheries and mining (sand), fisheries and coir manufacturing, fisheries and forestry (mangroves), fisheries and transport, fisheries and tourism, fisheries and urban development, tourism and power, tourism and transport, etc. On the 'water side' also conflicts exist between fishing and port, port and defence, port and power and between other sectors.

It is worth recalling here that the multiple use conflict potential of the coastal zones has been noted in chapter four, while discussing the rationale for coastal zone management. The inter-use conflict potential of many of the activities as reported in the literature has been presented there. Some of the industries/activities that have impacted on other activities in the coastal zones of Kerala in recent times is worth noting here. Table 7.18 gives a list of industries/activities that have led to inter-use conflicts in Kerala in recent times.

Table 7.18 indicates that almost all the coastal activities impact on other industries and lead to inter-use conflicts. It is well known that agriculture (paddy cultivation) causes considerable pollution of water bodies through pesticide residues and fertilizer deposits carried by water channels and flooding of farms. The impacts are felt maximally in the fisheries sector. Aquaculture has its impacts on capture fisheries through water pollution, bio-diversity loss and stock depletion. It also leads to the conversion of the coastal wetlands into aquaculture farms, resulting in intense inter-use conflicts as seen taking place in the *Pokkali* paddy fields in Vypeen, in the *Kari* lands in Kuttanad, in the *Kole* lands in Thrissur and in the *Kaippad*

Table 7.18

List of industries/activities that have led to inter-use conflicts in Kerala in recent times

S. No.	*Industry/ activity*	*Location*	*Industry activity affected*	*Nature of impact*
1.	Agriculture	Kuttanad	Fisheries	Pollution
2.	Aquaculture	Kuttanad, Vypeen	Paddy cultivation	Reclamation of paddy land for aquaculture
3.	Fishing (capture)	Marine and inland	Coastal fishing, natural resource conservation	Pollution, mangrove destruction, loss of biodiversity, stock depletion
4.	Fish processing	Kuttanad	Paddy cultivation	Land use changes, food insecurity
5.	Agriculture (cash crops)	Kochi, Kollam	Fishing, sanitation	Pollution
6.	Coir retting	Kuttanad, Kollam	Fisheries	Pollution, loss of biodiversity
7.	Mining (mineral sand)	Kollam, Alappuzha	Water supply sanitation	Salnity incursion, soil leaching, etc
8.	Mining (river sand)	River stretches	Agriculture, fisheries, water supply, tourism	Soil erosion, sedimentation, siltation, saline water incursion, etc.
9.	Mining (lime shell, clay)	Vembanad, Kuttanad, Thrissur	Fisheries, agriculture	Sedimentation, water logging, etc.
10.	Tourism	Kovalam, Kumarakom, Pathiramanal	Fisheries	Dislocation of fishermen

(*Contd.*)

(Table 7.18 contd.)

S. No.	Industry/ activity	Location	Industry/ activity affected	Nature of impact
11.	Water transport	Alappuzha	Tourism	Obstruction to water sports
12.	Urban development	Gosheree (Cochin)	Fisheries	Land reclamation, loss of habitat
13.	Oil (petroleum) industry	Punnamada lake	Fisheries, tourism	Oil pollution, displacement of water sports, tourism and recreation in Vembanad
14.	Chemical industries	Udyogamandal, Ambalamugal	Fisheries, agriculture, water supply, housing, health, sanitation	Pollution, loss of biodiversity, quality of life, aesthetic value
15.	Port	Vallarpadom	Navy	Expected to affect the landing and take off of naval planes by the huge cranes on the flight path
16.	Defence	Cochin, Ezhimala	Fishing, agriculture	Other activities are prohibited

Source: Newspaper reports, Cochin, 2000-02.

lands in Kannur. It also leads to encroachments and pressures to convert the coastal common property waters into private property enclosures to promote intensive aquaculture. This has already resulted in social tension at several places in the state. The crisis in Kuttanad was reported on several occasions (Ajithkumar 1993; Byju, 2001, 2002).

The capture fisheries, though not directly affecting any activity in the coast has its impact on nearby port facilities, either through congestion in the shipping channel as in the Cochin port area or in the Neendakara region. It can also impact on tourist attraction to the port or the beach as at Kovalam, Vizhinjam, Thankassery, Kannur and at many other places.

The impact of fish processing is also like wise felt in the beach front or the backwater front where the fish processing plants discharge their effluents. The impact is mainly on the water front users, predominantly the local residents and other users of the coast. The inter-use conflicts in these cases are mostly local, confined to the main centres of fish processing in the state at Neendakara, Kochi and Kozhikode.

The inter-use conflicts arising from the coir industry is from coir retting causing pollution in the nearby water bodies affecting fishing and water supply. Such conflicts prevail at several places in Kollam, Alappuzha, Ernakularn, Thrissur and Kozhikode districts.

Mineral sand mining along the coast is likely to impact on coastal agriculture, aquaculture, water supply, etc. Major areas likely to be affected by this issue are the Alappuzha—Kollam stretch of the coast. The recent move by the Government of Kerala to privatise and promote sand mining in the Alappuzha coast following the Global Investor Meet in 2002 has led to widespread protests from the local public, forcing the Government to postpone the decision (*The New Indian Express,* Cochin, 3.5.2003).

Mining of river sand has its impact on agriculture, fisheries, water supply, water transport (inland navigation) and tourism, through land subsidence, soil erosion, sedimentation, siltation, etc. The impact is felt all along the coast through deposition of silt and water pollution.

Lime shell mining also has similar impacts; the effects being concentrated primarily in the Ashtamudi, Vembanad and Kozhikode regions.

Tourism development had its impact on fisheries at Kovalam/ Vizhinjam, Kumarakom, Pathiramanal, etc. Dislocation of fishermen was reported at all these places. Extensive development of tourism in the coast (beach tourism and backwater, tourism) can impact fishing activity through pollution and competition for space and amenities. The backwater fisheries of the Vembanad might need special attention in this regard. The crisis at Pathiramanal is deep rooted (Anonymous, 2001 and 2002). The potential for water transport affecting tourism, recreation, etc. is reported from Alappuzha, where the development of the west coast canal system and the setting up of container cargo terminals are expected to interrupt the famous Nehru trophy boat race and damage the tourism potential of the area (Krishna Kumar, 2002).

The pressure from urban development is felt predominantly by agriculture and fisheries, where wetland reclamation leads to displacement of farmers and fishermen. This has happened all along the coast where urbanisation is fast taking place. The latest example is the Goshree project at Kochi. Instances of wetland reclamation for urban development were reported from Thalassery and Kozhikode earlier (Annonymous, 2000 and Rajeev, 2000).

The threat from the oil (petroleum) industry, apart from contamination at the port while transhipping, is felt to become manifest at the proposed Punnamada lake oil terminal in Alappuzha district where it is feared to cause damage to the tourism prospects of the region.(Annonyrnous, 2002 a and 2000 b).

The greatest threat to the coastal zone of Kerala is felt to be from the chemical industries which discharge the toxic effluents into the rivers, backwaters and the sea. Its impact is felt maximally by fishermen, agriculturists and the local residents. The greatest threat is from the industrial units operating from the Udyogamandal and Ambalamugal areas in Ernakulam district, the Veli area in Thiruvananthapuram district and the Chavara-Kundara belt in Kollam district. The inter-use conflict, prevailing in these regions is quite acute and it has led to long agitation by fishermen at Thumba, Cochin and elsewhere in the past.

Activities of the port also cause inter-use conflicts, especially with fishing and naval exercises. Ports, apart from causing marine-pollution in the port mouth and affecting fisheries, also prohibit fishing in the navigation channels. Naval activities are also constrained oy the port services. Recently, fears were expressed about the impact of the expansion of the Cochin port to the Vallarpadom container terminal, where the installation of tall cranes is expected to impede the exercises by naval aircrafts in the region (Das, 2002). Oil slick in the inshore waters of the north of Cochin Port channel was reported in 1999 (Kaladharan, *et.al.* 1999).

What is apparent from the above cursory note on inter-use conflicts in the coastal zones of the state is their potential to impede the harmonious development of the coast. Preventing or minimising the level of inter-use conflicts is vital for the sustainable development of the coast. Viewed in this perspective, the task before ICM in Kerala is to prevent the occurrence of inter-use conflicts and to harmonise the working of various coastal activities for producing maximum aggregate value.

7.3.4. Stagnation (unsustainable development)

Another major economic issue facing the coast, as in other parts of the state, is the difficulty in sustaining the process of development (unsustainability) or the stagnation in the economy. The tendency for the economy to stagnate has already been noted in the last chapter while analysing the position of various coastal activities. The role of ICM in sustaining these activities were also noted. The unsustainability of development in the coast, however, needs some elaboration.

It is worth recalling here the meaning of the central concept of 'sustainable development'. The World Commission on Environment and Development (Brundtland Commission) in 1987 has defined it as 'development that meets the needs of the present without compromising the ability of future generations to meet their own needs' (WCED, 1987, p. 8). Cicin-Sain and Knecht observe that 'sustainable development can be seen as a continuous process of decision making guided by a basic philosophy emphasising development that improves the quality of human life (ensuring equity in the distribution of benefits flowing from development) and development that is environmentally appropriate, making proper use (and sometimes non-use) of natural resources and protecting essential ecological processes, life support systems, and biological diversity. A necessary element of sustainable development is an integrated decision-making or policy process. Other elements that enhance the likelihood of sustainable development, as suggested by the World Commission on Environment and Development, include a political system that secures effective citizen participation in decision making, an economic system that can generate surpluses and technical knowledge on a self-reliant and sustained basis, a social system that provides for solutions to tensions arising from disharmonious development, a production system that respects the obligation to preserve the ecological base for development, a technological system that fosters sustainable patterns of trade and finance, and administrative system that is flexible and has the capacity for self-correction' (Cicin-Sain and Knecht, 1998, pp. 85-86).

A frequently suggested method of measuring the sustainability of development is to assess the development process by applying the three essential criteria of sustainability, viz. the environmental (ecological) sustainability, economic sustainability and social sustainability.

Environmental (ecological) sustainability demands that the natural resource base (ecological basis) for economic activity is sustained for future use as well. This requires that all developments take place without impairing the environment and allowing the ecological processes to continue with minimum disturbance. But, while taking note of the ecological issues outlined in the last section, it would appear that the development path followed in the state was not sustainable and there are constraints for promoting growth and even for maintaining status quo in many activities in the coast.

Economic sustainability expects the industry (activity) to produce some surplus to keep the resources tied to the industry. Non-viability of many of the activities of the coast, for example, paddy cultivation, coconut cultivation, etc., make them unsustainable. As a matter of fact, economic sustainability of most activities will be at stake when all costs are internalised and the negative externalities caused by them are taken into account. This will be of particular importance for the polluting industries when the cost of pollution abatement are taken into account, or the 'polluter pay' principle is applied.

Social sustainability seeks to ensure that the development path followed is socially acceptable. It requires that society accepts the development process as 'just' and 'equitable' and fulfilling the ends of social justice, both in the present and in the future. It postulates that intra-generational and inter-generational equity in resource use are maintained.

Judged in the light of these criteria, and looking at the intra-use and inter-use conflicts in the coastal zone and the ecological threats to development, it would appear that the development achieved by the state is quite unsustainable.

7.4. Socio-cultural issues

The socio-cultural issues of the coast are vast. These issues may be considered at the primary level of meeting the socio-economic needs of the community like fulfilling the need for housing, health and sanitation, water supply, waste disposal, etc. and at the higher level of providing for cultural and recreational needs. A brief review of these issues is attempted here.

7.4.1. Housing

Poor housing is one of the most critical problems of the coast. It is critical due to several factors. Some of the major factors are: (1) the growing demand for housing from the growing population, (2) limited space in the coast, (3) high cost of construction and (4) coastal hazards. Among all these factors the last one has been a matter of great concern for the state and the coastal population, each year, especially during the monsoon season. Housing and colonisation of fishermen have always been a major component of the government's programme for fisheries development in Kerala. Providing better housing to all vulnerable sections of the coastal population certainly merits the attention of an ICM programme in Kerala.

7.4.2. Poor health and sanitation

Along with insufficient housing, poor health and sanitary facilities form the twin social issues of the coast. With poor drainage facilities, environmental pollution and over crowded settlements, health and sanitation are the biggest threat to community life in the coastal areas. The critical situation on this front has been reported on several occasions in the past (Shaji, 2001).

Frequent onslaughts of diarrhoea and cholera are chronic issues of the coast which an ICM mode of development planning in the state has to tackle.

7.4.3. Shortage of water supply

Yet another highly agitating problem of the coast is the lack of potable water for the teaming population. Water shortage, especially for drinking and other domestic uses has been agitating the coastal community for years. It has given vent to this problem by organising mass agitation at frequent intervals. The agitations in Kochi has highlighted the intensity of the problem in the islands of Vypeen, Kadamakudi, Varapuzha, etc. and the coastal, stretches of Kumbalangi, Chellanam, etc.

An approximate representation of the water supply shortage in selected coastal municipalities and corporations of Kerala is given in table 7.19.

Table 7.19
Water shortage problem in selected coastal municipalities and corporations of Kerala in iitres per capita per day (LPCD)

S.No	*Name of Municipality/ corporation*	*Projected population in 2000*	*Demand for water as per norms (LPCD)*	*Supply of water (LPCD)*	*Supply gap (LPCD)*
1.	Thiruvananthapuram Corporation	544006	200	140	60
2.	Varkala	44737	150	20	130
3.	Kollam	148942	150	135	15
4.	Kochi Corporation	654923	170	75	95
5.	Paravoor	32371	120	70	50
6.	Kodungalloor	34898	125	87	38
7.	Chavakkad	42286	110	7	103
8.	Ponnani	58275	125	45	80
9.	Kozhikode Corporation	453417	253	80	173
10.	Vadakara	84023	140	83	53
11.	Thalassery	123784	135	67	68
12.	Kannur*	75670	135	135	—
13.	Payyannur	76813	70	3	67
14.	Kanhangad	66978	125	26	99
15.	Kasargode	58727	125	78	47

* The population in Kannur seems to be an under estimate.
Source: State Planning Board, 2001, p. S. 249.

Table 7.19 indicates a major demand-supply gap in most of the municipalities and corporations. The gap is found to be the highest in Kozhikode corporation followed by the municipalities of Varkala, Chavakkad and Kasargode. The corporation of Kochi also had a significant shortage of water supply. It may be noted here that the problem of water shortage is likely to be more acute in the coastal panchayats where rural water supply schemes are less developed. The role ICM in filling this gap is explicit.

7.4.4. Waste disposal

With the growing concentration of population both in the urban and the rural areas of the coast, the disposal of solid as well as liquid waste is a gargentuan task for coastal planners. Its impact on coastal ecology, health and hygiene has already been noted. The fact that the coastal zone is increasingly being used for waste disposal is a matter of great concern for the coastal community and town planners and the task before ICM is to harmonise this use of the coast without adversely impacting on other uses. This issue is further looked in chapter nine.

7.4.5. Cultural and recreational issues

One of the dominant criteria of sustainable development is the preservation and protection of indigenous cultures as a form of 'social capital'. Preservation of this culture or 'cultural capital', in an economic sense, as noted by Throsby 'can provide a means of representing culture which enables both tangible and intangible manifestations of culture to be articulated as long-lasting stores of value and providers of benefits for individuals and groups' (Throsby, 2001, p.44). Throsby also points out that 'an over arching principle of sustainability is the proposition that no part of any system exists independently of other parts. In this respect it can be suggested that cultural capital, makes a contribution to long-term sustainability which is similar in principle to that of natural capital. It is now well understood that natural ecosystems are essential to supporting the real economy, and the neglect of natural capital through over use of exhaustible resources or unsustainable exploitation of renewable capital stocks may cause such systems to break down, with consequent loss of welfare and economic output. A parallel proposition can be put in regard to cultural capital ... it is becoming clearer that cultural 'ecosystems' underpin the operations of the real economy, affecting the way people behave and the choices they make. Neglect of cultural capital, by allowing heritage to deteriorate, by failing to sustain the cultural values that provide people with a sense of identity and by not undertaking the investment needed to maintain and increase the stock of both tangible and intangible cultural capital, will likewise place cultural systems in jeopardy and may cause them to break down, with consequent loss of welfare and economic output. Thus this final principle, in essence draws together the entire concept of sustainability when applied to cultural capital, providing an overall framework within which the more specific principles can be seen to operate' (ibid, pp. 57-58).

Considering this point of view and the developments (changes) in the coast, especially in the cultural milieu of the coast, one is inclined to think that the cultural capital of many communities has been seriously eroded. This must be typically the case with indigenous communities of fishermen, farmers, coir workers and many others. With the collapse of the natural (ecological), economic (financial) and social (cultural) capital, these communities are facing the threat of eviction or extinction from their 'heritage'[1] zone and increasingly being replaced by new industrial, urban, commercial cultures.

It is also worth noting here that this trend (process) is further reinformed in the coasts with the development of new industries/ activities. Along with the conversion of wetlands (paddy fields, mangroves, etc.) into aquaculture fields and real estate business, a new industry using the cultural landscape of the coast is also now developing in the state. It may be called as 'cultural tourism' or 'heritage tourism'. The problem with this type of industry, however, has been summarised by Throsby. Throsby remarks that 'the principal issues lying at the intersection of the economic and cultural aspects of tourism have to do with possible conflicts between the economic incentives driving the tourist industry and the cultural values upon which tourism impinges or relies. While it is true that tourism provides an economic stimulus and financial support for much cultural activity, it may also have adverse cultural impacts. Damage to cultural sites, congestion of cultural facilities, inappropriate hotel or resort development in culturally sensitive areas and so on, are all examples of ways in which pursuit of the financial rewards from tourism provision may have negative cultural ramifications. Thus tourism strategies which seek to maximise the economic gains from tourist expansion, as proposed, for example, by regional development authorities and other public agencies, may require consideration of such cultural impacts if they are to be successful ... in fact, there is a close parallel between tourism that can be judged sustainable with respect to environmental amenity and that which is sustainable in cultural terms' (ibid, pp.129-130).

Sustainable development of the coast demands sustaining the ecological, economic and cultural ecology of the coast. It is doubtful whether the Tourism Preservation and Trade Bill floated by the

Government of Kerala as a tourism promotion measure has any provision for protecting the indigenous culture of the coastal communities. Current developments indicate that the coastal communities are under pressure to surrender many of their natural amenities and privileges to new entrants to the coast. The fact that coastal areas are being subjected to tremendous ecological, economic and cultural traumas, especially in the wake of globalisation of the economy, necessitates an ethical commitment to protect the economic, social and cultural values of the indigenous communities of the coast as a first charge on development and as agreed in international conventions (Rio-agreements). It, however, impinges on ICM in Kerala to follow a culturally sustainable development policy to make it truely sustainable.

7.5. Summary

This chapter outlined the major ecological, economic and socio-cultural issues facing the coast. The ecological issues noted included (1) coastal pollution, (2) over-exploitation of natural resources, (3) habitat destruction and biodiversity loss and (4) natural hazards. Among the economic issues discussed are (1) population growth and unemployment, (2) low incomes, (3) intra-use and inter-use conflicts and (4) stagnation (unsustainable development). The socio-cultural issues of the coast have been considered at the primary level of meeting the housing, health and sanitation, water supply and waste disposal needs of the community and at the higher levels of providing for the cultural and recreational needs of the population.

All along, this chapter observed that the problems of the coast are quite critical and needing an ICM approach for solving them and for making the development sustainable.

8

Coastal Zone Management in Kerala—Past and Present Initiatives

8.1. Introduction

Managed use of the coastal zone is vital for sustainable development, the objective being to fulfil the current and future needs of the society.

The attempt in this chapter is to give an outline of the past and present efforts for the management of coastal zones in Kerala. This is important for two main reasons. In the first place, as pointed out by Kay and Alder 'history provides a framework for understanding how current approaches to the planning and management of coastal resources have evolved, and the constraints these approaches are operating within' and in the second 'by looking back at how coastal planning and management have developed, trends become evident. Projecting such trends provides an insight into the possible future development of coastal management and planning' (Kay and Alder, 1999, p.8). As a matter of fact, a knowledge of the past can be a guide for the future. Accordingly, this chapter presents a brief account of coastal management efforts in Kerala. It is presented in three sections: (1) pre-colonial period, (2) colonial period and (3) post-colonial period. A fourth section is devoted for a critique of the coastal zone management plan of Kerala since 1995. A final section notes the summary of points discussed in this chapter.

8.2. The pre-colonial period

As pointed out by Kay and Alder, 'humans have deliberately modified the coastal environment and exploited its resources for thousands of years. Ancient civilizations throughout the world built ports and seawalls, or diverted river water flowing into the sea; they also evolved various management systems for their fisheries, use of rich coastal soils for agriculture, trading through ports, and other coastal resources' (ibid, pp.8-9). This description of the ancient communities' efforts to manage their coastal resources seems to be very well applicable to the context of Kerala as well. Referring to the achievements made in managing the fishing industry of Kerala in ancient times, the Directorate of Fisheries of Kerala notes 'the fishing industry in Kerala has a hoary tradition. Scattered evidence of the immensity of its fisheries, the abundance of its fish trade and the importance of the fishing community in its social structure are found in the songs of the Sangam Age (i.e., 1st to 4th century A.D.) and in the diaries and records of travellers to India, like Pliny and the anonymous author of the 'Periplus of the Erythrean Sea' both of whom wrote in the first century A.D.' (Directorate of Fisheries, 1969, p.4).

The importance of the coast and its management was not confined to fisheries. The prosperity of the coast was revealed in the presence of numerous ports in ancient times. The Kerala State Gazetteer notes: 'early writers like Strabo (A.D. 19) and Pliny, the elder (A.D. 77) have mentioned about several minor ports like Musiri, Tundi, Naoora, and Nalkunda as to have been, situated on the Kerala coast. The anonymous author of the 'Periplus of the Erythrean Sea' (A.D. 80-89) has furnished many details about these ports, which were flourishing in trade and other tertiary activities ... The references about these ports contain stadia distances between one port and another as well as other physical and cultural identifications. The classic literature in Tamil has gone a step ahead indicating the geomorphological unit *(tinai)* in which these places were situated. In spite of all these hints, the historians have not arrived at a consensus in locating them' (Gazetteers Department, 1986, p.72).

A more detailed description of the ports of Kerala in their historical setting has been given by Sreedhara Menon. Menon noted that 'the ports situated on its long coast have given to Kerala a place of pre-eminence on the commercial map of India and the world from time immemorial. Muziris (modern Kodungallur) was the foremost port of foreign trade, the *primum Emporium Indiae,* since the early centuries of the Christian era. The classical writers of Rome mention some other ports like Tyndis, Barace, Nelcynda, Balita, Naura, etc. While the Tamil Sangam works refer to such ports as Tondi, Vakaie, Pantar, etc. ... Quilon, the capital of Venad, served as an important port from the 9th century A.D. It was the chief centre of Chinese trade at the time of the visit of Sulaiman (84 A.D.), Marco Polo (13th century) and Ibn Batuta (14th century). Calicut came into prominence by the 13th or 14th century and at the time of the landing of Vasco da Gama in 1498 A.D. it was already a major port. However, with the exception of Quilon, almost all the other ports mentioned above had become forgotten ports by this time' (Sreedhara Menon, 1999, p. 261).

Referring to the rise of Cochin (in the pre-colonial period), Menon writes: 'a new port came into existence on the west coast in Central Kerala 'in the 14th century. This was the port of Cochin. It is believed that the Cochin Port was formed in 1341 A.D. when as a result of the heavy floods in the river Periyar during the year the mouth of Muziris got silted up and this ancient port became almost a mere geographical expression with none of its old commercial glory. Cochin now took the place of Muziris and soon became a rival to Calicut ... Cochin figured prominently in the wars of the European powers for the commercial supremacy of the Kerala coast. From the time of the arrival of Cabral in 1500 A.D., till its capture by the Dutch in 1663, the Portuguese were dominant at the place. Caesar Frederick, a Venitian merchant who visited Kerala in the latter half of the 16th century refers to Cochin as 'the chiefest place the Portuguese have in India next unto Goa'. Cochin remained a Dutch stronghold till it was captured by the English in 1795 but the early years of British rule proved ruinous to the town as there was a lot of wanton destruction' (ibid, pp. 262-263). 'The early history of Cochin under British rule' says Whitehouse 'is not calculated to reflect credit upon the Hon. E.I. Company. Utterly neglected for a long period, with a declining trade and an impoverished population generally deprived of all religious and commercial advantages, one cannot wonder that it gradually sank, lower and lower, commercially, socially and morally,'..(ibid, p. 263).

Writing about the prosperity and growth of Calicut port in the early times, Sreedhara Menon notes that 'under the patronage of the Zamorins, Calicut developed before long into a major seaport on the Kerala coast' (Sreedhara Menon, 1998, p.166). Menon further quotes Krishna Iyer and says 'the rise of Calicut is at once a cause and a consequence of the Zamorin's ascendency in Kerala. Its trade filled his coffers and enabled him to extend his authority. And the expansion of his empire in turn increased its commerce. Originally a barren strip covered all over with thorny jungle, the genius of the Manavikramans converted it into a mighty sea port, where the Arabs and the Chinese meet to exchange the products of the west with those of the east. Kerala's exports of pepper, cardamom and textiles were shipped from here in bulk to foreign countries. The Zamorin declared Calicut a free port where even foreign ships not bound for it could call at any time and enjoy the facilities provided for taking fresh water or reinforcing depleted provisions. This helpful attitude of the Zamorin towards all foreign traders coupled with his reputation as a tolerant and fair minded monarch attracted foreign traders to Calicut in large numbers and made it the chief emporium of Malabar trade. The Chinese and the Arabs were among the most important of the foreign nationals who traded with Calicut' (ibid, pp.186-187).

Some of the more striking account of Calicut, given by foreign travellers was recounted by Sreedhara Menon. Menon reports that 'the earliest notice we have of Calicut is from the pen of Ibn Batuta (1342-1347) who visited the place at least six times. He describes Calicut as one of the great ports of the district of Malabar where merchants from all parts of the globe are found ... Ma Huan, a Chinese Muslim was the next important foreigner to visit Calicut. He was impressed by the large scale cultivation of pepper and coconut in the Zamorin's Kingdom ...

At the time of Abdu Razak's visit in 1443 there was a preponderance of trade with Arab countries at the port of Calicut, Chinese trade having declined in volume. He says, Calicut is a perfectly secured harbour, which like that of Ormuz, brings together merchants from every city and from every country. In it are to be found abundance of precious articles brought hither from maritime countries and especially from Abyssinia, Zirbad and Zanzibar. Security and justice are also firmly established in the city, that the most wealthy merchants bring thither from maritime countries considerable cargoes, which they unload and unhesitatingly send into the markets and bazars, without thinking in the meantime of any necessity of checking the account or of keeping watch over the goods. The officials of the Customs House take upon themselves the charge of looking after the merchandise, over which they keep watch day and night. When a sale is effected they levy a duty on the goods of one fortieth part; if they are not sold, they make no charges on them. In other parts, a strange practice is adopted. When a vessel sets sail for a certain point, and suddenly is driven by a decree of

Divine Providence into another roadstead, the inhabitants, under the pretext that the wind has driven it there, plunder the ship. But at Calicut every ship, when it puts into this port, is treated like other vessels, and there has no trouble of any kind to put up with.

Nicolo Conti (1444) and Athanasius Nikitin (1468-1474) who came later have alluded to the rich trade in pepper, ginger, cinnamon and other spices at Calicut. The latter was particularly impressed by the 'big bazar' of Calicut city (ibid, pp.194-196).

The above descriptions give a fairly good picture of the commercial glory and the attendant economic prosperity of the area prior to the arrival of the Portuguese, the first colonialist power to India. The predominance of the coastal zone of Kerala in the pre-colonial times is further reflected in the naval superiority of its people. A shocking discription of the fishermen of Purakkad in Alappuzha district by Duarte Barbosa reveals this. Barbosa wrote that 'Porcad has a ford of its own. Here many gentle fishermen reside, who do nothing and have no other occupation than that of fishing during the winter, and of plundering on the sea during summer such as fall in their way. They possess certain small boats like brigantines which they row skillfully, and collecting many of these together, they themselves being armed with bows and arrows, they surrounded any ship becalmed and after forcing it to surrender by means of their arrows, they proceed to plunder the crew and the ship. The booty they divide with the lord of the country who countenanced them' (Barbosa, Reprint, 1970, p.157). The exploits of Kunjali Marakkars, the Admirals of Kozhikode during the presence of Portuguese in the sixteenth century are also well known.

It may appear that the coastal zone of Kerala in the precolonial period was largely a zone of peaceful interaction with foreign traders with no major intra-use or inter-use conflicts. The acts of the fishermen of Purakkad may be an aberration.

8.3. The colonial period

This period witnessed the conquest of the coast by various European powers and the establishment of European 'industry and culture' in the coast. Referring to this development, Tharakan notes that 'Europeans were involved either through organisational or financial control or even directly in areas like production of spices in Kerala. A little later they were also involved in cotton production in other parts of India as well. In various European enclaves like Anjuthengu, Purakkad, Kochi, Chettuwai, Kozhikode, Mayyazhi, and

Thalassery, labour was incorporated into the European economy through production or collection of goods for trade to Europeans. In other words, the fact that this era, that is the three centuries before the 19th, was also the period when European world–economy fully grasped the opportunities offered to it by the world beyond the Mediterranian, had far reaching implications not only for Europe but also for the rest of the world' (Tharakan, 1999, pp. 333-334). Speaking about the English acquiring control of certain parts of Travancore, Sreedhara Menon notes, 'the acquisition of Anjengo was a substantial gain to the English, for the place commanded a line of water communication to the north and provided ample facilities for trade ... Anjengo developed into the most important English possession on the west coast, next only to Bombay. It also provided a convenient foothold from where the English East India Company could extend its sphere of influence in South and Central Kerala' (Sreedhara Menon, 1998, p. 319).

Referring to the English factory at Tellicherry, Menon writes 'while the English were steadily building up their influence in south Kerala, they took steps to safeguard their interests in north Kerala as well ... When the English companies were united in 1702, Tellicherry was along with Kannur, Calicut and Anjengo, one of the affiliated factories of Bombay. Its affairs were administered by a Chief and a Council called 'Factors" (ibid, p. 390).

The colonial powers consolidated their command over the coast by the force of military power. Referring to this factor, Tharakan notes that 'another factor behind colonial supremacy is the implication of the invention and diffusion of military drill ... the colonial army was already professionalised around 1830 ... they strengthened by mercenaries, and local recruits would be used more effectively and flexibly in most situations. The early colonial armed interventions were backed by plundering and looting. Indian forces also indulged in looting. But as far as the English was concerned the loot went into their capital accumulation and reinforced both processes, that is their military might and their financial capacity to back such interventions, mutually. In this sense the colonial army served indistinguishably as an integral part of early colonial commercial policy. The most visible evidence of this was the war indemnities that were charged upon Indian powers. The English who enlisted the support of the Kerala Kingdoms in their fight against Tippu, finally charged them, Thiruvitankur being the best example, heavy 'reimbursements' of the so called expenses for war and maintenance of the army. Through several networks of such policies the English gradually built up an unequal balance of power in their favour which was used to extract tribute. At least in the case of Kochi, the relatively smaller Kerala Kingdom, the unequal balance of power was used nakedly to extract tribute payment' (Tharakan, 1999, pp. 339, 347-348).

The colonial period was also characterised by the ruthless exploitation of the local community, including fishermen/ferry men through the land revenue extraction system. Referring to this, Tharakan notes that 'an elaborate administrative system was introduced in the directly administered region of Malabar to extract revenue. With the failure of indirect extraction through local chiefs, the responsibility of collection was vested in the hands of Joint Commissioners appointed initially by the British Government of Bombay. At a later date they were operating under a supervisor, which position still later merged with that of Principal collector ... In the meantime Tiruvitamkur and Kochi were incorporated into the colonial empire as princely states with certain amount of autonomous authority. Nevertheless there were the same kind of pressure or demand from the supreme colonial power for surplus, in all the three regions. Such demand had differential impact upon the three regions, on their institutions and on land policy. In Tiruvitamkur the monarchy followed a policy not two divergent from the earlier centralised regime. Therefore in this region there were gradual reduction of powers and control of traditional *janmies* or landlords and a relative strengthening of the position of upper strata of tenants.

In Malabar region, a more radical disturbance of agrarian structure occurred, leading to relative deprivation among some, particularly those who benefitted by the Mysorean rule. This led to further intensification of internal contraditions in that society leading to frequent agrarian rebellions and revolts.

According to the terms of the treaty which the governments of Tiruvitamkur and Kochi entered into with the British, Tiruvitamkur had to pay a sum of Rs 8,00,000 per annum from 1805 onwards, while Kochi which formed less than one-fifth of the area of Tiruvitamkur had to pay Rs 2,70,000 per annum from 1809 onwards. In Malabar a new scheme for collection of land revenue was devised. According to this, 20 per cent of the gross produce was regarded as sufficient to meet cultivational expenses. Out of the rest, 33.3 per cent was to be the cultivator's share, 26.7 per cent that of the *Janmies* and 40 per cent' of the colonial state. The annual assessment for Malabar, where the extent of cultivated land was much less than in Tiruvitamkur, was Rs.16,00,000 from 1800 onwards. The intensification of extraction under direct colonial administration is evident from this differential rates. Apart from the general characteristics of the system, the failures of the English to sufficiently respect time-tested privileges and traditions led to two formidable revolts, one led by Pazhassy Kerala Varma of Kottayam and the other by Kurichias. Both these revolts were suppressed militarily within the framework of the collector's regime.

Tiruvitamkur and Kochi remained under constant threat of direct colonial intervention. An agent of the colonial government called the Resident with vast amount of 'undefined' powers was attached to these governments from 1788 onwards. The interface between the Resident and local groups tended to alienate some of the latter leading to the revolt of Veluthampi and Paliath Achan in 1809. After the suppression of these revolts, there was a phase of 'disguised' intervention in the internal affairs of these two states'(ibid, pp. 349 351).

In pursuance of the colonial policy of extracting revenue from land and taxes and tolls from other trades, the colonial period witnessed marked changes in the coastal economic and social organisation of production. Some of the notable changes brought about in the economic front was the large scale reclamation of water bodies (*Kayal*) for agriculture (paddy cultivation), which was noted in chapter six. Another outstanding development in the coastal zones made during this period was the construction of a large number of navigation canals connecting the three regions of erstwhile Malabar, Cochin and Travancore.

In the Malabar area, the first known excavation of an artificial canal is the Sultan's canal, 3.8 km long completed in 1766. This was constructed by Ali Raja of Cannanore, to connect Peruvamba and the Kuppam (Thaliparamba) rivers. In 1822, a canal from Kavvayi to Chetwai was investigated but was subsequently dropped. In 1845, the Elathur-Kallai canal, the Tanur canal connecting Tirur and Kadalundy rivers, the Ponnani-Chetwai canal and the Badagara canal were taken up. All these were completed by 1848.

In the Cochin area, the Karanchira-Trichur canal was constructed during 1840-1850. The Edathuruthy canal was deepened to provide through traffic between Ernakulam and Trichur. The Thevara-Kundannur canal connecting Ernakulam and Tripunithura was also completed during this period. In 1870, the Munayam-Thiruvanchikulam canal was constructed. The Edappalli and Parur canals were constructed by one of the Namboodiri chieftains of the period to provide water-ways to Thiruvanchikulam.

In the Travancore area, the importance of connecting the backwaters by canals in order to provide, as far as practicable, an uninterrupted water route from Trivandrum to the northern districts was first appreciated and acted upon during 1860-1880. The first canal opened was the one from Channamkara at the southern tip of Anjengo lake to the landing place, Vallakadavu, at Trivandrum, and this made communication possible from Trivandrum to Varkala cliff. The second was the Paravoor canal connecting the backwaters of Edava and Paravoor. The canal connecting the Ashtamudi and the Paravoor lakes was also taken up by about the same time. Then came the Chavara canal connecting the Ashtamudi lake with the Panmana backwaters. Another canal of importance formed was the commercial canal, connecting the Alleppey town with the backwaters. In the meantime a scheme for connecting Trivandrum with Kanyakumari and thereby extending the water way to the extreme south of India was conceived. The Anantha-Victoria-Marthandam (AVM) canal, an extension of the T.S. canal from Trivandrum to the south formed the beginning of this system and this was started in 1860. The reach between Poovar and Colachel was completed by 1867. The Varkala barrier canal was intended to complete the water communication system from Trivandrum to the railway station of Beypore (Chaliyam) in the north, a distance of 367 km. It consisted of open cuttings and two tunnels. The former was open to traffic in 1877 and the latter in 1880. Work on the Alleppey-Shertallai canal was begun in 1912, but was subsequently given up.

Thus starting from 1766, the chain of canals was completed by 1880, having thorough traffic between Malabar and Travancore through Cochin. This route came to be known as the west coast canal (Public Works Department, 1974, pp. 73-74). The extent of these canals in different stretches has been given in table 5.34. During this period and thereafter, many cross canals and link canals connecting the midland towns and industrial centres were also constructed (ibid, p.74). The canal system thus proved as the most effective infrastructure for transporting the natural resources and products of the Kerala coast to the international markets. The products transported included spices, coir, timber, etc.

Another major development in the coastal zone of Kerala during the colonial period was the construction of the railway network. Logan reported that the railway line from Madras was extended from Podanur to Calicut on 12th May 1862. From 1861 to 1888, the terminus was at Chaliyam on the southern bank of the Beypore river. The line was extended to Calicut in 1888. In 1901 and the two following years it was opened for traffic as far as Badagara, Tellicherry and Cannanore respectively and in 1907 it reached Mangalore. In 1927, a new line from Shornur to Nilambur via Angadipuram - a distance of 41.5 miles was opened.

The introduction of a railway into Travancore was taken up by the Travancore Government in 1876. Through communication from Quilon to Tirunelvely was opened on the 26th of November 1904. The Cochin-Shornur railway line was opened for goods traffic on the 2nd of June 1902 and for passenger traffic on the 16th of July 1902. The extension of the railway from Quilon to Trivandrum was completed in 1917 and the line opened for traffic on the 1st of January, 1918. In 1926 the extension of this line from the Trivandrum beach to Thampanur in the heart of the town was sanctioned and in 1931 the line was opened for traffic.

The railway line from Shornur to Cochin was opened for goods traffic on the 2nd of June 1902 and for passenger traffic on the 16th of July 1902. The line was extended from Ernakulam to Cochin Harbour Terminus on the 1st of July 1940 with the opening of the bridge head and pier (Gazetteer Department, 1989, pp. 631-634). The railways, like the canal system helped the state in linking it with the ports and thereby to the international markets. The railways also helped in the transport of fish, especially cured fish from the coast to domestic and international markets. It may be noted here that the colonial administration and their appendages in the various parts of the state had taken pains to encourage those activities and industries which suited the colonial economic interests by way of land revenue and from merchandise exports. Interestingly, the colonial period witnessed the suppression of such activities of the coast, like manufacturing of salt, cloth, etc. and promotion of their import by which the colonial powers sought to maximise the colonial profits. Portraying this policy of the British, with respect to fisheries, a major coastal activity of Kerala, the Department of Fisheries, Government of Kerala, states that 'the administration of the British was one of disregard of the social welfare of especially those communities that were involved with natural produce. The various fishing harbours became silted up by default, lack of attention and maintenance. This was hastened by soil erosion as a result of the fast deforestation. The boat building industry for which Kerala was famous dwindled very much. When the world marched fast in the flush of new technological knowledge, the fishing industry stood untouched by all these. As the world bypassed Kerala, its fishing industry stood still and on the eve of independence, it was primordial in comparison ..." (Department of Fisheries, 1969, p.5).

During the colonial period, some efforts were made for the protection of the coast. The first attempt to protect a vulnerable coastal section in Kerala was made in 1890 at Chilakkoor near Varkala. Here the T.S. canal runs through tunnel, close to the sea. The work was mainly intended to safeguard the canal from a possible attack of the sea. The protection was offered by a set of 18 rubble groynes, normal to the coast. The effect of this has been found to be satisfactory. The next effort was made in 1910, twenty years later, when a sea wall was constructed for a length of three km to protect the Vypeen foreshore, north of the Cochin outlet. This seawall is known as the 'Campbell Bund'. This consisted of a sand core with a casing of laterite and granite rubble in cement mortar. This has helped to protect the strip of land behind it.

During 1936-1949, sea walls for a length of eight km were constructed at Manassery, Pallithodu and Nayarambalam. These subsequently failed. The fourth attempt was made in 1940, at Tellicherry to protect the lower portion of the laterite cliffs by toe revetments (Public Works Department, 1974, p. 94).

It may not be out of context to note here that the social/cultural organisations of the coast were also moulded to play second fiddle to this colonial policy of extraction of surplus from foreign lands. Referring to this instrument of appropriation of wealth by the British, Tharakan notes that 'using his powers, Munro (British Resident) struck effectively at the social premises of possible Nayar revolts in Tiruvitamkur by taking over the properties of all important temples of the state. Following the footsteps of his predecessor, Macaulay, Munro also sought to create a group within these two states who are friendly to colonial dispensation, by encouraging active interaction between the Anglican Missionaries and the non-Roman Catholic

Syrians. Though in the sense of a formal break between the Syrians and Anglicans, this policy immediately had a set back; it along with his active patronising of evangelical activities of Christian missionaries in general 'helped to wean at least a small group to be uncritically in favour of the colonial dispensation' (Tharakan 1999, p.351, words in parenthesis added). The Department of Fisheries also corroborates this view. It noted that 'with the advent of western domination in India from the 16th century the fisherfolk was subjected to heavy proselytisation' (Department of Fisheries, 1969, p.5).

In summing up this section it is noted here that the colonial period witnessed the successful moulding of the coastal economy and culture to subserve the interests of the colonial masters.

8.4. Post-colonial period

This period consists of the period after independence, marking the era of planned development of the country. This period witnessed the implementation of nine five year plans, the objective of these plans being to promote the socio-economic development of the coast by tapping the natural, human and physical resources of the coast. Such an approach was considered vital for national economic development and for national integration. National integration legitimately and truely called for regional development. The coastal zones were considered vital for the development of the country. This was particularly true of Kerala, with the majority of the population residing in the coastal districts and the coastal plains being the hub of the state's economy. Naturally, the focus of the government's programmes for the economic development of the coast was centering on coastal activities like, fishing, agriculture, aquaculture, mining, manufacturing (coir, cashew, chemicals, etc.), tourism, transport, etc.

The economic development achieved by these sectors is state's contemporary economic history. Part of the achievements made by these sectors and their critical problems have been noted in chapter six. A detailed examination of the development/management of those sectors in the post-colonial/post-independence period is not in the scheme of analysis of this study. Nor is it in the scheme of ICM proposed in the next chapter. Accordingly, the attempt in this section is only to look at the notable regulatory or protective measures introduced by the Government of Kerala, which incidentally are considered as coastal zone management measures in Kerala/India and in many general contexts. This approach to coastal zone management or to any management, i.e., the practice of referring exclusively to the regulatory part and excluding the more important synchronised development (use) of all economic and non-economic activities of the coast, is anathema to the concept and practice of ICM. The synchronised use of coastal resources is the crux of the issue of ICM in Kerala. This issue will be discussed in the next chapter. Here, the limited efforts for the regulation or protection of coastal resources and their use since independence are discussed. This is done in two sections: (1) pre-1991 period and (2) post-1991 period.

8.4.1. Pre-1991 period

This period covered the time span from 1947 to 1991, i.e., the period prior to the issuance of the Coastal Regulation Zone (CRZ) notification by the Government of India in 1991. As already noted, only the regulatory or protective measures taken during this period are discussed here. Such protective measures were a continuation or extension of the then existing shore protection works in the state.

A major programme for the protection of the vulnerable coastal zone was launched in 1959. The programme was designed by the Central Water and Power Research Station, Poona, based on model studies. It consisted of building a system of rubble groynes and sea wall. The groynes were 61 metres long spaced at 122 metre intervals. The seawall was given a top width of 1.2 metres and 2:1 slope on the seaside and 1:1 slope on the landside. Granite stones of size 80 to 140 dm^3 were used for the formation of groynes while for the seawall 20 to 40 dm^3 size stones were used. About 40 km length of the coast was thus protected by the groyne and seawall system.

In 1962 and 1963, the coast of the state was subjected to sea erosion on an unprecedented scale. The catastrophe was so widespread that many portions of the coast were simultaneously attacked by the sea. This forced the state and central Governments to seek the advice of some foreign experts to find out a lasting and economical solution to the problem. Accordingly the services of Mr. George M. Watts, of the U.S. Army Corps of Engineers was sought, who visited the state in 1963 and inspected the affected places during the month of October and November. As advised by him, the groynes were dispensed with and the seawalls were given flatter slope of 4:1 (instead of 2:1 as per the original design) on the seaside and the land-side slope was retained as 1:1. Armour stones of size 110 to 170 dm^3 covering a core made of 20 to 40 dm^3 size stones were suggested for the formation of sea walls. A total length of 35 km was protected adopting this modified design. Table 8.1 gives details of shore protection works completed till August 1973.

Table 8.1
Shore protection works completed till August 1973

S. No.	*Location*	*Period of construction*	*Type of construction*	*Other details***	
				Seawall length in km	*Groynes No.*
1.(a)	Padne Kadappuram (near Kasargode)	1964-65	seawall	0.300	–
(b)	Chandragiri river mouth	1965-68	seawall	0.150	–
2.	Azhikkal (Valapatnam river outlet)	1959-62	seawall and groynes	0.450	8
3.(a)	Cannanore (bluff zone)	1960-62	seawall	0.300	17
(b)	Cannanore	1960-62	seawall and groynes	1.780	–
(c)	Cannanore	1965-67	seawall	0.180	–
4.(a)	Thayyil	1960-64	seawall and groynes	1.200	5
(b)	Thayyil	1962-65	seawall	0.600	–
5.	Thottada	1967-68	seawall	0.350	–
6.	Dharmadom	1967-68	seawall	0.250	–
7.(a)	Tellicherry (bulff zone)	1959-62	seawall and groynes	1.900	2
(b)	Tellicherry (Chalil Gopalapetta area	1960-63	seawall and groynes	0.840	4
8.(a)	Thalayi	1963-66	seawall	0.210	–
(b)	Thalayi	1961-62	seawall and groynes	0.850	6
(c)	Thalayi	1965-68	seawall	1.000	–
9.	Mahe-Azheekal	1965-68	seawall	0.600	–
10.	Kollam beach	1962-63	seawall and groynes	0.850	1

(*contd.*)

(Table 8.1 contd.)

S. No.	Location	Period of construction	Type of construction	Other details	
				Seawall length in km	Groynes no.
11.(a)	Quilandy	1961-63	seawall and groynes	0.250	3
(b)	Quillandy	1965-67	seawall	2.450	–
12.	Calicut	1960-63	seawall and groynes	4.680	15
13.	Kallai (Kallai river mouth)	1964-65	seawall	0.500	–
14.	Beypore (Beypore river mouth)	1963	groynes	–	4
15.	Parappanangadi	1962-63	seawall and groynes	0.700	5
16.	Veliyangode	1963	seawall	0.100	–
17.	Nattika	1964-65	seawall	0.100	–
18.	Azhikode (Periyar river mouth)	1964-65	seawall	0.500	–
19.(a)	Vypeen (North of Cochin)	1956-63	seawall and groynes	8.200	–
(b)	Vypeen	1961-67	seawall	4.600	57
20.(a)	Chellanam (South of Cochin)	1954-63	seawall	14.460	114
(b)	Chellanam (South of Cochin)	1964-66	seawall (modify design)	1.600	–
21.	Campbell's bund (North of Cochin*)	1914	seawall and groynes	2.150	12
22.	Anthakaranazhi	1960-63	groynes	–	19
23.(a)	Purakkad	1964	artificial nourishment	0.500	–
(b)	Purakkad	1964-67	seawall (modified design)	3.000	–
24.	Thottapally-Purakkad	1959-64	seawall and groynes	5.000	33

(contd.)

(Table 8.1 contd.)

S. No.	Location	Period of construction	Type of construction	Other details	
				Seawall length in km	Groynes No.
25.	Pallana	1958	seawall and groynes	1.000	9
26.	Thrikunnapuzha and Arattupuzha	1960-62	groynes	–	45
27.	Alapad	1960	groynes	–	31
28.	Cheriyazheekal	1960	seawall and groynes	2.000	21
29.	Panmana	1960	groynes	2.800	–
30.	Chavara	1962	seawall	–	9
31.(a)	Neendakara	1966-68	seawall and groynes	1.180	–
(b)	Sakthikulangara Thirumullavaram	1960	seawall	2.500	37
32.	Odayam	1964	groynes	0.600	–
33.	Chilakkare*	1890	groynes	–	19
34.	Varkala to Poonthura	1959-62	seawall and groynes	8.00C	69
35.	Kovalam	1964	beach fill	–	–
36.	Alapadu Kuzhithira to Parayakadavu	1972	seawall	0.304	–
37.	Neendakara	1972	seawall	1.185	–
38.	North of Paravur Bar in Mayyanad panchayat	1972	seawall	0.450	–
39.	Front of the Factory, Chavara	1972	seawall	0.500	–
40.	South of Narakkal	1972	seawall	1.060	–
41.	Sinkarathope at Poonthura (Chirayinkil)	1972-73	seawall	0.335	–
42.	Sinkarathope to Muthalapozhi (Poonthura in Chirayinkil)	1972-73	seawall	1.463	

(contd.)

(Table 8.1 contd.)

S. No.	Location	Period of construction	Type of construction	Other details	
				Seawall length in km	Groynes no.
43.	Thankassery	1972-73	seawall	0.400	–
44.	Near IRE Factory Chavara	1972-73	seawall	1.000	–
45.	Neendakara	1972-73	seawall	0.625	–
46.	South of Chetwai	1972-73	seawall	0.240	–
47.	Azhikode in Kodungalloor taluk	1972-73	seawall	0.300	–
48.	Elathur river mouth	1973	seawall	0.335	–
49.	Cheriyamangad to Valiyamangad in Quilandy	1973	seawall	0.210	–
50.	Manjeswaram	1973	seawall	0.275	–
51.	Kizhunna beach in Edakkad	1973	seawall	0.285	–
52.	Manayad in Tellicherry	1973	seawall	0.616	–
53.	Dharmadom	1973	seawall	0.080	–
	Total length	–	–	88.343	–

* Work completed before independence..

** Construction of groynes was stopped from 1964. From 1965 onwards construction of seawalls was as per modified design wherever seawalls were recommended.

Source: Public Works Department, 1974, pp. 97-98.

The shore protection programme was continued during the Fifth Five Year Plan. The Fifth Five Year Plan document of Kerala noted that 'there are at present 114 schemes and a programme for Beach Erosion Studies is under implementation: ... As Government of India has accepted the state's ten year programme for coastal protection costing Rs 40 crores, an outlay of Rs 2 crores is proposed for Fifth Plan' (State Planning Board, 1973, p. 220).

Referring to the anti-sea erosion programmes of the Sixth Five Year Plan, the Sixth Five Year Plan document of Kerala noted that 'the state has a coastline of 560 km and a large part of this coast line is subjected to severe erosion at several places during the monsoons. Loss of valuable lands and buildings along the coast line and loss of human life have been the outcome. Sometimes the coastline is subjected to tidal overflow and adjoining low lying lands are submerged resulting in damages to paddy lands and dwelling units and pollution of inland freshwater lakes' (State Planning Board, 1980, p.80). It also states that 'a coastline of nearly 320 km is subjected to erosion which requires protection. Of this 250 km of coastline is subjected to severe erosion. Till March 1980, an amount of about Rs 40 crores has been spent to protect 227 km of coastline. Work is in progress over a length of 40 km. Out of the 227 km of coastline protected, about 70 km requires reformation and repairs. There are 87 spill-over schemes' (ibid, p. 80).

The Sixth Plan document further notes that 'the length of the coastline requiring protection within the next decade is about 95 km. Besides, the beaches adjacent to the inlet need stabilisation and areas of head-land bay formation need protection. The outlay for anti-sea erosion made in the plan is for the above mentioned works. The physical targets envisaged during this period is the protection of a length of 85 km of coastline and reformation and repairs of about 70 km seawall already constructed' (ibid, p. 80). The plan proposed an outlay of Rs 15.50 crores by the state and Rs 31 crores as special assistance by the centre since sea erosion has to be viewed as a national calamity (ibid, p. 80).

The anti-sea erosion programmes of the state were continued during the Seventh Five Year Plan. The draft Seventh Five Year Plan report noted that 'under anti-sea erosion,priority is given for completing the phase-1 programme which consists of construction of new seawalls of 18.3 km and reforming 46.6 km of old damaged seawalls ... Phase-1 is to be completed by the third year of the Seventh Plan; phase-II which consists of construction of seawalls for 143 km of beaches and reforming of 10 km of damaged seawalls is proposed to be taken up on completion of phase-1' (State Planning Board, 1984, p.107).

The plan document makes it further clear that 'for anti-sea erosion scheme central loan assistance in the ratio of 2:1 (central and state respectively) is provided to the state Government since the Fourth Plan period for implementation. This has been modified from 1983-84 onwards in respect of reformation of damaged seawalls. Only assistance in the ratio of 1:1 is provided for this, whereas for the new works old ratio is retained ... As phase-II programme is only a continuation of phase-I programme, assistance of Government of India may be continued in the same pattern as existing now. The programme of Anti-Sea Erosion Works during 1984-85 includes 70 schemes spilled over from 1983-84 with balance commitment of Rs 1295 lakhs for their completion and 64 new works with an estimated cost of Rs 1734 lakhs ... The physical target is construction of 11 kms of new seawalls and 13 kms of reformation works' (ibid, p.107). This plan also spoke of the need for extensive dredging for protecting the fishing harbours and minor ports. It noted that 'a number of coastal inlets in Kerala are to be developed as fishing harbours and minor ports. Large quantity (3.5 million m^3) of beach material is to be dredged by capital dredging and maintenance dredging in the near future' (ibid, p.107).

It appears from the above plan reports that anti-sea erosion/shore-protection work was the main component of the coastal management programmes of the state in the pre-1991 period. Nonetheless, the operation of a couple of regulations introduced during this period and which seeks to regulate, restrict or prohibit fishing in the coast, or control the coastal land/water use, and prevent conflict in the coastal zone may be noted here. These include:

1. The Indian Fisheries (Madras Amendment) Act, 1929, applicable to the Malabar district of the erstwhile Madras Presidency.
2. The Travancore-Cochin Fisheries Act of 1950 applicable to the former Travancore-Cochin region.
3. The State Act for the Prevention and Control of Water Pollution.
4. The Kerala Land-Use Control notification of 1974.
5. The Kerala Marine Fishing Regulation Act 1980.

8.4.2. Post-1991 period

This period witnessed the continuation of the anti-sea erosion programmes and the initiation of certain measures to regulate, restrict or prohibit certain activities in demarkated zones of the coast following the publication of Coastal Regulation Zone (CRZ) notification by Government of India in 1991 and the Supreme Court judgement on cases relating to the non-implementation and violation of CRZ rules in the country. The measures taken during this period were largely in response to the global demand and compulsions. The attempt in this section is to outline the anti-sea erosion programmes and the regulatory proposals and measures taken by the Government of Kerala following the CRZ notification.

8.4.2.1. Anti-sea erosion programmes since 1991

The anti-sea erosion programme was a continuing programme launched in 1959 and carried forward in each successive five year plan. During the Eighth Five Year Plan (1992-97), the major emphasis under this programme was on the 'completion of the spill-over works as per phase-I programme, completion of 30 per cent of the phase-II programme, stabilisation of inlets and protection of coasts adjacent to inlets, carrying out coastal erosion studies, data collection and evaluation and experimental studies' (State Planning Board, 1991, p.60). This was a centrally assisted programme and central assistance upto 66.66 per cent of the cost of works is available for original seawall construction and 50 per cent of the cost of work for the reformation of old seawall. The total outlay proposed for this work during the Eighth Plan was Rs 7950 lakhs, of which Rs 4650 lakhs were central support and Rs 3300 lakhs, state's share' (ibid, p. 60).

The total coastal line identified as vulnerable for erosion during Eighth Pian was 448.226 km. Out of this, till the end of March 1996, the construction of 347.6 km of new seawall have been reported as completed (State Planning Board, 1997, p. 81).

It is interesting to note here that in the Ninth Five Year Plan, for the first time, the anti-sea ercsion programme of the state has been stylised as 'coastal zone management'. The plan document states that 'during the Ninth Plan coastal zone management will receive a different perspective for eco-preservation in the light of the Coastal Zone Regulations now ordered by Government of India. A multi-pronged approach integrating engineering, eco-restoration, regulatory and management measures will have to be followed for the Coastal Zone Management. The outlay envisaged is for the protection of the sea coast on the above lines based on the broad guidelines issued for the purpose' (ibid, p. 81). The total outlay proposed for the programme during this plan was Rs 5000 lakhs.

8.4.2.2. Coastal Regulation Zone notification of 1991

In view of the dynamic changes taking place in the Indian coasts and the growing threat of environmental pollution, the Government of India issued the Gazette notification [No.S.Q.114(E)] declaring the Coastal Regulation Zones of India on 19.2.1991. It noted that 'in exercise of the powers conferred by clause (d) of sub-rule (3) of Rule 5 of the Environment (protection) Rules, 1986, and all other powers vesting in its behalf, the Central Government hereby declares the coastal stretches of seas, bays, estuaries, creeks, rivers and backwaters which are influenced by tidal action (in the land ward side) upto 500 metres from the High Tide Line (HTL) and the land between the Low Tide Line (LTL) and the HTL as Coastal Regulation Zone, and imposes with effect from the date of this notification, the following restrictions on the setting up and expansion of industries, operations or processes, etc. in the said Coastal Regulation Zone (CRZ)' (Ministry of Environment and Forests, 1991). For the purpose of this notification, the High Tide Line means the line on the land upto which the highest water line reaches during the spring tide. The High Tide Line shall be demarcated uniformly in all parts of the country by the demarcating authority or authorities authorised by the Central Government in accordance with the general guidelines issued in this regard by the Government.

It further stated that the distance from the High Tide Line shall apply to both sides in the case of rivers, creeks and backwaters and may be modified on a case by case basis for reasons to be recorded while preparing the coastal zone management plans. However, this distance shall not be less than 100 metres or the width of the creek,river, or backwater whichever is less. The distance upto which development along rivers, creeks, and backwaters is to be regulated shall be governed by the distance upto which the tidal effect of sea is experienced in rivers, creeks and backwaters as the case may be, and should be clearly identified in the Coastal Zone Management Plans.

8.4.2.2.1. Prohibited activities

As per the 1991 notifications and the various amendments, the following activities are declared as prohibited within the Coastal Regulation Zone, namely:

(1) Setting up of new industries and expansion of existing industries, except those directly related to water front or directly needing foreshore facilities;

(2) Manufacture or handling or storage or disposal of hazardous substances as specified in the notifications of the Government of India in the Ministry of Environment and Forests, No.S.O.594(E) dated 28th July 1989, S.O. 966(E) dated 27th November 1989 and GSR 1037(E) dated 5th December 1989, except transfer of hazardous substances from ships to ports, terminals and refineries and vice versa in the port areas, provided that (i) facilities for storage of the petroleum products as specified in Annexure III appended to the notification, may

be permitted within the said Zone in areas not classified as CRZ-1, (ii) subject to implementation of safety regulations including guidelines issued by the Oil Safety Directorate in the Government of India, Ministry of Petroleum and Natural Gas and guidelines issued by the Ministry of Environment and Forests and subject to such further terms and conditions for implementation of ameleorative and restorative measures in relation to the environment as may be stipulated: (a) by the Government of India in the Ministry of Environment and Forests to facilities for storage that are wholly or partially outside the existing port limits of existing ports and to the dedicated storage facilities which form part of an integrated project, irrespective of falling within or outside the port limits, and (b) by the Government of India in the Ministry of Environment and Forests or the Ministry of Surface Transport to facilities for storage that are within the existing port limits of existing ports;

(3) Setting up and expansion of fish processing units including warehousing (excluding hatchery and natural fish drying in permitted areas); provided that existing fish processing units for modernisation purposes may utilize twenty five per cent additional plinth area required for additional equipment and pollution control measures only subject to existing Floor Space Index/Floor Area Ratio norms and subject to the condition that the additional plinth area shall not be towards seaward side of existing unit and also subject to the approval of State Pollution Control Board or Pollution Control Committee;

(4) Setting up and expansion of units/mechanism for disposal of waste and effluents, except facilities required for discharging treated effluents into the water course with approval under the Water (Prevention and Control of Pollution) Act, 1974, and except for storm water drains;

(5) Discharge of untreated wastes and effluents from industries, cities or towns and other human settlements. Schemes shall be implemented by the concerned authorities for phasing out the existing practices, if any, within a reasonable time period not exceeding three years from the date of this notification;

(6) Dumping of city or town waste for the purpose of land filling or otherwise; the existing practice, if any, shall be phased out within a reasonable time not exceeding three years from the date of this notification;

(7) Dumping of ash or any wastes from thermal power stations;

(8) Land reclamation, bunding or disturbing the natural course of seawater except those required for construction of ports, harbours, jetties, wharves, quays, slip ways, bridges and sea-links and for other facilities that are essential for activities permissible under the notification or for control of coastal erosion and maintenance or clearing of water ways, channels and ports or for prevention of sand bars or for tidal regulators, storm water drains or for structures for prevention of salinity ingress and sweet water recharge;

(9) Mining of sands, rocks and other substrata materials, except those rare minerals not available outside the CRZ areas; provided that in the Union Territory of Andaman and Nicobar Islands, mining of sands may be permitted by the Committee which shall be constituted by the Lieutenant Governor of the Andaman and Nicobar Islands consisting of Chief Secretary, Secretary, Department of Environment; Secretary, Department of Water Resources; and Secretary, Public Works Department. Committee may permit mining of sand from non-degraded areas for construction purposes from selected sites, in a regulated manner on a case to case basis, for a period upto the 30th September 2000. The quantity of sand mined shall not exceed the essential requirements for completion of construction works including dwelling units, shops in respect, of current year and 2000-2001 annual plans. The permission for mining of sand may be given on the basis of a mining plan from such sites and in such quantity which shall not have adverse impacts on the environment;

(10) Harvesting or drawal of groundwater and construction of mechanisms thereafter within 200 m of HTL. In the 200 m to 500 m zone, it shall be permitted only when done manually through ordinary wells for drinking, horticulture, agriculture and fisheries; provided that drawal of groundwater is permitted, where no other source of water is available and when done manually through ordinary wells or hand pumps, for drinking and domestic purposes, in the zones between 50 to 200 m from High Tide Line in case of seas, bays and estuaries and within 200 m or the CRZ, whichever is less, from High Tide Line in case of rivers, creeks and backwaters subject to such restrictions as may be deemed necessary, in areas

affected by seawater intrusion, that may be imposed by an authority designated by State Government/Union Territory Administration;

(11) Construction activities in ecologically sensitive areas as specified in Annexure-1 of the notification;

(12) Any construction activity between the Low Tide Line and High Tide Line except facilities for carrying treated effluents and waste water discharges into the sea, facilities for carrying seawater for cooling purposes, oil, gas and similar pipelines and facilities essential for activities permitted under the notification; and

(13) Dressing or altering of sand dunes, hills, natural features including landscape changes for beautification, recreational and other such purposes, except as permissible under the notification.

8.4.2.2.2. Regulation of permissible activities

All other activities, except those prohibited as noted above are regulated by the following norms.

(1) Clearance shall be given for any activity within the Coastal Regulation Zone only if it requires water front and foreshore facilities.

(2) The following activities will require environmental clearance from the Ministry of Environment and Forests, Government of India, namely:

(i) Construction activities related to defence requirement for which foreshore facilities are essential (e.g., slip ways, jetties, etc.), except for classified operational component of defence projects for which a separate procedure shall be followed (Residential buildings, office buildings, hospital complexes, workshops shall not come within the definition of operational requirements except in very special cases and hence shall not normally be permitted in the CRZ);

(ii) Operational constructions for ports and harbours and light houses and constructions for activities such as jetties, wharves, quays and slip ways; provided that for expansion or modernisation of existing ports and harbours including fishing harbours, operational constructions for ports and harbours and construction of jetties, wharves, quays, slipways, single point mooring and single buoy mooring and for reclamation for facilities essential for operational requirements of ports and harbours in areas within the existing port limits, except the areas classified as category CRZ-1(1), shall require environmental clearance from Government of India in the Ministry of Surface Transport, which shall take decision on these activities on the basis of Environment Impact Assessment Report; provided further that reclamation for commercial purposes such as shopping and housing complexes, hotels and entertainment activities shall not be permissible;

(iii) Exploration and extraction of oil and natural gas and all associated activities and facilities thereto;

(iv) Thermal power plants (only foreshore facilities for transport of raw materials, facilities for intake of cooling water and outfall or discharge of treated waste water/cooling water); and

(v) All other activities with investment exceeding rupees five crores except those activities which are to be regulated by the concerned authorities at the State/Union Territory level in accordance with the provisions of paragraph 6, sub-paragraph (2) of Annexure-1 of the notification.

8.4.2.2.3. Preparation of coastal zone management plans

The CRZ notification prescribed that the coastal states and union territory administrations shall prepare, within a period of one year from the date of this notification, coastal zone management plans identifying and classifying the CRZ area within their respective territories in accordance with the guidelines given in Annexure-1 and II of the notification and obtain approval (with or without modifications) of the Central Government in the Ministry of Environment and Forests.

Within the framework of such approved plans, all development activities within the CRZ other than those noted in the above two sub-sections shall be regulated by the state governments, union territory administration or the local authority as the case may be in accordance with the guidelines for coastal area classification and development and the guidelines for development of beach resorts/ hotels in the designated areas of CRZ as given in Annexures I and II of the notification.

The notification also made it clear that in the interim period till the Coastal Zone Management Plans are prepared and approved, all development and activities within the CRZ shall not violate the provisions of this notification. It also prescribed that state governments and union territory administrations shall ensure adherence to these regulations and violations, if any, shall be subjected to the provisions of the Environment (protection) Act, 1986.

The Central Government had also notified the procedure for monitoring and enforcement of the CRZ rules. It noted that 'the Ministry of Environment and Forests and the Governments of State or Union Territory and such other authorities at the State or Union Territory levels, as may be designated for this purpose, shall be responsible for monitoring and enforcement of the provisions of this notification within their respective jurisdictions' (Ministry of Environment and Forests, 2001).

8.4.2.2.4. Coastal area classification and development regulation

For regulating development activities, the coastal stretches within 500 metres High Tide Line on the landward side are classified into four categories and the norms for their use prescribed. Table 8.2 gives the details of CRZ classification and norms of regulation as given in Annexure-1 of the notification.

Guidelines for the development of beach resorts/hotels in the designated areas of CRZ-III for temporary occupation of tourists/visitors, with prior approval of the Ministry of Environment and Forests were also issued as Annexure-2 of the CRZ notification.

It noted that construction of beach resorts/hotels with prior approval of MEF in the designated areas of CRZ-III for temporary occupation of tourists/visitors shall be subject to the following conditions.

1. The project proponents shall not undertake any construction (including temporary constructions and fencing or such other barriers) within 200 metres (in the landward side) from the High Tide Line and within the area between the Low Tide and High Tide Line; live fencing and barbed wire fencing with vegetative cover may be allowed around private properties subject to the condition that such fencing shall in no way hamper public access to the beach; no flattening of sand dunes shall be carried out; no permanent structures for sports facilities shall be

Table 8.2
Details of CRZ classification and norms of control

CRZ category	*Description of the zones*	*Norms for regulation*
CRZ I	(1) Areas that are ecologically sensitive and important, such as national parks/marine parks, sanctuaries, reserve forests, wild life habitats, mangroves, coral/coral reefs, areas close to breeding and spawning grounds of fish and other marine life, areas of outstanding natural beauty/historical/heritage areas, areas rich in genetic diversity, areas likely to be inundated due to rise in sea level, consequent upon global warming and such other areas as may be declared by the Central Government or the concerned authorities at the State/Union Territory level from time to time.	No new construction shall be permitted within 500 metres of the High Tide Line. No construction activity, except those listed under item 12 of prohibited activities above will be permitted between the Low, fide Line and the High Tide Line; provided that construction of dispensaries, schools, public rain shelters, community toilets, bridges, roads, jetties, water supply, drainage, sewage which are required for traditional inhabitants of the Sunderbans Biosphere reserve area, West Bengal, may be permitted, on a case to case basis, by an authority designated by the State Government.
	(2) Area between the Low Tide Line and the High Tide Line	

(contd.)

(Table 8.2 contd.)

CRZ category	*Description of the zones*	*Norms for regulation*
CRZ-II	The areas that have already been developed upto or close to the shore line. For this purpose, 'Developed' area is referred to as that area within the municipal limits or in other legally designated urban areas which is already substantially built up and which has been provided with drainage and approach roads and other infrastructure facilities, such as water supply and sewage mains.	(1) Buildings shall be permitted only on the landward side of the existing road (or roads approved in the coastal zone management plan of the area) or on the landward side of existing authorised structures. Buildings permitted on the landward side of the existing and proposed roads/existing authorised structures, shall be subject to the existing local Town and Country Planning Regulations including the existing norms of Floor Space Index/Floor Area Ratio. Provided that no permission for construction of buildings shall be given on landward side of any new roads (except roads approved in the coastal zone management plan) which are constructed on the seaward side of an existing road. (2) Reconstruction of the authorised buildings to be permitted subject to the existing FSI/FAR norms and without change in the existing use. (3) The design and construction of buildings shall be consistent with the surrounding landscape and local architectural style.
CRZ-III	Areas that are relatively undisturbed and those which do not belong to either category I or II. These will include coastal zone in the rural areas (developed and under developed) and also areas within municipal limits or in other legally designated urban areas which are not substantially built up.	(1) The area upto 200 metres from the High Tide Line is to be earmarked as 'No Development Zone'. No construction shall be permitted within this zone except for repairs of existing authorised structures not exceeding existing FSI, existing plinth area and existing density and for permissible activities under the notification including facilities essential for such activities. An authority designated by the State Government/ Union Territory Administration may permit construction of facilities for water supply, drainage and sewage for requirements of local inhabitants. However, the following uses may be permissible in this zone–agriculture, horticulture, gardens, pastures, parks, play fields, forestry and salt manufacture from sea water.

(contd.)

(Table 8.2 contd.)

CRZ category	Description of the zones	Norms for regulation
		(2) Development of vacant plots between 200 and 500 metres of High Tide Line in designated areas of CRZ III with prior approval of Ministry of Environment and Forests (MEF) permitted for construction of hotels/beach resorts for temporary occupation of tourists/visitors subject to the conditions as stipulated in the guidelines.
		(3) Construction/reconstruction of dwelling units between 200 and 500 metres of the High Tide Line permitted so long it is within the ambit of traditional rights and customary uses such as existing fishing villages and goathans. Building permission for such construction/ reconstruction will be subject to the conditions that the total number of dwelling units shall not be more than twice the number of existing units; total covered area on all floors shall not exceed 33 per cent of the plot size; the overall height of construction shall not exceed nine metres and construction shall not be more than two floors (ground floor plus one floor). Construction is allowed for permissible activities under the notification including facilities essential for such activities. An authority designated by State Government/ Union Territory Administration may permit construction of public rain shelters, community toilets, water supply, drainage, sewage, roads and bridges. The said authority may also permit construction of schools and dispensaries for local inhabitants of the area, for those panchayats, the major part of which falls within CRZ, if no other area is available for construction of such facilities.
		(4) Reconstruction/alterations of an existing authorised building permitted subject to (1) to (3) above.

(contd.)

(Table 8.2 contd.)

CRZ category	*Description of the zones*	*Norms for regulation*
		Andaman Nicobar Islands
CRZ IV	Coastal stretches in the Andaman and Nicobar, Lakshadweep and small islands, except those designated as CRZ-I, CRZ-II or CRZ-III.	(1) No new construction of buildings shall be permitted within 200 metres of HTL. (2) The buildings between 200 and 500 metres from the High Tide Line shall not have more than two floors (ground floor and first floor), the total covered area on all floors shall not be more than 50 per cent of the plot size and the total height of construction shall not exceed nine metres; (3) The design and construction of buildings shall be consistent with the surrounding landscape and local architectural style; (4) Corals from the beaches and coastal waters shall not be used for construction and other purposes. Sand may be used from the beaches and coastal waters, only for construction purpose upto the 30th day of September 2000 and thereafter it shall not be used for construction and other purposes. (5) Dredging and underwater blasting in and around coral formation shall not be permitted; and (6) However, in some of the islands, coastal stretches may also be classified into categories CRZ-I or II or III, with the prior aporoval of Ministry of Environment and Forests and in such designated stretches, the appropriate regulations given for respective categories shall apply.

(contd.)

(Table 8.2 contd.)

CRZ category	*Description of the zones*	*Norms for regulation*
		Lakshadweep and small islands
		(1) For permitting construction of buildings, the distance from the High Tide Line shall be decided depending on the size of the islands. This shall be laid down for each island in consultation with the experts and with approval of the Ministry of Environment and Forests, keeping in view the land use requirements for specific purposes vis-a-vis local conditions including hydrological aspects, erosion and ecological sensitivity;
		(2) The buildings within 500 metres from HTL shall not have more than two floors (ground floor and first floor), the total covered area on all floors shall not be more than 50 per cent of the plot size and the total height of construction shall not exceed nine meters;
		(3) The design and construction of buildings shall be consistent with the surrounding landscape and local architectural style;
		(4) Corals and sand from the beaches and coastal waters shall not be used for construction and other purposes;
		(5) Dredging and underwater blasting in and around coral formation shall not be permitted; and
		(6) However, in some of the islands, coastal stretches may also be classified into categories CRZ-I or II or III with prior approval of Ministry of Environment and Forests and in such designated stretches, the appropriate regulations given for respective categories shall apply.

Source: Ministry of Environment and Forest, 2003.

permitted except construction of goal posts, net posts and lamp posts; construction of basements may be allowed subject to the condition that no objection certificate is obtained from the State Ground Water Authority to the effect that such construction will not adversely affect free flow of ground water in that area. The State Ground Water Authority shall take into consideration the guidelines issued by the Central Government before granting such no objection certificate. It is noted that though no construction is allowed in the 'no development zone', for the purpose of calculation of FSI, the area of entire plot including 50 per cent of the portion which falls within the no development zone shall be taken into account;

2. The total plot size shall not be less than 0.4 hectares and the total covered area on all floors shall not exceed 33 per cent of the plot size, i.e., the FSI shall not exceed 0.33. The open area shall be suitably land scaped with appropriate vegetal cover;
3. The construction shall be consistent with the surrounding landscape and local architectural style;
4. The overall height of construction upto highest ridge of the roof, shall not exceed nine meters and the construction shall not be more than two floors (ground floor plus one upper floor);
5. Ground Water shall not be tapped within 200 m of the HTL; within the 200 metre - 500 metre zone, it can be tapped only with the concurrence of the Central/State Ground Water Board;
6. Extraction of sand, levelling or digging of sandy stretches except for structural foundation of building or swimming pool shall not be permitted within 500 metres of the High Tide Line;
7. The quality of treated effluents, solid wastes, emissions and noise levels, etc. from the project area must confirm to the standards laid down by the competent authorities including the Central/State Pollution Control Board and under the Environment (Protection) Act, 1986;
8. Necessary arrangements for the treatment of effluents and solid wastes must be made. It must be ensured that the untreated effluents and solid wastes are not discharged into the water or on the beach; and no effluent/solid waste shall be discharged on the beach;

9. To allow public access to the beach, at least a gap of 20 metres width shall be provided between any two hotels/beach resorts; and in no case shall gaps be more than 500 metres apart;
10. If the project involves diversion of forest land for non-forest purposes, clearance as required under the Forest Conservation) Act, 1980 shall be obtained. The requirements of other Central and State laws as applicable to the project shall be met with; and
11. Approval of the State/Union Territory Tourism Department shall be obtained.

The Guidelines also made it clear that in ecologically sensitive areas (such as marine parks, mangroves, coral reefs, breeding and spawning grounds of fish, wild life habitats and such other areas as may be notified by the Central/State Government/Union Territories), construction of beach resorts/hotels shall not be permitted.

8.4.2.3. Coastal zone management plan of Kerala

As already noted the Coastal Regulation Zone notification of the Government of India contemplates the preparation of a Coastal Zone Management Plan, identifying and classifying the CRZ areas within the respective territories in accordance with the guidelines given in the notification and obtain approval (with or without modifications) of the Central Government in the Ministry of Environment and Forests. As per the Supreme Court of India decision dated 18.4.1996 on the non-implementation and violation of CRZ notification in the country, states were directed to file the state plans by 30.6.1996. The Central Government was also directed to finalise and approve the State regulation plans, with or without modifications within three months thereafter.

The Coastal Zone Management Plan of Kerala State (COZMAP) was prepared by the Centre for Earth Science Studies (CESS), Thiruvananthapuram, for the Department of Science, Technology and Environment of Government of Kerala during December 1995. This plan was considered by the Ministry of Environment and Forests in its meeting held on 19.6.1996 and recommended for approval subject to certain conditions. The Coastal Zone Management plan of Kerala was subsequently approved by the Ministry of Environment and Forests on 27th September 1996.

The highlights of the Coastal Zone Management Plan of Kerala as prepared by the CESS in 1995 are as follows:

1. The Coastal Zone Management plans (maps) for Kerala are prepared in 1:12,500 scale. The maps are spread over 109 plates. A 500 m regulation zone is identified along the sea coast and a 50 m (or width of the creek whichever is less) regulation zone along the water bodies affected by tide. The 50 m limit in the case of creek, river or backwater was later extended to include 100 m as set in the original notification of CRZ and as required by the Supreme Court in 1996.
2. The High Water Line (which is used synonymous to the High Tide Line as required in the notification) is measured with respect to the reference pillars and along the coast and demarcated in the CZM plans.
3. The HWL/HTL at the water bodies are fixed along the land-water boundary as obtained from the Survey of India topo sheets, which are updated/corrected using the satellite imageries of 1991. Further modifications observed in the boundaries were required to be taken into account while implementing the regulations and plans at such locations to be prepared in micro-scale using the guidelines given in the CZM plans.
4. The limited mangrove eco-system areas that occur in Ernakularn, Malappuram, Kozhikode, Kannur and Kasargode districts are classified as CRZ-I.
5. The filtration ponds, mangroves and tidal marshes are fish breeding centres and these areas are vulnerable to inundation due to sea level rise. Their adjoining 50 m are classified as CRZ-I.
6. Along the sea coast there are some laterite cliffs (Vizhinjam, Varkala, Paravoor, Bekal, etc.) which are areas of 'outstanding beauty'. Such sections are vulnerable to slumping, which will be accelerated by the sea level rise. At these locations a 50 m zone within the 500 m regulation zone is earmarked as CRZ-I.
7. All the urban areas (municipalities and corporations) and 'legally designated' urban areas (Thumba) are classified as CRZ-II.

Rest of the area in the regulation zone is categorised under CRZ-III.

8. It is estimated that Kerala has 88.006 sq.km. (including area between HTL and LTL) of CRZ-I, 68.748 sq.km. of CRZ-II and 341.825 sq.km of CRZ-III.
9. It is also estimated that a 13 km stretch of NH 47 (in Kottayam, Alappuzha and Ernakulam districts) and 27 km of NH 17 (in Malappuram, Kozhikode, Kannur and Kasargode districts) passes through the Coastal Regulation Zone. Moreover, a well developed PWD/Panchayat road network is available and it is better in southern Kerala than in the north.
10. Several areas of outstanding natural beauty, heritage/archaeological areas come under the Coastal Regulation Zone.

Table 8.3 gives details of area under CRZ in Kerala as contained in the CZM plan of Kerala.

Table 8.3
Area under CRZ in Kerala

S. No.	*Category*	*Area*
1.	Total Length of coastal at HTL	571.001 km
2.	Total area between HTL and LTL	30.787 sq. km
3.	Total area under CRZ-III	341.825 sq. km
4.	Total area under CRZ-II	68.748 sq. km
5.	Total area under CRZ-I	88.006 sq. km
6.	Total Area under CRZ	498.579 sq. km

Source: Baba, *et al.* 1995, p.76.

The district-wise and zone-wise distribution of the coastal areas of Kerala is given in table 8.4.

The extent of area of different categories of regulation zones in the coastal districts of Kerala is given in appendix 8.1.

The final report of the CESS titled as 'Coastal Zone Management Plan of Kerala' released in 1998 gives details of the area under various land use categories in the CRZ of all coastal panchayats, municipalities and corporations of the state. The land use pattern of the CRZ in the state is discussed in Volume I of the report, subtitled as 'coastal land use and resources'. The major land use categories considered in this volume are given in table 8.5.

Table 8.4
District-wise and zone-wise distribution of coastal stretches of Kerala

S. No.	*District*	*Coastal stretches in*		
		CRZ-I	*CRZ-II*	*CRZ-III*
1.	Thiruvananthapuram	Selected locations of historical/archaeological importance and areas of outstanding natural beauty of Anjengo Fort, Papanasam-Varkala, Edava, Kappil; laterite cliffs in Pozhiyur-Pulinkudi, Kovalam, Shangumugham, Veli, Puvar South, Kottukal, Vettukad.	Thiruvananthapuram Corporation, Varkala Municipality	Pozhiyur-Pulinkudi, Vizhinjam-Beemapalii, Valiathura-Veli, Thumba-Puthenthura, Channakara-Parumathura, Mudalapozhi-Anjengo, Kadakkavur-Chilakkoor, Vettur-Edava.
2.	Kollam	The historical, heritage or beautiful areas of Pozhikkara, Mundakkal (Johnapuram), Thirumullavaram, Palliyamthuruth, Neendakara, Karunagappally, Thangassery.	Kollam and Paravur Municipalities	Kappil-Mayyanad, Thenni-Asramam,Nedungolam-Pilakkad, Thangassery-Neendakara, Kuppanabhagam-Uliyakovil, Neendakara-Kovilthottam, Kanjaveli-Munrothuruthu, Perinad-Kumbalam, Panmana-Alumkadavu, Mullikkala-Kallribhagom, Thekkekara-Pazhayur

(contd.)

(Table 8.4 contd.)

S. No.	District	Coastal stretches in		
		CRZ-I	CRZ-II	CRZ-III
3.	Alappuzha	Selected area of Thaikkal-Kadappuram, Anthakaranazhi-Chellanam, Pallipuram-Puchakkal, Panavalli-Vaduthala, Kulasekharamangalam-Puthodu, Arthungal-Ambalapuzha	Kayamkulam, Alappuzha and Cherthala municipalities	Al appad-Tharayilkadavu, Perumpally-Arattupuzha, Mangalamthura-Thottappally, Kuruttur Vandanam, Punnapra-Omanapuzha, Mararikulam-Ayramtal, Thaikkal-Kadapuram, Thanneermukkom-Pallipuram, Pallipuram-Puchakkal, Panavalli-Vaduthala, Kulasekharamangalam-Puthodu
4.	Kottayam	Vaikom lake side	-----	------
5.	Ernakulam	Selected historical or beautiful areas of Fort Cochin, Mattancherry, Chennamangalam, Parur and Cherai; land adjoining filtration ponds, on the banks of Kottapuzha and Kathapuzha; kayals around Manasseri, Panangad and Kumbalam islands, and Kundannur, Puthuvaipu, Vypeen and Mangalavanam, Chellanam-Kumbalangi, Kannamali-Palluruthi, Arur-Nettur, Thoppumpadi-Murukkumpadam, Kundannur-Elamkulam, Elamkunnapuzha-Njarakkal, Pachalam-Pizhala, Nayarambalam-Kuzhipilli	Cochin corporation, Tripunithura and Parur municipalities	Chellanam-Kumbalam No. 1, Kannamali-Palluruthi, Arur-Nettur,Peramballi-Kandanadu, Thoppinpadi-Murukkumpadan Elankunnapuzha-Njarakkal, Pachalam-Pizhala, Nayarambalam-Kuzhipilli, Varapuzha-Kottuvalli, Iyyampilli-Pallipuram, Chennamangalam- Kaitaram

(contd.)

(Table 8.4 contd.)

S. No.	District	Coastal stretches in		
		CRZ-I	CRZ-II	CRZ-III
6.	Thrissur	Munambam, land adjoining filtration ponds at Chombalthodu, North-East of Chettuvayi, Munambam-Vakadappuram, Chapra, Pattay - akadu-Perinjom, Chervu-Arippalam, Manalur-Mullasseri	Kodungallur and Chavakkad municipalities	Munambam-Vakadappuram, Vadakkupuram-Chapra, Pattyakadu-Perinjom, Chervu-Arippalam, Panaparambu-Chandrappini, Edamuttorn-Nattika, Edathuruthi-Kizhupillikara, Thalikulam-Vadanapalii, Engandiyur-Aditirutti, Manalur-Mullasseri, Mada-Tiruvetta, Elakkazhiyur-Edakkara, Veliyangod-Kappirikkad.
7.	Malappuram	Parasseri-Niramaruttur	Ponnani and Tirur municipalities	Puthiya Ponnani-Kottathara, Purathur-Padiyam, Parasseri-Niramaruthur, Kalatkadapuram-Ullanam, Pottingal-Ariyallur.
8.	Kozhikode	Kuthirakada, Mangad-Kollam, Chemencheri-Quilandy	Kozhikode corporation and Badagara municipality	Vattikunnu-Chaliyam, Velimuk-Thuzhi-Palam, Karuvanthiruthi-Panniyamkara, Ramanattukara-Kadal, Kallayi-Kacheri, Olavanna-Iringallur, Mannankadavu-Perumana, West Hill-Elattur, Thalakulattur-Kadalur, Ichchanur-Annasseril, Mannamangalam-Kadalur, Mangad-Kollam, Thuvakkad-Mannankavu, Vanmugam-Ayinikad, Kodakkad-Turayur, Iringal-Badagara, Mattungal-Mahe.

(contd.)

(Table 8.4 contd.)

S. No.	District	Coastal stretches in		
		CRZ-I	*CRZ-II*	*CRZ-III*
9.	Kannur	Thalassery Fort and mangrove system adjacent to Eranjoli; Edannur-Eranjholi, Dharmadam-Eddakkad, Kavumbhagam-Vadakumpad, Palliyamoola-Azhikkal, Valapattanam-Narath, Pazhyangadi-Thekkumpad, Pattuvam-Kuppam.	Thalassery, Kannur and Payyannur municipalities .	Onchiyam-Putiyamambram, Edannur-Eranjholi, Iringannur-Menapram, Dharmadom-Edakkad, Kavumbhagom-Vadakkumpad, Adikadalayi-Chalad, Kizhunna-Kizhathalli, Palliyamoola-Azhikkal, Valapattanam-Narath, Puthiyangadi-Ettikulam, Mattul South-Mattul North, Kalliasseri-Kuttikol, Pattyam-Kodallur, Cuttad-Vadakkumpad, Pazhayangadi-Thekkumpad, Pattuvam-Kuppam.
10.	Kasargode	Bekal	Kanhangad and Kasargode municipalities	Kavayi-Vedelekkad, Ayitti-Orumukku, Taikadappuram, Ozhinjavalappu, Cheruvathur-Ramanchira, Punchavi-Kanhangad, Kalavayal-Agasarahole,Thrikunnad-Chimmanad, Nellikkunnu-Kumbala, Arkadi-Uppala gate, Manjeshwar-Karnataka border.

Source: File //A: Intercoast. htm 8/15/01.

Table 8.5
Land use categories identified by CESS in the CZMP of Kerala

S. No	Land use categories: Major head	Land use categories: Minor head
1.	Forest	1. Reserve forest
		2. Social forestry
2.	Agricultural land	1. Paddy
		2. Coconut palms
		3. Mixed vegetation
		4. Waste land
		5. Others
3.	Water bodies	1. Estuary
		2. Rivers/stream
		3. Freshwater body
4.	Wetlands	1. Beach
		2. Tidal flat with mangroves
		3. Tidal flat without mangroves
		4. Filtration ponds
		5. Marsh/swamp (non-tidal)
5.	Built up land	1. Clustered settlement
		2. Settlement with vegetation
		3. Industrial area
		4. Other major establishments
6.	Transportation	1. Road (High way)
		2. Other roads
		3. Railway
7.	Coastal structures	1. Harbour/port
		2. Fish landing centres
		3. Seawall/groynes
8.	Other features	1. Rocky cliff
		2. Laterite cliff
		3. Sand dune areas with vegetation
		4. Sand dune areas without vegetation
		5. Reclaimed areas
		6. Mining areas
		7. Waste dumping, drains and effluent discharge sites
		8. Vacant/open land
		9. Areas of outstanding natural beauty
		10. Historical areas
		11. Heritage area

Source: Baba, *et. al,* 1998, pp.4-10.

The land use pattern of the CRZ at the district level worked out by CESS is given in appendix 6.2.

8.4.2.3.1. Coastal zone management plan of Iravipuram panchayat

The final report of the CESS carrying the CZMP of Kerala also contains a section (Volume II) on 'Coastal Zone Management of Iravipuram Panchayat', located in Kollam district. Part three of this volume gives details of the panchayat in relation to land form, soil, water availability, transport network, population, marine related activities, land use, nearshore waters and inland water bodies. Part four of this section identified and discussed the coastal zone management issues and management plans of the panchayat. The 'Major problems of concern' noted in the Report are:

(a) Pressure for settlement in the regulated zones and the desire of the fisherman to live close to the sea
(b) Coastal erosion and damages to property and seawalls especially in Thekkumbhagom, A and B wards
(c) Scarcity of potable water
(d) Siltation in the canal and kayal and the need for dredging
(e) Pollution of the canal due to the dumping of domestic wastes by people living close to the canal
(f) Need for developing 'free' beach into public recreational centres
(g) Shortage of boat launching areas and landing centres
(h) Land reclamation
(i) Desire of the people in the coastal wards to have better infrastructure facilities
(j) The need to incorporate the local community's requirements into the CZM plan.

The 'main' elements (recommendations) of the draft ICZM for the coastal wards of Eravipuram panchayat noted by CESS (Baba *et.al.*, p.102) are;

(a) Double storeyed and multistoreyed settlement colonies with necessary infrastructure facilities be established in Thekkevila, C and Vadakkumbhagom wards to accommodate future settlement needs of coastal communities
(b) Rehabilitate the people staying close to the canal (between the canal road and the canal) to these new colonies
(c) Passages across the canal be provided close to the settlement colonies for easy access to the beach
(d) Water supply to the coastal areas be strengthened through the Kerala Water Authority's proposed World Bank aided scheme

(e) Desilt and clean the canal so that country crafts and fishing boats can reach the new settlement colonies

(f) Protection measures be strengthened through appropriate measures only along the eroding sector of the shore line. Maintain the frontal beach along the stable sectors through proper management

(g) Improve domestic recreational facilities by maintaining the cleanliness of the wide beach on the northern sector.

8.4.2.3.2. District coastal management plan for the ashtamudi estuary

The proposal for a district coastal management plan for the Ashtamudi lake in Kollam district was made by ASR Ltd., a consultant company of New Zealand and sponsored by the Asia Development Assistance Facility of the New Zealand Official Development Assistance Programme in 2000. The project is directed and led by ASR Ltd. The project profile states that 'it will be carried out with the participation of CESS and CDS, Kerala Government, district administration, local panchayats surrounding the Ashtamudi Estuary, NGOS, social groups and other local stakeholders will also be involved in the project' (Black and Baba, 2000). It also notes that the proposal, was 'prepared in consultation with the STEC Chairman, State Planning Board Secretary, Kollam District Collector, 21 Grama Panchayats surrounding the Ashtamudi Estuary, District Tourism Promotion Council, CESS, CIFFS and other stakeholders' (ibid, p.4).

Referring to the background of this project, the note states that 'the shores of Ashtamudi estuary are home to thousands of Kollam district's population. Their future - be it poverty or sustainable prosperity - will be significantly affected by decisions made today concerning the estuary's resources and its sustainable management. There are no localised 'District Coastal Management Plans' which can guide the future of the estuary and its surrounds. Thus there was a need to 'fill the gaps' in meso-scale and create a localised 'management plan 'for the Ashtamudi Estuary' (ibid, p.4).

Pointing to the objectives of the project, the ASR Ltd. Consultants noted that 'taking account of the Ashtamudi Estuary's deteriorating conditions and the potentially far-reaching implications of catastrophic degradation, the assignment aims primarily to provide the basis for and development of a District Coastal Management Plan for Sustainable Management of Ashtamudi Estuary; thereby enhancing the sustainability of the water resources' (ibid, p.4).

The complementary objectives noted are:

(a) Provide the skills and information needed to build counterpart technical capacity for environmental monitoring and management, thereby enhancing institutional capacity;

(b) Provide training for local NGOs, community groups and government representatives in estuarine behaviour, environmental management, technical, socio-economic and gender issues to empower and enable them to have input to the coastal management plan;

(c) Facilitate community participation in the sustainable environmental management of the estuary;

(d) Enhance women's access to public decision making forums through their active role in a Steering Committee for coastal management;

(e) Provide effective communication as a means to share results so that the environmental education for the NGOs and community representatives can be passed onto the local people, thereby increasing the environmental awareness and natural resources management skills of the community.

The key outputs planned by the project are the preparation of (1) residence time and flushing map, (2) social use map, (3) estuarine use and resource map, (4) bathymetric chart, (5) numerical model, (6) water level and current map, (7) video films, and (8) report (ibid, p. 9).

The project also aims at capacity building including (1) improving the knowledge base for effective decision making, (2) enhancing research, (3) enhancing management practices and techniques, (4) enhancing the transfer of coastal/estuarine resource management and decision making to users and (5) strengthening the institutional framework for coastal management (ibid, p.10).

8.4.2.3.3. Integrated coastal zone management plan for the panchayats of Alappad, Panmana, Chavara and Neendakara in Kollam district

The Centre for Earth Science Studies (CESS) is reported to have undertaken the task of drawing up an integrated coastal zone management plan (ICZMP) for the panchayats of Alappad, Panmana, Chavara and Neendakara in Kollam district (CESS, 2001, p. 3).

The report states that 'the vulnerable nature of the coastal ecosystems, high density of population and the stress on resources were the prime driving force behind developing an ICZM for these panchayats. Unhygienic slum conditions, scarcity of safe drinking water and shrinkage of open space make life miserable. During monsoon, people live under the threat of high levels of coastal erosion. Seawalls are constructed all along the coast. Experience has shown that these walls are of limited use as the beach is lost ... The commercial mining of heavy minerals, started in 1920's, is a subject of major conflict between the local communities and the industry. Another major concern is the possible impact of human health due to high radiation exposure levels from heavy minerals. Comprehensive assessment of the scenario has shown that an approach based on Integrated Coastal Zone Management (ICZM) giving due consideration to different stakeholders only can ensure sustainable development' (ibid, p. 3).

The methodology followed for preparing this plan was outlined in the report. It states that 'physico-environmental data were generated for each panchayat with a view, to create conservation and environmental appraisal maps. Conservation area map identifies such sites as water bodies, mangroves, religious/cultural institutions, etc. Environmental appraisal map brings out the dominant environmental issues and their spatial extent including coastal erosion, reclamation and mining sites. These two maps along with the socio-economic information of each panchayat are synthesised in a GIS environment for generating ICZMP. Sites for different activities like mining, settlement, development, agriculture, coastal protection, aquaculture, etc. are identified based on social and demographic requirements and environmental feasibility. In view of the importance of having settlement zones in hazard free areas and protecting sensitive coastal ecosystems, a special approach based on various factors like conservation zones, coastal erosion, availability of space and concentration of heavy minerals was evolved. A limited resettlement is proposed for future mining areas' (ibid, p. 3).

The above exercise, the report states, is done after a 'discriminative evaluation of problems and prospects of the area are carried out concurrently in close association with experts and specialists in various disciplines' (ibid, p. 3).

Highlighting the features of the ICZMP for Alappad panchayat, the report notes 'Alappad with a total land area of 7.3 sq.km. is a modified barrier island with a high density of settlement (>600 houses per sq.km.). Placer mineral deposits are a major resource and the dominant land use of the region is coconut with settlement. Land form exerts perceptible high control over the development pattern of the panchayat. A 'Coast Conservation Zone' of 50 m or the area seaward of the main road is proposed for Alappad. Mangrove zones, estuaries, lagoons, and canals are the habitats for conservation in this panchayat. It has many temples, sacred groves, schools and hospitals which are also to be conserved. Areas having more than 50 per cent heavy mineral concentration are kept as conservation zone. Marshes, swamps, water bodies and areas affected by erosion are categorised as hot spots. Zones for development, settlement, mangrove propagation and potential mining, cultural and tourism development, fish processing and aquaculture are earmarked' (ibid, p.3).

It is also suggested in this report that 'this ICZMP can be proposed to replace the CRZ regulation for the area with the approval of the Ministry of Environment and Forests, Government of India' (ibid, p.3).

So also 'artificial surf reefs and such other offensive protection schemes which can help rebuilding of beaches in this land starved panchayat, are recommended as a viable option for the protection of highly eroding coastal sectors' (ibid, p.3).

Finally it is stated that 'the ICZMP is slated for further discussion at different levels with various stake holders before implementation with support from funding agencies. Experts in different fields like fisheries, town planning, etc. are being consulted for projectisation of action plans. Linkage with development programmes of the local bodies will provide the key in institutional arrangements for ICZMP implementation. This is a worthy model that can be emulated in the coastal areas of the country[1] (ibid, p.3).

8.4.2.3.4. Integrated coastal zone management plan of Thrissur district

An integrated coastal zone management plan for Thrissur district was being prepared by the Kerala Sasthra Sahitya Parishat. The Parishat had conducted village level studies during the last couple of years to identify the coastal issues and to evolve management programmes. It had also organised a couple of seminars to discuss the coastal issues and to evolve consensus on management solutions. The focus of this effort seems to be on preparing a framework for planning for coastal hygiene and employment generation.

8.4.2.3.5.Coastal zone management committee of Kerala

Considering the responsibility of the Department of Science, Technology and Environment (STED) as the nodal agency designated for monitoring and enforcement of the provisions of the CRZ notification, and with a view to enhancing the capability of STED in advising Government on issues related to CZM, Government of Kerala constituted the state level CZM Committee in November 1997 [G.O. (M.S.) No.I33/97/STED, dtd. , Thiruvananthapuram, 28th November 1997]. The Committee was vested with the power to coordinate, monitor, and implement coastal zone management regulations. The Committee has the Chairman of the Science, Technology and Environment Committee (STEC) as its Chairman, Director of STED as convener and Directors of the Departments of Fisheries, Ports, Tourism, Industries and Panchayat and the Director of CESS as members.

The major responsibilities of the Committee (as per terms of reference) are the following.

1. To assess whether there is justification for locating the proposed project in the coastal zone.
2. To see that the project constructions and activities do not violate the provisions of Coastal Regulation Zone notification.
3. Considering the development needs of the state, whether there is any need for recommending any relaxation in Coastal Regulation Zone rules for specific projects.
4. To assess the EIA submitted with the proposal and to see that it covers all relevant environmental aspects and to recommend any further studies with respect to EIA.
5. To look into the merit of complaints with respect to environmental aspects of the Coastal Regulation Zone from the public or other organisations, and recommend necessary corrective steps, if needed.
6. To recommend projects for CRZ clearance by the Government.
7. To review post-implementation monitoring of the environmental parameters and recommend corrective measures, if needed.

8. To look into complaints on general violation of CRZ rules and recommend redressal, if needed and
9. To look into any other issues connected with the management of Coastal Regulation Zone.

8.4.2.4. Coastal zone management plan of Kerala—A critique

The Coastal Zone Management Plan (map) of Kerala prepared by CESS in 1995 may be considered as the starting point of a new strategy for ICM in Kerala. It may be considered as the first attempt to demarcate and regulate coastal land/resource use as per the CRZ notification of 1991. Its primary aim was to identify the CRZ of Kerala. This has been acknowledged by the CESS in its first report on 'Coastal Zone Management Plan of Kerala' (Baba, *et.al.* 1995). It noted that 'the main objective of the work is to identify the Coastal Regulation Zone with its boundaries and categories' (ibid, p. 1).

The final report of the CESS carrying the same title also make this point clear. This report notes that 'in accordance with the notification, and as instructed by the Government of Kerala through Department of Science, Technology and Environment, CESS has prepared the Coastal Zone Management Plan maps for Kerala and was submitted in December 1995. As per the Government instructions, modified plans were also submitted in August 1996 and September 1996. In the present study, i.e., in the second phase of the project, a detailed inventory of present land use and resources in the panchayat/municipalities and corporations having either a sea frontage or bordering a tidal river/creek/estuary are made ... This study is expected to turn out to be a forerunner in identifying critical areas and evolving their management strategies, with an ultimate goal of achieving the sustainable development of the coastal zone' (Baba, *et.al.* 1998, p. 3).

Notwithstanding the above admission by CESS, and the inclusion of a 'model' of a management plan for the Iravipuram Grama Panchayat in Kollam district, the concept of ICZM and its practice in Kerala seems to be simply dithering in the realm of academic/technical studies, consultancy, etc. This is evident from the protracted and piecemeal efforts for the preparation of an ICZM plan for Kerala. The pioneering efforts initiated by CESS at the state level during 1995-98 seems to be dissipated by fragmented efforts at local/regional level carried out since then.

The delay/failure in bringing out a comprehensive plan for ICM in Kerala conforming to the standards/criteria of a master plan seems to be the result of limited academic/scientific inputs and the lack of social/political commitment to promote ICZM for sustainable development of the coast in Kerala. The lack of political commitment has been amply alleged by the Kerala Swathanthra Matsyathozhilali Federation in 1996 (Trivandrum District Fishermen's Union, November 1996, p. 2). The Federation has gone to the extent of alleging that the successive administrations in the state have soft pedalled the idea of ICM in the state with the explicit objective of favouring the hotel, tourism and construction lobby at the cost of local fishermen and other coastal people (ibid, p. 3). The rationale of this approach to ICM in Kerala buttressed in the 'unique' exemption arguments will be highlighted in the next chapter.

8.5. Summary

This chapter outlined the basic features of the approach to coastal zone management in Kerala during the pre-colonial, colonial and post-colonial periods. It noted that the pre-colonial period was a period of peaceful interaction with foreign traders with no major intra-use or inter-use conflicts in the coast.

The colonial period, on the other hand, witnessed the conquest of the coast by various European powers and the establishment of European 'industry and culture' in the coast. This period succeeded in moulding the coastal economy and society to subserve the interests of the colonial masters.

The post colonial period, which consisted of the pre-1991 period and the post-1991 period as two distinct phases, found that the focus of coastal zone management in the first phase was to promote coastal development as part of the national economic development programme. But considering this aspect of coastal development as part of the contemporary economic activity of the coast which was discussed in the last chapter, it focused on the coastal regulatory or protective measures taken by the Government during this period. The major coastal protection measure taken during this period was the anti-sea erosion/shore protection works. The existence of certain relevant rules/legislations concerning fisheries, land use, mineral mining, water pollution, etc. was also noted.

The post-1991 period marked the introduction of CRZ rules and the preparation of so-called ICZM plans for Kerala. A review of ICZM efforts made during this phase showed the deficiency of academic/scientific inputs and dearth of socio-political will as reflected in the absence of a master plan for ICZM in Kerala.

9

Coastal Zone Management in Kerala—The Political Economy of Sustainable Development

9.1. Introduction

The ultimate objective of ICZM in Kerala is to promote sustainable development of the coast. The realisation of this goal, however, requires the understanding and application of the principles and methods of ICZM or the strategies and techniques (programmes) of ICZM. The essential technique of ICZM consists of the preparation of a master plan with clear statement of objectives, strategies and programmes for implementation. The plan should be integrated vertically, horizontally and spatially. Successful implementation (practice) of the master plan requires financing, capacity building, building of constituency, ensuring people's participation, compliance, etc. A precautionary approach with provision for regular evaluation of the plan is also a precondition for the success of this plan. The attempt in this chapter is to first present the need for ICZM in Kerala, a general framework of objectives, strategies and techniques of ICZM and to examine these with respect to Kerala and to prescribe the need for financing, capacity building, building constituency and ensuring people's participation and compliance. The relevance of a precautionary approach is also suggested. The final section gives the summary of points discussed in this chapter.

9.2. Need for ICZM in Kerala

A review of coastal issues made in chapter seven has made the need for integrated coastal zone management in Kerala quite clear. The intra-use and inter-use conflicts prevailing in the coast and their impact on the ecological, economic and social sustainability of the coastal society were pointed out there. The coastal crisis will become quite apparent from a simple scanning of local daily newsppers, some of which have been listed in chapter seven. A close examination of the fortnightly, 'Alakal', a vernacular publication of the Kerala Swathanthra Matsyathozhilali Federation (Federation of Kerala Independent Fishermen's Unions, a major stakeholder's association of fishermen in Kerala coast), will also point to the severity of the crisis in the Kerala coast, especially in the southern parts of the coast.

One of the major crises (intra-use conflict) reported in the coast, all along, has been the conflict between traditional fishermen and mechanised boat operators. This problem has been resolved to some extent with the rigorous implementation of some of the provisions of the Kerala Marine Fishing Regulation Act of 1980, especially since 1988 when a seasonal ban on monsoon trawling began to be introduced in the coast. This intra-use conflict has, however, taken a new dimension with the traditional fishermen improving their craft with better equipment and power all leading to further intensification of fishing effort and greater pressure on the natural resource base. This crisis is now affecting the sustainability of the industry, ecologically, economically and socially. Another conflict of the intra-use form now brewing and threatening the sustainability of the fishery sector is the conflict between the local fishermen and migrant fishermen from other states. The resource crisis, economic crisis and social crisis, all seem to have forced the local fishermen to organise a protest blockade of Cochin Fishing Harbour, quite recently (City Express, Cochin, 4.10.2003).

Another intra-use conflict in the coast is the conflict between the fishermen and aquaculturists. Intensive aquaculture, although prohibited by the Supreme Court judgement of 11.12.1996, (Fishing Chimes, January, 1997, pp.15-16), is believed to be posing a serious threat to the coastal fisheries by destroying the coastal ecosystem. Large scale destruction of coastal mangroves affecting the breeding grounds of fish and the biodiversity of the coast are reported at Cannanore, Tellichery and other parts of the coast. Some of these have been noted in chapter seven. The impact of coastal aquaculture on water quality and the resultant spread of fish disease all over the coastal water bodies is now well documented and noted in chapter seven. The damage to the coastal economy caused by coastal aquaculture is summarised by Nandakumar and Muraleekrishna. They report that 'the rapid growth of extensive and semi-intensive aquafarms all over the country is affecting the social, economic and ecological aspects of the coasts and has led to people's protests and culminated in the Supreme Court order banning such activity' (Nandakumar and Muraleekrishna, 1998, p.65).

The inter-use conflicts threatening the sustainability of coastal zone activities in Kerala are umpteen. Some of these conflicts have been noted in chapter seven. It is worth recalling here that the conflicts between the mining, manufacturing (chemicals, fertilizers, etc.), tourism and power sectors are significant and they have reached flash points on several occasions in the past. The magnitude of the conflict was severe at Valiathura-Veli in Thiruvananthapuram, where the Travancore Titanium Product is wreaking havoc on the coastal fishermen; at Eloor-Udyogamandal-Ambalamugal belt where FACT, Travancore Cochin Chemicals (TCC), etc. are causing water pollution and mass fish kill; at Kovalam, Kumarakom, Kasargode (Bekal),etc. where tourism development is transgressing the rights of the local community; at Kayamkulam where the power project is set to displace local population and at Vypeen near Ernakulam where city development and land reclamation for Goshree project have ruined local inland (backwater) fishermen. The conflicts in the coast arising from sand mining, mineral extraction, land reclamation (urban development) municipal waste dumping, etc. are also severe and many of these have been noted in chapter seven.

The magnitude of the coastal crisis arising from intra-use conflicts, even after the introduction of CRZ notification in Kerala has been reported by Nandakumar and Muraleekrishna (Nandakumar and Muraleekrishna, 1998, *op. cit.*). Referring to the state of CRZ implementation and the nature of CRZ violations in Kerala, these authors noted that 'though Kerala has a well-prepared CZM plan (map), the state's interest is to relax the notification so as to accommodate the 'development' in the state. Different committees were constituted to dilute the present accepted plan, but to no avail, thanks to the resistance put up by people's groups' (ibid, p.56). Pinpointing the CRZ violations in Kerala, they observed that 'of the 377 violations recorded, a major chunk, 39.59 per cent is industrial related (sic) activity. Tourism constitutes about 28.12 per cent of the total, which concentrates in certain pockets like Kovalam, Bekal, Cherai, etc. Of this, 26 per cent is in the NDZ which is representative of what is happening to coastal Kerala. Within this category, out of 106 violations, 73 are 'new' constructions. Industrial activity includes large projects like the Naptha based power projects at Kannur and Vypeen and small scale units, both 'new' and 'polluting' ones. 11.67 per cent reclamation is reported which are (sic) taking place along the back water systems, from the waterbodies or in the mangrove marshes. Mining ... comes to 4.77 per cent. Infrastructure contributes 5.77 per cent, all within the NDZ. All the 21 infrastructure violations mapped are in the 'new' category and of these, three are in CRZ-1. This takes place in the beaches and in the river beds in the coastal stretch' (ibid, p. 56. Words in parentheses added). Table 9.1 gives details of CRZ violations reported by Nandakumar and Muraleekrishna.

Table 9.1
Details of CRZ violations in Kerala reported by Nandakumar and Muraleekrishna in 1998

Activity	*Number of violation in*	
	0-200 m (NDZ)	*200-500 m*
Tourism	99	7
Industry	146	3
Infrastructure	21	Not recorded
Reclamation	44	"
Aquaculture	39	"
Mining	18	"

Source: Nandakumar and Muraleekrishna, 1998, p. 56.

The above authors have also highlighted the threat to the coastal ecosystem expected to emerge from four mega projects in the state which are either operating or in the offing. The four projects noted are the Bekal Tourism Project at Kasargode, Enron Thermal Power Plant at Irinavu in Kannur district, Goshree Island Development project at Vypeen, near Ernakulam and the Seasin project, a naphtha based power plant at Vypeen (ibid, pp. 65-66). All these projects are in clear violation of the CRZ notification and without fulfilling the sustainability criteria. One may also anticipate significant impacts on the coastal zones of Ezhimala near Payyannur in Kannur district following the establishment of the Naval Academy at Ezhimala. More dangerous may be the impact of joint naval exercises off the coast of Kerala, the so called 'Malabar 2003', to the coast in the long run. The threat perception has been expressed by many including political party leaders (*The New Indian Express, Cochin*, 8.10.2003). It is not surprising in view of the historical experience that expansion of colonial trade was followed by strategic military control of administration. It is quite possible that the coastal zones of Kerala may again become the 'level playing ground' for global business interests.

The general threat to the coastal zone and the unsustainability of the development path that is being promoted in the country since 1991 is partly conveyed in a personal communication sent by Bittu Sehgal, member, Coastal Task Force to the additional secretary, Ministry of Environment and Forests in 1998. It noted that the 'land developers around the country are working overtime with state government officials to encash, literally, thousands of crores of rupees worth of public lands. There is a similar move afoot for forest lands and together the attack on coastal belts and forest belts will alter the survival ecology of over 300 million people within the next three to five years. To my mind, this represents a more serious threat than any other development project or anti-people initiatives ever initiated on the Indian subcontinent in the past 50 years. The net effect of both changes will be the creation of vast monocultures in both forest and coastal belts. In forests, teak, eucalyptus, acacias, wattle and poplars will clothe the commons. In coastal areas, salt marshes, wetlands, sand dunes, corals, mudflats and mangroves-which are the breeding grounds of fish upon which coastal communities survive-will be replaced by prawn farms, five star hotels, thermal plants, chemical and petroleum complexes, copper smelters, coastal highways and urban sprawl' (Quoted by Nandakumar and Muraleekrishna, 1998, pp. 7-8).

The need for an ICZM plan for the coast of India was unequivocally raised by the Supreme Court of India in 1996. Its judgement in the related case on 18.4.1996 directed the coastal states to submit the master plan for coastal zone management to the Central Government before 30.6.1996 and the Central Government to give detailed report on the approved plans to the Supreme Court before 30.9.1996. It is quite apparent, from the above and the nature of CZM efforts in the state as noted in the last chapter, that there is a clear need for a master plan approach to ICZM in Kerala.

9.3. The master plan

The overall purpose of an ICZM programme, as noted by Clark,is 'to provide for the best long-term sustainable use of the coastal natural resources and for perpetual maintenance of the most beneficial natural environment. In practical terms, the ICZM programme is intended to support the management goals and purposes ... by providing the basis for sustainable use of resources, bio-diversity preservation, protection against natural hazards, pollution control, enhancement of welfare, development of a sustainable economy and optimum multiple use' (Clark, 1996, p. 25). Referring to the Master Plan, Clark notes that 'the Master Plan is the framework of the ICZM programme. It identifies the options for human progress in the coastal area and recommends governmental and private actions to accomplish beneficial and sustainable change, change that is economically sound and socially just and that maintains the natural resource base. Depending upon the degree of comprehensiveness and multi-sectoral integration involved in the programme, the planning function of the programme may be either limited or extensive in subject and geographic coverage' (ibid, p. 55).

Clark further observes that "the strength of an ICZM comes from the Master Plan which is the operative basis for the programme. Its components reflect the need for the programme, the method and legislative basis, rule making, implementation strategy, staffing and financing, public participation, coastal zone boundaries, permits and environmental assessment, and other relevant aspects' (Clark, 1997, p. 210).

It is also noted by Clark that 'the particular form of any ICZM programme will depend upon the national and regional issues it is meant to address' (Clark, 1996, p. 25). It is, however, said that the essential purpose of the programme remains the same, i.e. to create an inter-agency coordination mechanism and regulatory programme to promote sustainable multiple use of renewable resources within the defined coastal area.

Clark makes the further observation that 'while each country's programme will be unique, there are several basic stages in the generation of an ICZM programme that will be found to be common to all, in one form or another' (ibid, p.26). These stages include (1) policy formulation, (2) strategy planning, (3) programme development and (4) implementation.

Referring to the typical stages in developing an ICM programme, Cicin-Sain and Knecht noted that 'as with any other public policy, the policy for integrated coastal management generally goes through a number of predictable stages of development, issue identification and assessment, programme preparation or formulation, formal adoption and funding, implementation, operation, and evaluation' (Cicin-Sain and Knecht, 1998, p. 58).

9.3.1. Preparation of the plan

A master plan for ICZM should be an integrated plan for the sustainable development of the coast. It should be a comprehensive plan for the all round development of various coastal activities to produce maximum social benefit. It is quite likely that the master plan will be a long term plan or a perspective plan with long term objectives, strategies and programmes. An Integrated Coastal Area Management plan (ICAM) according to FAO, 'should be viewed as long term, continuous and iterative'(Nadia,1998, p. 58). The major principles (sequences) noted by it are (a) inception, (b) performance review, (c) data collection and research, (d) analysis, (e) strategy formulation, (f) plan formulation/absorption in the sectoral plans, and (g) plan implementation (ibid, p. 60). Olsen, *et.al.*, have described the ICM process 'as a cycle with the same features of other institutional endeavours' (Olsen, *et.al.*, 1997, p. 160). This process begins by identifying and analysing the issues in the stretch of the coast in question, and then proceeds to set objectives, and prepares a plan of policies and actions. The next step is formalisation through law, decree or inter-agency agreement and the securing of funds for implementation of some selected set of actions. Policy implementation is the next step, in which procedures and actions planned in the policy formulation stage are made operational. Mechanisms for this may include public meetings, conflict resolution, and enforcement procedures, while actions for this span the building of physical infrastructure, the strengthening of institutions and dissemination of appropriate forms of resource use. The final step, said to be too often ignored or poorly executed, is formal evaluation. In this step, the results of the policy-making process are compared with the desired outcomes.

Table 9.2
Details of actions to be taken at every stage (step) of the ICM process

Step		Actions
1.	Issue identification and assessment	Rapid assessment of existing conditions, consult key stakeholders and identify priority issues
2.	Programme preparation	Select issues to be addressed and geographic focus. Conduct sustained public education programme. Define boundaries of management area. Define management objectives, strategies and actions. Carry out early implementation actions
3.	Formal adoption and funding	Adopt formal management plan and governance process, secure adequate funding for implementation
4.	Implementation	Construction/operation of infrastructure Promote compliance to regulations and agreements; implementation of sustainable development practices
5.	Evaluation	Evaluation of governance process and outcomes, reassess issues and strategies, select adjustments to plan and governance process

Source: Adapted from Olsen, *et al.* 1997, p.161.

Pernetta and Elder have noted that any coastal management programme or plan must have the following basic set of elements in order to be successful: (1) policies and goals, (2) plans, activities and projects, (3) institutional arrangements, (4) legislation, (5) training, (6) implementation plan, (7) public education, (8) monitoring and education (Pernetta and Elder, 1993). These writers have also put forward a seven stage iterative process of ICM which consists of the following: (1) problem definition, (2) assessment and analysis, (3) definition of issues and options, (4) formulation of management plans, (5) adoption of plans by all interested parties, (6) implementation, (7) monitoring and evaluation (ibid). The ICZM planning process as given by Chua (1993) is given in appendix 9.1.

The major components of a perspective master plan for ICZM are outlined in the following sub-sections.

9.3.1.1. Objectives of the plan

The master plan ought to make the objectives of the plan explicit. The over all objective of an ICZM programme as noted by Bower and Turner is to 'produce overtime a socially desirable mix of coastal zone products and services' (Bower and Turner, 1998, p.45). This mix is likely to change overtime with changing demands, changing knowledge and changing pressures.

The goal of ICM as put forward by the Joint Group of Experts on the Scientific Aspects of Environmental Protection (GESAMP) 'is to improve the quality of life of human community who depend on coastal resources while maintaining the biological diversity and productivity of coastal ecosystem' (Olsen, *et. al.*. 1997, p.157).

The general objectives of ICZM have been summarised by Clark thus: 'ICZM has its central purpose the organisation of an integrative, holistic system for ensuring sustainability of coastal resources, the perpetuation of biodiversity, socio-economic improvement and security from natural hazards. A major objective is to overcome the consequences of an uncoordinated sequence of coastal development projects, the result of which is resource degradation and fore-closure of future options for resource use. ICZM attempts to avoid these by broad multiple sector planning and integrated project development, by future.oriented resource analysis, and by applying the test of sustainability to each development initiative' (Clark, 1996, p.31). The 'typical objectives' of ICZM as put forward by Clark are the following:

1. *Maintain a high quality of coastal environment.* This is important because the coast is a major resource, providing commerce, food, recreation, spiritual refreshment and security. The need for ICZM arises because the productive state of the resource is not guaranteed to last longer and the coast could easily become polluted, ugly, and unproductive along much of its length if development safeguards are not applied.
2. *Protect species diversity.* Maintenance of a natural coastal environment, as provided by general regulatory means is considered favourable to most species. However, many species are believed to need the special protection and extra safeguards that can be provided by designating their habitats as nature reserves or natural parks.
3. *Conserve critical habitats.* Certain ecosystems are of such outstanding diversity and ecological value that they should be set aside and protected from alterations by development; these include many of the productive estuaries and islands along the

coast and their adjacent shorelands. Specific habitats of importance include mangrove forests, seagrass meadows, sand beaches and dunes, and certain tideflat habitats. Whenever these occur on the coast, they are presumed to be 'critical habitats', the loss of which would reduce productivity, species well-being and ecological balance.

4. *Enhance critical ecological processes.* Certain ecological processes are considered critical to the productivity of coastal ecosystems, for example, light penetration through the water (which can be blocked by excessive turbidity) and water circulation (which can be blocked by infils and cause ways). These critical processes need protection through regulation of development and appropriate planning.
5. *Control pollution.* Pollution from specific 'point-sources and from land run off can foul coastal habitats and waters causing human health problems as well as ecological disruption and reduced productivity. Accidental spills of oil and chemicals can be most damaging. Strong pollution control regulations are needed to keep the coast clean and productive.
6. *Identify critical lands.* Certain areas of the coast are said to have a special potential for recreation, housing, nature protection, economic development, and so forth. The objective of ICZM is to identify such lands for optimum development and for nature conservation.
7. *Protect against natural hazards.* Protection from hazards is an essential part of an ICZM programme.
8. *Restore damaged ecosystems.* Restoring the area and productivity of coastal ecosystem like the wetlands, mangroves and marshes is an important objective of ICZM.
9. *Encourage participation.* An important objective of ICZM is to create public awareness of the coast and of the need for coastal conservation.
10. *Provide planning guidance.* Another objective of ICZM is to provide guidelines and advice to planners to regulate coastal development.

The above objectives of ICZM may be condensed to three fundamental goals of achieving ecological sustainability, economic sustainability, and social (cultural) sustainability. These three goals correspond to the objectives of utilising and maintaining the natural, physical and social (cultural) capital. In sum, they aim at the sustained use of these resources by fulfilling the criteria of sustainable development, defined as 'development which meets the needs of the present without compromising the ability of future generations to meet their own needs' (WCED, 1987) or 'the management and the conservation of the natural resource base and the orientation of the technological and institutional change in such a manner as to ensure the attainment and continued satisfaction of human need for present and future generations' (Nadia, 1998, p.235) The ultimate objective of ICZM in Kerala should correspond to these goals of maximising the value of the coastal social product by maintaining suitable environmental, economic and social climate for sustainable development.

9.3.1.2. Strategy of the plan

The fundamental strategy of the plan is to link the policies and programmes with the objectives and to devise institutional mechanisms for implementing the programmes. Clark observes that it is the 'process that explores options and develops an optimum strategy for a management programme. It examines the facts, considers the issues, suggests possible solutions, and proposes legal and institutional arrangements' (Clark, 1996, p.28). It is also considered as 'the key step in the process of organising an integrated coastal zone management (ICZM) programme', where the 'policies and objectives are chosen and methods determined* (ibid, pp. 28-29).

Some of the common tools, which are strategically used by ICM planners and administrators, as noted by Clark are (a) permits for building, land clearing, etc. (b) environmental assessment (EA), (c) natural area protection (marine reserves), (d) zoning (use allocation), (e) set back (buffer areas) (f) environmental standards and guidelines, (g) infrastructure control, (h) land-use regulations, (i) land use planning, (j) watershed management, (k) pollution regulations, (l) community participation, (m) conflict resolution, (n) rural assessment, (o) remote sensing and geographic information systems (ibid, p. 26).

Olsen and others link the strategy with the governance of the coast which 'refers to the method of coastal management and includes the laws, institutions, policies and processes that affect how coastal resources are utilised and allocated[1] (Olsen, et al., 1997, p.158).

The governance process is the means by which we test and improve ICM strategies in order to move away from socially and environmentally unsustainable forms of development and towards more sustainable forms of development. Some of the strategies and principles that support the ICM process as noted by Olsen, *et.al.* include the following (Olsen, *et. al.*, 1997, p.158).

(1) work at both the national and local levels with strong linkages between levels (the two track approach),
(2) build programmes around issues that have been identified through a participatory process,
(3) build constituencies and political support for resource management through public education programmes,
(4) develop mechanisms for sustained learning on how to improve the efficiency and effectiveness of integrated coastal management,
(5) develop an open, participatory and democratic process, involving all stakeholders in planning and implementation,
(6) build capacity at the national, regional and local levels to practice integrated, community based management of coastal resources through training, learning by doing and cultivating host country colleagues who can forge long-term partnerships based on shared values.
(7) complete the loop between planning and implementation as quickly and frequently as possible, using small projects that demonstrate the effectiveness of innovative policies,
(8) adopt policies that lead to economically and ecologically sustainable and equitable resource management,
(9) strengthen or introduce mechanisms for cross-sectoral action,
(10) adopt an incremental, adaptive and long term approach to integrated coastal management, recognising that programmes undergo cycles of development, implementation and refinement, building on prior success and adapting and expanding to address new or more complex issues.

9.3.1.3. Implementation of the plan

As already noted, the strategy of the plan interlinks the objectives and the sequence of implementation of the policies and programmes by different layers of administration to produce the projected result over time. Accordingly, implementation of the master plan assumes great priority in integrated coastal zone management, just as in any other planned effort. It, however, remains to be noted here that implementation of the master plan with structural balances and integrations are vital for producing the anticipated results.

Structural balances are vital for the smooth implementation of the plan just as horizontal, vertical and lateral integration are needed to produce harmonic outcomes and maximum value to the society. The advantages of integration have been noted in chapter four.

Implementation of the master plan is usually done in stages, through annual plans and five year plans. It may be noted here that the global literature, which is quite critical of 'central planning' as practised in socialistic-communistic or democratic countries like India, did not make the duration of the plan explicit. It should, however, be apparent to the 'global' writers that the master plan is a long term plan which is implemented in stages, through annual plans and five year plans. This has been the practice in planned economies while planning 'for national economic development, with sectoral programmes and targets. This was the norm notwithstanding the new found charge by the ICZM writers that 'central planning' had failed in integrating 'sectoral' programmes.

The failure of planning with poor implementation and lack of integration has been frequently highlighted by many ICZM writers. Vallejo, for instance, notes that 'in the majority of countries, CZM has evolved in isolation from the mainstream of national development process, has not been integrated in national development plans and has not commended substantial institutional or financial commitment' (Vallejo, 1993, p. 164). It is also pointed out by Vallejo that 'coastal zone management and national development planning have evolved in parallel without benefitting from a cross-fertilization of knowledge, experience and expertise' (ibid, p. 172). The same writer is, however, confident that both types of planning are now 'going through a period of transition and adaptation to new and challenging demands' and 'it is not difficult to immediately perceive not only the urgent need for integration, but the large benefits that can be accrued from this 'marriage of experience', where both types of planning can complement each other and the results account for much more than the sum of the parts' (ibid, p. 172).

It is significant to note here that the global literature on ICZM is now quite categoric about the need for integrating and interlocking of the very many components of ICZM, such as vertical and horizontal integration, integration of disciplines, building of partnerships, capacity, constituency and institutions and financing. Indeed, the success of ICZM programmes is deemed to depend on the synchronised working of the various CZM components.

Referring to the critical importance of implementation in ICZM programmes, Chua notes that 'implementation of projects and programmes is a critical stage of ICZM. In the past, many ICZM initiatives ... were not able to proceed beyond the planning phase. There are many reasons for this. ICZM programmes developed outside the government planning or concerned line agencies have the tendency of being ignored by these organisations and often end up shelved, irrespective of the comprehensiveness of the programmes. On the other hand, if the planning and line agencies were involved right at the initial stage of ICZM programme development, there is a greater likelihood of the programme being integrated totally or partly into the respective development plans of the relevant agencies' (Chua, 1993, p. 97).

The relevance of funds and human resources for successful implementation of the plan is also noted by Chua. The author observes that 'funds and human resources are the most important ingredients needed for programme implementation. Government funds could be used only if the policy makers are convinced of the programme's potential economic and social benefits. The success of project implementation primarily depends on the project design and capability of the implementing agencies. The coordinating body should ensure sufficient technical back stopping for programme implementation' (ibid, pp. 97-98).

Chua also observes that 'not all projects and programmes of ICZM developed must be implemented at any one time. In fact, they are best implemented in stages over the proposed time frame' (ibid, p. 98).

Highlighting the significance of implementation of master plan for fisheries development, Korakandy noted that 'the master plan, once it is accepted, should be implemented ... The master plan will be implemented in phases as annual plans and five year plans. Certain targets would be fulfilled in the short run itself and others, only in the long run ... Implementation of the plan on the basis of clear priorities and necessary revisions will help in fulfilling the objectives to the maximum extent ... The failure of most plans is attributed to faulty or poor implementation' (Korakandy, 1996, p.134).

9.3.1.4. Monitoring and evaluation

Monitoring aad evaluation of the plan is important for understanding the achievements and shortcomings of the plan. It specifically helps in measuring the extent of fulfilment of objectives of the plan and any gap prevailing therein. It also helps in identifying the constraints or bottlenecks that prevent the achievement of the targets. Based on the evaluation, it will be possible for the planners to take remedial measures for improving the performance of the plan. Evaluation of the plans should be made at all successive stages of plan implementation, and also necessary corrections made in the ensuing periods. Interim or mid-term appraisals of the plan may be made by the planning agency or by the implementing department.

Pointing to the significance of monitoring and evaluation in ICZM planning, Chua notes that 'this important component of the management process should be incorporated into the ICZM programme at the planning and implementation stage. Monitoring of progress and evaluation of impacts should be undertaken annually by the respective implementing and coordinating agencies. The purposes are to see how the projects and programmes are doing, determine what could be done for better performance, find out opportunities that could be explored and developed, and assess the impacts and lessons learned. The ultimate objective of this exercise is to ensure timely intervention to assist projects and programmes in meeting set objectives. Monitoring and evaluation provides opportunities for refinement or for increase or decrease in financial and logistic support' (Chua, 1993, p. 98).

It is also noted that it 'measures the changes that have occurred in relation to the set objectives within the time frame given and also assesses the impacts of outputs against the values of inputs. Monitoring and evaluation also identifies the strength and weaknesses of programme implementation with respect to efficiency and effectiveness'(ibid, p. 98). Chua has further suggested that 'external reviews of the progress and impacts of the programme should also be encouraged in the middle of programme implementation and at the termination of the programme phase' (ibid, p.98).

Referring to monitoring and evaluation, Kay and Alder note that 'monitoring and evaluation are processes which assist in answering the question, 'is the plan working? and, if it is not working, what future actions are needed to make it work. If a coastal plan has included measurable objectives and criterion to evaluate the plan's ability to meet those objectives, ongoing monitoring may provide some of the information required to evaluate the effectiveness of the plan. Monitoring and evaluation also contribute to decision making' (Kay and Alder, 1999, pp. 332-333).

Clark has identified two basic types of evaluation: (1) process evaluation, which examines the means by which goals are achieved and (2) outcome evaluation, which measure the extent to which the programme's goals or objective are achieved. Specific indicators to evaluate the 'process' and 'outcome' have also been given by Clark (Clark, 1996, p. 62). The 'process' indicators given by Clark are:

(a) Budget allocation per year
(b) Number of permits issued, denied, conditional
(c) Consistency of law dealing with coastal management
(d) Number of agreements relating to inter agency cooperation
(e) Availability of appropriately trained and educated staff
(f) Number of subnational programmes initiated or approved
(g) Quality of information used in programme development.

The 'outcome' indicators given by Clark are grouped into:

1. *Instrumental factors consisting of:*
   (a) Cost and length of time for permit review
   (b) Number of procedures and steps eliminated (streamlining)
   (c) Public participation–number of individuals and groups
   (d) Geographic scope and issue coverage of information base
2. *Environmental or socio-economic conditions covering:*
   (a) Water quality (toxics, oxygen, nutrient levels, etc.)
   (b) Fishery yields
   (c) Food, income, provided by coastal fisheries
   (d) Amount (linear distance) of coastal fisheries
   (e) Kilometres of coast in public ownership
   (f) Number of tourist user days
   (g) Number of coastal species under special protection
   (h) Acreage of wetlands protected or restricted
   (i) Amount of special housing provided within the coastal zone
   (j) Tonnage and value of commodities handled in ports
   (k) Employment derived from fisheries and tourism sectors
   (l) Natural hazard effects; amount of lives and property saved.

9.4. An ICZM framework for Kerala

The fundamental issues of the Kerala coast, indeed the very basis of this study, have been pointed out in chapter seven and section two of this chapter. The crucial objective of this and the following sections is to present an ICZM framework for the sustainable development of the Kerala coast.

9.4.1. Preparation of master plan for ICZM in Kerala

The futility of a sectoral approach to coastal zone management has been pointed out by several authors and noted in earlier chapters. Accordingly, the preparation of the master plan is the first major step in the ICZM strategy. A master plan for ICZM for Kerala should consider the complex issues of the coast emanating from multiple uses of the coast and suggest integrated policies, programmes and solutions. An ICZM programme for Kerala, which is problem solving in nature, should first of all focus on the objectives of the plan.

9.4.1.1. Objectives of the master plan

The fundamental objectives of the master plan should be to minimise or overcome the various problems that the coast is now facing and to guide it to the trajectory of sustainable development in the future.

Keeping in view of this broad objective and the various coastal issues of Kerala, noted in chapter seven, the specific goals of an ICZM plan for Kerala may be listed under the following categories.

1. *Ecological objectives*
    - (a) prevent or minimise coastal pollution
    - (b) prevent over-exploitation of natural resources
    - (c) prevent habitat destruction and biodiversity loss
    - (d) protect the coast from natural hazards
2. *Economic objectives*
    - (a) control population growth and unemployment
    - (b) promote income
    - (c) prevent or minimise intra-use and inter-use conflicts
    - (d) remove stagnation and promote sustainable development
3. *Socio-cultural objectives*
    - (a) promote better housing
    - (b) provide better health and sanitary facilities
    - (c) enhance water supply
    - (d) control waste disposal
    - (e) protect cultural/recreational values

The above listed objectives of ICZM for Kerala needs some elaboration, especially in view of the complexity of these problems. First of all, the ecological objectives may be highlighted.

9.4.1.1.1. Ecological objectives

Among the ecological objectives noted, the most outstanding and ubiquitous one is the need to prevent or minimise coastal pollution. The intensity of the pollution problem has been noted in chapter seven and the need for an ICM solution to the problem was indicated. The major industries/activities that cause pollution in the coast are agriculture, aquaculture, fish processing, coir retting, mineral/sand mining, petro-chemical industries, shipping and port, tourism, municipal waste dumping, etc.

Another very important ecological problem threatening the very sustainability of the coastal economy is the overexploitation of the coastal natural resources, especially the fish stock. The over-fishing problem in the state has been highlighted in chapter seven and it is only natural that conservation of the natural resource base or prevention of their over-exploitation is considered as a primary goal of an ICZM plan for Kerala. Likewise, preventing the over-exploitation of the coastal mineral sand resources, even while promoting global investment in the state should be considered a significant objective of an ICZM plan for Kerala.

Yet another objective of ICZM for Kerala on the ecological front, is the need to prevent the destruction of the habitat of fish and other wild life in the coast and to protect the biodiversity of the coast. This need has been amply explained in chapter seven and it only needs to be emphasised here that habitat (mangroves, tide flats, etc.) protection and biodiversity conservation be made the core of an ICZM programme for Kerala.

An equally important ecological goal of an ICZM plan for Kerala shall be the protection of the coast from natural hazards. This, indeed, has been the chief or perhaps the only goal of coastal zone management (protection) programme in the past when seawalls were constructed to protect the coast from sea erosion.

It may be noted in favour of the various ecological objectives of ICZM for Kerala that they are rooted in the fact that the ecological (natural) resources of the coast form the material foundation upon which the coastal society (economy and culture) is built and the preservation of the ecological basis is vital for the sustainable development (sustainability) of the coastal civilization.

9.4.1.1.2. Economic objectives

The most outstanding economic objective of an ICZM programme for Kerala noted earlier, but seldom finding any mention in the global literature on ICZM programmes world wide, is the need to control population growth and to ease the unemployment problem. The high density of population and the severity of the unemployment problem in the coast has been highlighted in chapter seven. The twin problems were found to be acute among the fishermen community. Disguised unemployment among coir and cashew workers hypothesised was believed to aggravate the coastal unemployment problem. The problem was also found to have regional overtones, with higher concentrations of non-working (marine) fishermen population in districts like Kannur, Kozhikode, Thrissur, Ernakulam and Kollam. Similar trends in population growth and unemployment among inland fishermen, agricultural workers and other groups also demand that control of population growth and unemployment be made a major objective of an ICZM plan for sustainable development of Kerala coast. It is ironical that the global literature did not pay much attention to this problem. This was perhaps due to the lower priority attached to this goal by the 'global' writers and their preoccupation with the resolution of 'multiple use conflicts' especially in the wake of 'globalisation of the coastal commons'.

A very desirable economic objective of an ICZM plan for Kerala is to enhance the earnings of the coastal population, especially the fishermen' coir workers and others whose per capita income is believed to be quite below the state average. The per capita income of coastal districts like Kasargode, Kannur, Kozhikode, Malappuram and Kollam was found to be much below the state average. Sustainable development of the coast demands intra-generational equity, especially in meeting the minimum needs of the community and this calls for an improvement in the earnings of the community which accordingly should be made an objective of ICZM for Kerala.

The most powerful argument for ICZM in Kerala, as anywhere else is found in its potential to prevent or resolve intra-use and inter-use conflicts. Prevention of conflict, accordingly, has been noted as the most important economic objective of ICZM for Kerala, where both intra-use and inter-use conflicts are rampant. The magnitude of this conflict has been indicated in chapter seven. Intra-use conflict has been noted as prevailing in the fisheries sector for quite long and even now between operators of different craft-gear combinations, between full-time and part-time fishermen, between subsistence, commercial and recreational fishermen and between local and migrant fishermen.

Inter-use conflicts are widespread, both on the land-side and the water-side. Such conflicts are noted to prevail between agriculture and fisheries (aquaculture), agriculture and mining (clay), fisheries and mining (sand), fisheries and coir manufacturing, fisheries (aquaculture) and forestry (mangrove), fisheries and manufacturing, fisheries and transport, fisheries and tourism, fisheries and urban development, tourism and power (thermal), tourism and transport (container), port and defense, etc. The ultimate economic objective of ICZM being to maximise the value of the coastal product, any programme for ICZM in Kerala should be backed by prevention of intra-use and inter-use conflicts as an objective of ICZM in the state.

An equally powerful argument, which epitomises the very basic objective of ICZM in Kerala is to prevent 'stagnation' in the coast and to promote 'sustainable development' of the coast. Chapter seven has proved beyond doubt that the development path followed in the state, especially in the coastal zone was unsustainable. It was found to be unsustainable when the predominant ecological, economic and social criteria were applied. The various coastal zone activities were found failing in fulfilling the major ecological criteria of maintaining the natural resource base, or the economic criteria of satisfactory returns or the social criteria of community acceptance. Overwhelmed by intra-use and inter-use conflicts, the objective of any ICZM programme for Kerala should be to bring back sustainability by harmonising the multiple uses of the coast and its environment.

9.4.1.1.3. Socio-cultural objectives

The socio-cultural objectives of ICZM for Kerala noted included improvements in housing, health and sanitation, water supply, waste disposal and cultural/recreational values. The real compulsions of the coast on these fronts have already been noted in chapter seven. It only needs to be emphasised here that addressing these socio-cultural problems receive the requisite priority in any ICZM programme for Kerala.

9.4.1.1.4. Prioritising the objectives

Prioritising the objectives of ICZM is essential in view of the multiplicity of goals and the constraints of time and resources available to the ICZM planner. This is in fact a crucial decision making problem as in all decision making contexts. It, however, can be overcome by making use of the available information and through rapid appraisal technique. Of course, the planner can give greater priority to 'public good' or social interests, rather than to private good or private profit. Sustainability of the goals demands social approval.

9.4.1.2. Strategy of the plan

The ICZM strategy for Kerala should ensure that the several ICZM goals put forward are realised during the period envisaged. It, however, requires that sectoral plans are prepared for each and every coastal activity and they are integrated with the master plan, keeping consistency in objectives, targets, policies and programmes. It also calls for sufficient funding, staff, training, research, 'capacity building', building constituency, 'partnerships' and 'public-private' cooperation. This strategy should ensure that sustainable development of the coast is not a mere vision but a mission fulfilled.

9.4.1.2.1. Implementation of the plan

Implementation of the master plan is the second major step in the realisation of the goals of ICZM in Kerala, The master plan should be implemented in stages as successive components of a cumulative plan to fulfil the various goals as prioritised and as corresponding to the various coastal issues. Implementation of the plan can be spread over years as annual plans and five year plans. The master plan being a perspective (long term) plan, it can extend to longer time periods spreading over 15-20 years. Implementation of the master plan should be the responsibility of an apex coordinating department, with 'line' agencies (departments) doing the sectoral job. It is significant to note here that the success of the master plan will very much depend on the careful implementation of the plan with proper horizontal (sectoral), vertical (administrative) and spatial (geographic) integration of objectives and programmes.

9.4.1.2.2. Evaluation of the plan

As pointed out in the earlier section, evaluation of the master plan in the course of its working at successive stages is vital for ascertaining the outcome, successes and failures. Interim or mid-term appraisals are quite essential for the success of the master plan, as it is a long range plan and necessary timely corrections are to be made to prevent bottlenecks in the course of implementation of the plan. Constant review of plan performance can impart the master plan the required flexibility to incorporate the evolving concerns of the coastal system into the plan structure. This is especially important in the ICZM context where intra-use and inter-use conflicts are rampant and most coastal activities have irreversible impacts on the external environment.

Interim evaluations are also useful for making necessary changes in policy, strategy, institutions, and financing of the plan.

9.4.1.2.3. Criteria for evaluation

Evaluation of the ICZM plan should be based on sound criteria. These criteria should serve as 'reference points' referring to which the performance of the plan is evaluated. Fundamentally, these criteria should refer to the goals of the plan and they should be formulated as corresponding to the specific goals of the master plan and the sectoral components. Broadly, these criteria may be noted as relating to the ecological, economic and socio-cultural objectives of the plan. At the core, they should correspond to the objective of sustainable development of the coast or the sustainability criteria. It is necessary that the planning agency formulate the relevant criteria for evaluation even while planning for ICZM.

9.4.2. Financing of the plan

Financing of the master plan for ICZM in Kerala needs special attention and priority. It requires the careful consideration of the finance department since the sustainability of the coastal zone economic activities is vital for the survival of the Kerala economy. The multiple activities of the coast, small and big, ranging from agriculture to aquaculture, fishing, forestry, mining, manufacturing (coir, chemicals, fish processing, cashew processing, etc.), power production, petroleum, port (shipping and transport), tourism, defense, municipal waste dumping, etc. have economic impacts which are quite unsurpassed by any other sector or region of the state's economy. In view of the region's contribution to the state's domestic product, employment, foreign exchange earnings and other spill over benefits, it is only appropriate that the state earmark the requisite funds for the proper management of coastal zone activities and make them sustainable.

It is significant to note here that the requisite fund for ICZM in Kerala can be raised by transferring the corresponding allocations in the budgets of the 'line' ministries or departments.

Funding from international sources may be available in abundance, but their costs may also be high in real terms, both social and economic.

9.4.3. Need for capacity building

With the rising tide of globalisation, it is now fashionable to talk of 'capacity building' in all contexts. It is significant to note here that the global literature on ICZM is quite explicit about the need for capacity building in developing coastal states to equip them to implement the ICZM plan. Referring to the issue, the ASEAN noted that 'professional and technical support staff of organisations must be given appropriate formal education and training in CAM, dealing with issues and problems, and developing effective strategies, among others. Their capability must be further enhanced based on knowledge of the coastal resources and the environmental, social and cultural and economic systems; and understanding of present and future solutions through an integrated management approach' (Chua Thia, 1991, p. 83). The need for capacity building (human and institutional capacity) has been identified in Agenda 21 of the UNCED as well as by a number of international institutions as essential for integrated coastal management and sustainable development in developing coastal nations.

The global position has been summarised by Crawford *et. al.*, thus: 'The UNCED Earth Summit identified coastal management as a priority issue for the near future. Meeting this demand will require significant emphasis to be placed on institutional strengthening and human resource development. Coastal management already has become a priority for many low-income nations, where planning and implementation efforts are underway. Even modest estimates for the demand for individuals and organisations indicate that a large investment in capacity building is required to meet the objectives of Agenda 21.

The experience of the URI/USAID suggests that an integrated strategy of training and institutional strengthening can be successful. Assessing the strengths of individuals and organisations, as well as the development of coastal management in the country is a key to success. In training courses, the participatory, adult learning model has worked well. International training courses have attracted many participants. On-the-job learning can be facilitated by the joint development and implementation of projects by collaboration of staff at two or more organisations where one, with more experience, can provide useful advice. Education and training programmes also need to be established in institutions within low-income countries in various regions of the world' (Crawford, *et. al.* 1993, p. 333).

These writers further observed that 'current global capacity in coastal management is in a more formative stage of development than in other fields such as public health and agricultural development which have a much longer history of international experience. Coastal management is barely two decades old in the USA and most projects in developing countries have only emerged over the last 5-10 years. Hence, while there is a significant pool of experience within the USA, the pool of experienced ICM practitioners in developing countries is considerably smaller. To expand the pool of ICM expertise to the many individuals and organisations needed within a decade to meet the mandates of Agenda 21 presents a challenging goal' (ibid, p. 334).

Referring to the capacity building exercise, Sicin-Sain and Knecht noted the need for four types of capacity which included:

(a) Legal and administrative capacity – to designate a coastal zone, to develop and carry out coastal plans, to regulate development in vulnerable zones, and to designate areas of particular concern.

(b) Financial capacity – adequate financial resources to carry out the planning and implementation of coastal management efforts.

(c) Technical capacity – information gathering and monitoring of coastal marine ecosystems and processes, patterns of human use, and the effectiveness of government coastal management programmes, establishment and maintenance of coastal data base and information system.

(d) Human resource capacity – personnel with inter-disciplinary training in social sciences (including law and planning), natural and physical sciences and engineering. Also public awareness, and understanding of the coastal ocean environment and the problems and opportunities it offers (Sicin-Sain and Knecht, 1998, pp. 60-61).

The FAO observes in this regard that 'the institutions contributing to ICAM should have the collective capacity to allocate resources according to the goals and strategic approach adopted.

The engine to drive the process includes well-trained and experienced staff. The capacity to manage the process can be developed as part of the strategy. Not all individual participating organisations will - or should be able to satisfy this requirement, but it is important that the system as a whole is able to deliver the following services:

(a) an equitable and efficient decision-making process;
(b) use of best available knowledge about how the relevant ecosystem function;
(c) participation of resource users, and all those affected by management decisions, in the decision-making process;
(d) capacity to resolve differences of interests;
(e) ability to employ economic policy instruments strategically;
(f) integrated, simple and effective regulatory instruments;
(g) public investment for the protection of coastal ecosystems and management of renewable resources' (Nadia, 1998, pp. 48-50).

It also made it explicit that 'because coastal problems involve a range of actors and a multiplicity of complex interrelated issues, an institutional capacity to resolve conflicts and institutional supervision will be required to manage the participation and relationships of interested parties and the different interests represented, as well as to identify suitable options and agree on objectives and means to attain them. Depending on local circumstances (traditional practices and principles), consideration should also be given to establishing funding mechanisms for conflict resolution (in order to cover the costs of appointing mediators or experts, or simply of running negotiations) and providing training and education for third parties to mediate, facilitate or arbitrate in disputes. Administrative procedures and dispute resolution offices or commissions might also be established to anticipate and resolve conflicts arising within and between institutions' (ibid, pp.50-51).

Notwithstanding the above observation by the global writers, it will be illuminating to look at the domestic capacity for ICM in Kerala. The state, alongwith the nation, with long experience in planned development, is not devoid of personnel for plan preparation and implementation and this experience can easily be pooled for ICZM planning. Kerala, with 100 per cent literacy and a strong network of socio-political institutions is not lacking in capacity for decision making for ICZM. What it probably lacks is the political will or faith in the mission.

It is also interesting to note here that the state has now attracted global agencies in engaging in capacity building exercises to promote ICZM efforts. The Delft University of Netherlands has already established a collaboration centre for Integrated Management of Coastal Zones in the Cochin University of Science and Technology. Similarly, the ASR Ltd., a consultant company from New Zealand has also entered into ICZM capacity building exercises in collaboration with the Centre for Earth Science Studies, Thiruvananthapuram and started implementing ICZM plans at Ashtamudi estuary in Kollam district (Black and Baba, 2000). It is also heartening to note that Kerala, with its growing concern for environmental protection is attracting global networks like the Green Peace to fight coastal pollution and the capacity building exercise is gaining momentum in the state with the local press also contributing its mite to the ICZM drive (Dixit, 2003). More enthusing is the fact that the nature conservation movement in the state has been finally able to facilitate the entry of the three Kerala wetlands - Ashtamudi, Shasthamkotta lake and Vembanad kol into the Ramsar list (Rahman, 2003). This is notwithstanding the steady fall in the coastal wetland ecosystem.

9.4.4. Need for partnerships

Just as ICZM capacity building is considered vital for the adoption and success of ICZM in developing coastal states, developing global partnerships in this field is also considered valuable for the success of ICZM, world wide. The partnership advocated is predominantly at the academic level between Universities in the developed and developing countries. Notwithstanding the merits of such partnerships in promoting the goal of sustainable development in poor countries, the negative impacts of such partnerships on local governments and domestic industries have eroded the credibility of the academic relations of the present (Vijayachandran, 2003). The pervading spirit was evident during the World Summit on Sustainable Development (WSSD) held at Johanesburg in 2002. Faizi noted that 'the US and allies seek to use the Johanesburg process to open the UN up for the multinational corporations through a new provision called 'partnerships'. This is to trivialise the need for binding commitments on the part of governments and to legitimise the tyranny arising from the globalisation of western capital. The partnership syndrom has come here to stay and is likely to spread like an epidemic to other areas of UN endeavour' (Faizi, 2002).

Another variant of the partnership, now advocated is the partnership between the public sector and the private sector and between governments (bureaucracy) and business. This is considered ideal for reducing the transaction costs of business and for improving performance to make them economically sustainable. But considering the unholy nature of the alliance between bureaucracy and business worldwide, such partnerships will not be socially sustainable. This seems to have occurred in Kerala in the recent past when the controversy erupted following the government's move to permit large scale sand mining in the Alappuzha coast by the private sector and when the Government allowed a private firm to establish a cement clinkering plant at Azhikode near Kodungallur in Thrissur district (*The New Indian Express,* 7.10.2002 and 3.5.2003). Both the schemes, were proposed violating the provisions of the CRZ notification, and had to be shelved because of public protest which highlighted their environmental unsustainability. Here it is prudent to heed to the advise of Clark that 'taking sand from any part of the beach or the nearshore submerged zone can lead to erosion and recession of the beach front. The key to the natural protection provided by the beach front is the sand which is held in storage and yields to storm waves, thereby dissipating the force of their attack. Consequently, beach conservation should start with the presumption that any removal of sand is adverse and should be prohibited, unless it can be shown to be naturally replaceable; that is, if it is a sustainable use of a renewable resource' (Clark, 1996, p. 354).

It is also advisable for such partnerships to bear in mind that 'natural resource depletion in all sectors of development is aggravated by users concerned with short-term profits and by the absence of defined user rights ... Theoretically owned by all the people, the coastal commons is held in trust by the government and its uses decided by the government. Tenure systems are practically inadequate in the aquatic coastal area and will require strong efforts to establish them explicitly or revive them formally (traditional user rights)' (Clark, 1992, p.26). It is also worth recalling the OECD caution that the 'role of governments is to ... ensure that coastal resources produce goods and services, which are not produced by market forces (public goods), such as providing for conservation of natural areas, preservation of aesthetic beauty and a long term view is taken in contrast to the short-run profit maximisation criteria of the market' (OECD 1993 b). The partnership which the Global Investor Meet (GIM) of 2002 in Kerala sought to promote seems to have failed because of local resistance to the move to privatise the coastal commons.

It, nevertheless, needs to be noted here that the global academic partnerships and other cliques have succeeded in building 'networks' in the state and in the country to aid globalisation by providing strategic information about coastal natural resources, their hypothetical value (willingness to supply), major stakeholders in the coast, etc. through rapid rural appraisals and visual problem analyses. Referring to the kind of partnership now evolving, one newspaper commentator recently remarked that '...winning over intellectuals is the first step in the conquest of societies' (Vijayachandran, 2003). Here one may appreciate the fact that the post-modern global forces are quite sharp in choosing the academics as partners for facilitating their mission, just as the post-medieval merchants were smart in choosing the local chieftains as their immediate ally. Diplomacy has moved from courts and palaces to campuses. And the coastal zone continues to attract more and more people for forging new partnerships. It is upto the coastal people to accept or reject the new partnerships.

9.4.5. Building of constituency for ICZM in Kerala

The need for building constituency for ICZM has been highlighted in the global literature. It is considered as vital for the success of ICZM since the various programmes of ICZM have to be implemented in the coast and they should be accepted by the stakeholders. Educating the stakeholders about the need for ICZM and its advantages is the first step in building constituency for ICZM. As pointed out by FAO, 'successful management of natural resources requires a conviction on the part of those affected by management change that they can influence the process and that the proposed management measures are equitable and fair. Without this perception of legitimacy, or constituency building ... there is a strong likelihood that proposed management measures will fail. Indeed, those affected may even sabotage the measures (Nadia, 1998, p. 46).

The FAO also noted that 'creating a constituency for ICZM is one of the chief aspects of the policy process. Support from the private sector, including individual stakeholders, and from communities and special interest groups is essential. Accordingly, community leaders, members of the community and trade organisations should be targeted.

The full participation of resource users will often highlight conflicting interests affecting coastal resources that are difficult to reconcile. Through mediated dialogue, perceptions could be confronted and negotiated among stakeholders to define long-term patrimonial objectives in coastal areas' (ibid, p.46).

Cicin-Sain and Knecht noted that 'virtually all CZM programme require active and positive participation at the local or community level; ... Ideally, support at the community level should come from all quarters of society- coastal and ocean users, environmental and conservation groups, the private sector, educational and academic institutions, agricultural interests, aquacultural groups (if present) and the like. An active outreach programme specifically targeted to these groups is usually needed. An early task in this regard is development of a programme of regular newsletters, public meetings, and other events to keep every one informed about ICM effort, its current status, issues facing the programme, opportunities to provide input, ways of getting additional information and so forth. Openness and transparency will help lay the foundation of community trust needed for a successful ICM programme' (Cicin-Sain and Knecht, 1998, pp. 132-134).

Considering the above and the need for ensuring people's participation and compliance to ICM programmes, it may be noted here that the ICZM planners in Kerala should make efforts to build the constituency for ICZM in Kerala among the various stakeholders in the coast, ranging from fishermen to agriculturists, aquaculturists, people in coir industry, mining (sand, minerals), manufacturing (cashew, chemicals), port, shipping, transportation, defense, tourism, amenities (parks, water supply, waste-dumping), etc.

9.4.6. Need for ensuring people's participation and compliance

Highlighting the importance of public participation in ICZM planning, Clark writes that in most countries a priority goal of coastal management should be to arrange for the most extensive participation possible ... Consultations should be held with all relevant agencies of central and local government, with developers, with resource users and other interests that would be affected by ICZM (fishermen, farmers, etc.), environmental advocacy groups and investment sources (including international donor institutions).

Coastal areas and coastal resource systems are governmentally complex because of the degree of shared jurisdiction and the amount of common property resources involved. Therefore, resource management programmes need to involve all levels from national to village governments regardless of the particular institutional arrangement at the central level' (Clark, 1996, p.170).

Participation of the people is considered valuable for four specific reasons. Quoting Renard, Clark lists them as follows:

1. Participation is a way to ensure that popular knowledge and experience is indeed integrated into the planning and management process.
2. Participation gives a better guarantee for the quality of the solution identified and for the adaptation to a particular condition.
3. Participation in planning and problem identification promotes involvement in the actual implementation of decisions.
4. Participation ensures that all needs and priorities are taken into account in the formulation of management decisions (ibid, p.171).

Stressing the need for community participation for the success of ICZM programmes, Hildebrand notes that 'community-based coastal management represents a new form of partnership between government and community-based organisations. In essence, it is about 'power sharing' in the integrated planning and management of coastal zones. There is growing evidence of the desire, if not demand by local stakeholders to be more actively and meaningfully involved in what have been traditionally, government decisions. Traditional forms of 'public consultation' are no longer adequate. Yet there is still debate over the degree of public involvement that is desirable and feasible' (Hildebrand, 1997, pp.1-2).

Hildebrand also emphasised that 'genuine participation is only achieved when power is shared. This means that citizens, through community organisations, are making planning decisions with government that have meaningful consequences. Involvement in implementation and subsequent running of the management programme can give resource users and local stakeholders real power, if they play a central role in decision making about management actions' (ibid, p.2).

Referring to the need for people's participation in ICZM programmes, Clark notes that 'ICZM programmes require high levels of participation. Most likely, people who live along the coast and have traditionally used coastal resources will be greatly affected by any new rules and procedures. Therefore, if they are to support the programme, they must have a voice in the formation of coastal policies and rules on resource use. Broad participation will also provide an opportunity to resolve conflicting points of view among various shakeholders so that later the ICZM programme will meet lesser political-resistance' (Clark, 1996, p. 47).

Clark also points out that 'the stakeholders should be encouraged to go beyond dialogue and to participate to the maximum possible in goal setting, data collection, conflict identification, and so forth. The decision making and implementation process must be shared with the people and their organisers, requiring efficient communication and effective dialogue through participatory planning' (ibid, p. 47).

Quoting other sources, this author further argues that 'public participation is a tool available to the entire management community (resource users, public agencies, non-governmental organisations, etc.) to ensure the quality and effectiveness of the management solutions that will be implemented. Participation is also a duty because the issue remains, above all, one of human development and because people are not the object of that development, but the subject of development and the makers of their own history' (ibid, p. 47).

Some of the typical coastal sectors identified for the ICZM dialogue by Clark are (1) navy and other national defense operations, (2) port and harbour development, (3) shipping and navigation, (4) recreational boating and harbour, (5) commercial and recreational fishing, (6) mariculture, (7) tourism, (8) marine and coastal research, (9) shoreline erosion control.

Other sectors which are not 'coast specific' but having considerable impact on the coast and necessary to participate in the ICZM dialogue as noted by Clark are (1) agriculture, (2) forestry, (3) fish and wild life management, (4) parks and recreation, (5) education, (6) public health - mosquito eradication, (7) housing, (8) water pollution control, (9) water supply, (10) transportation, (11) flood control, (12) oil and gas development, (13) mining, (14) industrial development, (15) energy generation. It is absolutely necessary that all ICZM programmes in Kerala should invariably enlist the participation of the diverse coastal sectors and interests at all stages of programme planning, implementation and evaluation, especially in view of the great stakes involved and the trade-offs to be negotiated and settled.

9.4.7. Need for precaution

Referring to the need for precaution, Garcia notes that 'the concept of precaution requires management authorities to take pre-emptive action where there is a risk of severe and irreversible damage to human beings and, by extension, to the resources and the environment, even in the absence of certainty about the impact or the causal relationship. When there is doubt about the effect of a technology or (fishing) practice on the marine environment and resources, preventive or remedial action would have to be taken, erring on the safe side, with due consideration to the social and economic consequences' (Garcia, 1994, p.1, parentheses added).

The precautionary principle 'requires authorities at entrepreneurial, national, regional and international levels to take preventive action when there is a risk of severe and irreversible damage to human beings by technology. Its most characteristic attribute is that, in these circumstances, action is required even in the absence of certainty about the damage and without having to wait for full scientific proof of the cause-effect relationship. In addition, when there is disagreement on the need to take action, the burden of providing the proof is reversed and placed on those who content that the activity has or will have no impact' (ibid, p. 6).

The precautionary principle has evolved through the World Conference on Human Environment (Stockholm, 1972), the FAO Technical Conference on Fishery Development and Management (Vancouver, 1973), the United Nations Convention on the Law of the Sea (New York, 1982), the FAO World Conference on Fisheries Management and Development (Rome, 1984), the work of the Brundtland Commission from 1984 to 1987 (World Commission on Environment and Development, 1987), and the United Nations Conference on Environment and Development (Rio de Janeiro, 1992). The concept, when radically interpreted had the effect of curtailing all environmentally non-sustainable development, thus giving it a negative undertone (ibid, p. 6). Some writers even accused it of leading to a 'no decision' situation helping to maintain status quo and not contributing to 'problem resolution' (Kay and Alder, 1999, p. 160).

The concept has since undergone some transformation. The 'precautionary approach' as it is referred at the UNCED and now advocated, stipulates that 'in order to protect the environment, the precautionary approach shall be widely applied by states according to their capabilities. Where there are threats of serious or irreversible damage, lack of full scientific certainty shall be not used as a reason for postponing cost-effective measures to prevent environmental degradation' (Principle 15 of the UNCED Rio Declaration). Garcia observes that the above wording of the Approach' though superficially similar to that of the 'principle' is subtly different in that it reflects a softer requirement, recognising that there are differences in local 'capabiiities' to apply it and calling for 'cost-effectiveness', i.e., taking into account economic and social costs' (Garcia, 1994, p.7).

The need for taking a precautionary approach while implementing an ICZM plan for Kerala must be made clear now. It had become apparent from chapters five, six and seven that the coastal resources, activities and issues are quite diverse and complex and their resolution needs an ICZM effort. The precautionary approach prescribed above is applicable to Kerala in view of the uncertainty of the consequences of many of the actions and the limited information available to decision makers, be it in the state government or in other institutions. It is, however, significant to note here that the non-implementation of any CZM programme in Kerala since 1991 is by 'default' and not because of a 'precautionary approach' as prescribed by the ICZM planners.

The fact that Kerala did not implement the CRZ notification vigorously is not really indicating its adherence to the precautionary principles but the failure to anticipate the ecological, economic and social consequences of the 'no-decision' situation and the lack of political will to 'negotiate' between the various stake holders of the coast. The blanket argument of the state that implementation of the CRZ notification will thwart the economic development of the state was 'myopic' and without any knowledge of ICZM principles. The 'business as usual' (BAU) approach of the state has again become apparent in the recent controversy over mineral sand mining in the Alappuzha coast, where mining of mineral sand was advocated ignoring the precautionary principle and succumbing to global business pressures.

Yet another area where precaution is needed is with respect to the forging of 'spurious' partnerships for ICZM. Such partnerships,instead of promoting the ICZM goals, weaken the system. Referring to such a possibility, Vallega observes that 'these networks are not always beneficial, however. In many countries government agencies have a tendency to form elite internal groups that set up and maintain cooperative relationships only with each other. Interest groups and issue networks are inevitable features of any bureaucracy. However, they can, at times, become pathological when a group of powerful interests acquires sufficient power to co-opt the agency and pursue goals that conflict with the agency's programme or the wishes of the local community. This results in progressive segregation: the solidarity inside the agency increases at the expense of global solidarity and integrated management. It is imperative to design institutional mechanisms that guard against this tendency within the coastal management system[1] (Vallega, 1993, p.160). Here, while accepting Vallega's charge of complicity by the local/national bureaucracy in wrecking the 'global solidarity' in ICZM, the threat of a global hijacking of the ICZM mission for globalisation should also be anticipated and forewarned.

A precautionary approach to ICZM is prescribed for Kerala in view of its proclivity to neglect the ecological, economic and social impacts and the overzealous overtures to promote global investment in the state. The impact of globalisation on the economy, environment and culture of poor countries is well documented. Indeed the trade versus environment question has been at the base of all sustainable development debates and the ICZM debate in Kerala should also be considered as an offshoot of this argument. Precaution demands one to suggest that ICZM should not be made a vehicle for promoting global investment in the state but rather make it the gateway to promote balanced development of the coast.

9.5. Summary

This chapter considered the political economy of sustainable development of the coast. It argued that the sustainable development of the coast required the preparation of a master plan for ICZM for Kerala. Accordingly, it presented the basic framework of a master plan, starting with the preparation of the plan, identification of objectives, formulation of strategy, implementation, and finally the monitoring and evaluation of the plan. The master plan framework thus described was then applied to the ICZM context for Kerala. The ICZM master plan framework for Kerala discussed the fundamental objectives of a master plan, the need for prioritisation of objectives, strategy of the plan, implementation, evaluation, criteria for evaluation, financing of the plan, need for capacity building, need for partnerships, the dangers involved in it, need for building of constituency, need for ensuring people's participation and compliance, and finally the need for precaution.

The basic objectives of the ICZM plan for Kerala were grouped into three categories, each corresponding to the ecological, economic and socio-cultural dimensions of sustainable development. The need for a precautionary approach to ICZM was noted in view of the state's default in implementing the CRZ notification and its proclivity to neglect the ecological, economic and socio-cultural impacts of such inaction. Precaution is also suggested in view of its current overtures to global investment and global partnerships.

10

Summary of Findings and Conclusion

10.1. Summary of findings

Chapter one of this study made clear the theme and background of the study, the need for the study, its objectives, hypothesis and methodology. This chapter also specified the data base, scope, limitations and prospects of the study.

A scanning of the literature on coastal zone management made in chapter two made two things clear. First, it revealed that the domestic literature is quite underdeveloped and this was probably due to the lack of awareness among the scientific community about the need for coastal zone management. This is, however, considered to be quite anomalous when a large section of the academic and scientific community specialising in marine biology, fisheries and oceanography are thronging the national academic and scientific environment.

The second point that emerged from the review of literature was that the global literature on coastal zone management was quite extensive and fast growing. It found that this literature has evolved from national and regional concern for protecting the coastal environment and it has grown into a global concern for sustainable development of the coastal zone. The global literature has benefitted from regional and global programmes for coastal zone management promoted by the US, UN, World Bank and other national and international organisations. The global literature is now found nurtured by an exclusive journal, *Ocean and Coastal Management.* It is also being sustained by many 'inter-coast' networks.

The conceptual framework of ICM studied in chapter three highlighted many points. First of all, it recognised the prevalence of a plurality of phrases like Integrated Coastal Zone Management (ICZM), Integrated Coastal and Ocean Management (ICOM), Integrated Coastal Area Management (ICAM), Integrated Coastal Management (ICM), Coastal Resource Management (CRM), Integrated Marine and Coastal Area Management (IMCAM) and Community Based Coastal Resource Management (CBCRM). A scanning of the several definitions of ICZM, ICM, etc. revealed the commonality of their approach with regard to objectives, mode and sphere of management functions. It also noted a progressive widening of the spectrum of goals, methods and sphere of management actions contemplated in the literature.

A review of the evolution of the concept of coastal zone management made in this chapter led to the identification of four stages (sources), viz. (1) The US beginning, (2) The USAID led ICM programmes, (3) The European Initiatives and (4) International efforts. The US initiative, though considered primarily as an environmental protection measure has provided the basic framework for further evolution of the ICM concept, and through USAID led ICM programmes in the ASEAN and with the European and International efforts (predominantly supported by the UN) has culminated in the present concept and practice of ICZM for sustainable development of the coast.

This chapter also showed that the concept of ICZM is now a complex concept with multidimensional features combining ecological, economic, social and cultural aspects of development, transcending and integrating the spatial, horizontal and vertical dimensions of planning and administration of coastal activities. In this process, it is also found to call upon nations to use the knowledge of science, including social science and to build up the capacity for ICM on a global scale.

The rationale of coastal zone management as observed in the global literature and presented in chapter four focused on the ecological, economic, socio-political-cultural and other factors. The major ecological issues noted are pollution, threat to biological diversity and adverse natural processes. The economic argument for ICM made in this chapter focused on the multiple use conflicts arising from human settlements (housing), agriculture, aquaculture, fishing, forestry, mining, petroleum industry, other manufacturing industries, infrastructure, ports and marines, coastal tourism, waste disposal, water supply projects, shore protection works, national security, and marine excavation.

The socio-political-cultural arguments were fundamentally based on the notion of social equity as reflected in the criteria of intra-generational and inter-generational equity which are vital for sustainable development.

The other arguments favouring ICM are found to have their roots in 'globalisation', strategically planned through the instruments of the UN.

The holistic approach to ICM noted in this chapter, recognised the need for integrated solutions to the ecological, economic, social, cultural and political issues of the coast. It found that all coastal activities should be sustainable in terms of their ecological, economic, social, and cultural impacts.

A review of the coastal resources base of Kerala made in chapter five identified four categories of resources - natural, human, physical capital and infrastructure. The natural resources noted included the coastline, the continental shelf, fishing grounds, mineral sand, oil, backwaters and canals, mangrove areas and prawn filtration fields, areas of outstanding natural beauty, heritage sites and historical areas.

The human resources of the coast discussed in this chapter related to the total population, fishermen population, marine fishermen, inland fishermen, active fishermen, etc.

The physical capital available to the coast was discussed primarily in terms of the capital assets of the fishing industry in the form of fishing crafts and gears, boat building yards, net making units, fishing harbours, fishermen training centres, infrastructure for processing and marketing and coastal health facilities.

The other infrastructure considered included roads, railways, waterways, ports and lighthouses.

This chapter, by and large, recognised the critical resource base of the coast and their relevance for the sustainable development of the coastal zone.

A detailed description of coastal activities made in chapter six highlighted the complexity of the coastal economic system. It recognised the economic and non-economic uses of the coast and the activities of the 'water-side' and the 'land-side'. As a starting point, the land-use pattern of the demarcated coastal zone was examined.

The major activities of the coast and the corresponding values studied related to: (1) fisheries, (2) aquaculture, (3) agriculture, (4) mining, (5) manufacturing (coir, cashew processing, fish processing, fertilizers and chemicals), (6) tourism, (7) ports and harbours, (8) inland water transport, (9) urban development and (10) other uses. The first nine activities were considered as belonging to the category of economic uses while the last one was categorised as 'non-economic' or socio-cultural uses of the coast. This chapter while recognising the significant contribution of many of these activities to the coastal economy - to employment, earnings and output - noted the need for ensuring their sustainability.

The major coastal issues discussed in chapter seven placed the need for ICZM in Kerala in sharp relief. The various coastal issues facing Kerala were discussed in three major headings: ecological, economic and socio-cultural. The ecological issues discussed included (1) coastal pollution, (2) over-exploitation of natural resources (3) habitat destruction and bio-diversity loss and (4) natural hazards. Among the economic issues discussed are: (l) population growth and unemployment, (2) low incomes, (3) intra-use and inter-use conflicts and (4) stagnation (unsustainable development). The socio-cultural issues of the coast discussed included the 'primary needs' of meeting the housing, health and sanitation, water supply and waste disposal services, and the 'higher needs' of providing for the cultural and recreational needs of the population. All along this chapter placed the need for ICZM as very critical and vital for the sustainable development of the coast.

A review of coastal zone management efforts in Kerala in the past, attempted in chapter eight identified three periods; pre-colonial, colonial and post-colonial. It noted that the pre-colonial period was generally a period of peaceful interaction with foreign traders with no major intra-use or inter-use conflicts in the coast.

The colonial period, on the other hand, witnessed the conquest of the coast by various European powers and the establishment of European industry and culture in the coast. This period witnessed the moulding of the coastal economy and society to subserve the interests of the colonial masters.

The post-colonial (post-independence) period which included the pre-1991 period (prior to economic reform) and the post-1991 period, found that the focus of coastal zone management in the first phase was to promote coastal development as part of national economic development programmes. This phase, apart from carrying out the developmental programmes and coast conservation measures, also witnessed the introduction of certain sectoral controls on land use, fishing, mineral mining, water pollution, etc. The post-1991 period marked the introduction of CRZ rules and the preparation of the so-called ICZM plans for Kerala. A review of ICZM efforts made during this period, however, showed the deficiency of the programme with little or no academic/scientific inputs and the dearth of socio-political will as reflected in the failure to produce a master plan for ICZM in Kerala.

The political economy of sustainable development of the coast presented in chapter nine reiterated the unsustainability of present developments and showed that sustainable development of the coast needed the preparation of an ICZM plan for Kerala. Accordingly it first presented the basic framework of a master plan, starting with the general approach of the plan, identification of objectives, formulation of strategy, implementation, and finally the monitoring and evaluation of the plan. The master plan framework thus discussed was then applied to the ICZM plan for Kerala.

The ICZM plan framework for Kerala presented in this chapter discussed the fundamental objectives of the master plan, the need for prioritisation of objectives, strategy of the plan, implementation, evaluation, criteria for evaluation, financing of the plan, need for capacity building, need for partnerships, need for building of constituency, need for ensuring people's participation and compliance, and finally the need for precaution.

The basic objectives of the ICZM plan for Kerala were grouped into three categories; each corresponding to the ecological, economic and socio-cultural dimensions of sustainable development. The need for a precautionary approach to ICZM was also noted in view of the state's default in implementing the CRZ notification and its proclivity to neglect the ecological, economic and socio-cultural impacts of such inaction. Precaution is also suggested in view of its current overtures to global investment and 'partnerships', ignoring the fundamental criteria of sustainable development.

10.2. Conclusion

This study held the general hypothesis that sustainable development of the coast demands fulfilment of the ecological, economic and social criteria of sustainable development. It also noted that sustainable development of the coast is possible with ICZM efforts which will help in harmonising the ecological, economic and social basis of development. It examined the coastal issues of Kerala and found the current developments as quite unsustainable and lacking in any ICZM support. It suggested an ICZM programme which is precautionary in approach to promote sustainable development of the coast. This study also felt that ICZM is only a necessary condition for sustainable development of the coast and not a sufficient condition. The fulfilling condition for sustainability seems to be in the realm of the 'unknown'.

10.3. Post-script

A closer scrutiny of the theory and practice of ICZM, starting from the US Coastal Zone Management Act of 1972 makes one believe that the whole concept of ICZM has undergone drastic changes in its focus and intention. This has been noted in chapter three, earlier. What is not quite so apparent and what needs to be highlighted here is the inherent deficiencies in the concept.

The ICZM concept since UNCED 1992 has been focusing, on the goal of 'maximisation of the value of the coastal product' and linking it with sustainable development by harmonising the sectoral, regional and global interests. This idealised approach to ICZM and sustainable development is quite simple and undoubtedly the product of western liberal economic thinking. It will certainly help in projectising the 'coastal commons' with global partnerships and capacity building exercises. If present trends and approaches are any indication, it can certainly help the coastal economies to move in the direction of faster 'growth', maximising the value of production and consumption but with only scant regard for sustainability, ecological, economic, social and cultural.

'Sustainability' demands real commitment to the concept of 'deep ecology to preserve nature, and a policy for 'zero growth' in population and personal consumption. This requires mass adoption of what Boulding called the 'spaceman culture' of austerity and abandonment of the 'cowboy type' culture of rabid social consumption (Boulding, 1966). The ICZM concept, without incorporating these values will be merely projecting the mirage of 'sustainable development' and tacitly promoting unsustainable development. In such a situation, the ICZM appeal for harmonisation of multiple coastal interests and various kinds of integration will be just a lullaby for growth and a camouflage for globalisation. One possible response to this scenario as it exists today is to think that 'the achievement of sustainable development will involve a long struggle with many hard lessons learned by each country as it attempts to apply general principles to its specific circumstances' (Caddy and Griffiths, 1995, p. 3). Here one can be very sure that the poor country always learns 'new' lessons and quietly forgets the 'old' lessons. That makes ICZM quite 'novel' to third world academics, even while it explicitly rejects the socialistic and third world idea of central planning as practised in India in the past as 'sectoral or 'unintegrated' and implicitly accepts it as the starting point for its prescription of the master plan framework for ICZM as it emanated from the UNCED. What Kerala needs at present is an indigenous ICZM programme truely committed to preserve the ecology, economy and culture of the state and to enable it to call itself as 'God's own country'. Anything less than that will not be sustainable.

Appendices

Appendix 3.1
Participating organizations of ASEAN/US CRMP, 1986-1992

Brunei Darussalam
Department of Fisheries
Department of Forestry
Department of Town and Country Planning
Marine Department
Department of Public Works
Department of Agriculture
Brunei Museum
Universiti Brunei Darussalam

Indonesia
Indonesian Institute of Sciences
Directorate General of Fisheries
Research Institute for Marine Fisheries
Centre for Oceanological Research and Development
Centre for Agro-Economic Research
State Ministry of Population and Environment

Malaysia
Ministry of Science, Technology and the Environment Department of Fisheries
Ministry of Defence, Hydrography Section
Department of Agriculture
Drainage and Irrigation Department
Department of Town and Country Planning
Prime Minister's Department, Coordinating and Planning Unit
Department of Geology
Department of Survey and Mapping
Universiti Sains Malaysia
State Economic Planning Unit (Johore)

Forest Research Institute
Pusat Penyelidikan Ternak Air Payau
National University, Malaysia
SERES Sdn. Bhd.
Universiti Teknologi Malaysia

Philippines

Department of Science and Technology
Philippine Council for Aquatic and Marine Research and Development
University of the Philippines Marine Science Institute (UPMSI)
University of the Philippines College of Social Work and Community Development (UPCSWCD)
University of the Philippines in the Visayas
Bureau of Fisheries and Aquatic Resources
National Economic and Development Authority, Region 1.

Singapore

National Science and Technology Board
Primary Production Department
Department of Geography
National University of Singapore
Department of Zoology
National University of Singapore

Thailand

Office of the National. Environment Board
Ministry of Science, Technology and Environment
Brackishwater Fisheries Division
Department of Fisheries
Marine Fisheries Division
Department of Fisheries
Phuket Marine Biological Center
Department of Fisheries
Royal Forestry Department
Faculty of Forestry, Kasetsart University
Department of Marine Science
Chulalongkorn University
Faculty of Social Sciences and Humanities
Mahidol University

Source: Chua and Scura, 1992, p.77.

Appendix 3.2
Baguio Resolution on Coastal Resources Management issued by the Policy Conference on Managing ASEAN's Coastal Resources for Sustainable Development, 4-7 March 1990, Manila and Baguio, Philippines

Whereas, much of Southeast Asia's population lives in coastal areas, and the lives and reasonable aspirations for economic advancement of these coastal residents are inextricably linked to the sustained productivity of coastal resources; and coastal areas contain a diverse collection of natural resources within their interrelated ecosystems, and close linkages exist between these ecosystems and the socioeconomic systems in coastal areas; and fish and other aquatic resources are routinely captured and cultured in coastal areas, providing food, valuable chemicals and materials, employment and income for many coastal residents; and the region's unique coastal environments also provide many other economic opportunities for the private sector including oil, mineral and timber extraction, agriculture, shipping and tourism;

Whereas, many coastal environments within the Association of Southeast Asian Nations (ASEAN) have become seriously degraded, resource-use conflicts are escalating, and valuable coastal resources are being overexoloited; and the result is that the productivity of these coastal areas has diminished, and the prospects for continued economic prosperity in the region has been jeopardised,

Whereas, to maintain and enhance the livelihood of coastal communities within the ASEAN, coastal areas must be managed for sustainable development; and as population and economic pressures on these coastal resources increase, it becomes more difficult and challenging to achieve sustainable development in coastal areas in the absence of proper management; and effective management of coastal areas requires that the ecological and socioeconomic interdependencies that characterize these areas be taken fully into account; and this can best be done through development and implementation cf integrated coastal resources management plans;

Whereas, political leaders, and many groups and organizations have important roles in effective coastal resources management, and all of these can contribute to sustainable development; and government decision makers and the private sector can play a crucial role through their support of plan development and implementation, and their encouragement of coastal communities to act cohesively to enhance prospects for sustainable development of coastal areas; and donor agencies can likewise contribute meaningfully in setting the course of development of coastal areas by ensuring that all sectoral projects funded are congruent with multisectoral development plans that are conducive to sustainable development of coastal areas; and the mass media are important in increasing public awareness regarding the importance of coastal resources and the dependence of continued prospects for economic development in coastal areas on proper management of coastal resources;

Whereas, recognizing the need for effective strategies to manage coastal resources for sustainable development, the ASEAN, through its various mechanisms, has undertaken a series of cooperative programs, particularly the ASEAN/US Coastal Resources Management Project; and under this project, the following activities have been undertaken by various national institutions coordinated by the International Centre for Living Aquatic Resources Management:

- Analysis, documentation and dissemination of information on how coastal resources are being developed for economic purposes;
- Strengthening of existing management capabilities of local and national institutions within the region;
- Provision of technical solutions to resolve conflicts arising from competing uses of coastal resources; and
- Assistance to various organizations and agencies in the development of coastal area management plans ;

Whereas, the Policy Conference on Managing ASEAN's Coastal Resources for Sustainable Development recognizes the accomplishments of the Coastal Resources Management Project;

Therefore, we, the participants of the Policy Conference hereby resolve and further recommend that the ASEAN member-countries, donor agencies and all other groups and organizations give emphasis to the protection of these resources for the primary benefit of coastal communities by:

- endorsing policies that promote and enhance sustainable development of coastal resources;
- encouraging the development and implementation of integrated, inter-disciplinary and comprehensive coastal resources

management plans;

- further strengthening management capabilities of governmental and non-governmental organizations responsible for the management of coastal resources;
- undertaking measures to relieve human population pressures in coastal, areas;
- implementing and rigorously enforcing effective regulations and supporting incentive schemes to promote sustainable uses of coastal resources;
- increasing awareness of coastal populations regarding their critical dependence on the continued productivity of coastal resources;
- promoting community-based participation in coastal area management;
- adopting policies and programs to enable women to participate in and contribute more actively to the effective management of coastal resources for sustainable development;
- exploring ways and means by which the public and private sectors can cooperate and thereby benefit from efforts to sustain and develop ... coastal resources; and
- considering in coastal area management, the implications of possible climate change and sea level rise.

Adopted by acclamation in Baguio City, Philippines, on 6th March 1990.

Source: Chua and Scura, 1992, pp.4-6.

Appendix 3.3
Categories of lessons learned from ASEAN/US CRMP

The lessons learned through the experience of CRMP are related to:

Process

Desirable characteristics of the planning phase

- iterative process
- originate from within
- integrated with development agendas
- local participation
- full consideration of existing institutional and organizational arrangements
- research focused on identification of management priorities and opportunities
- management actions matched with management issues and goals

Essential features of management plans

- situation profile
- problems and opportunities
- philosophy, goals and objectives
- policies and strategies
- programmes and projects
- organization and management
- monitoring and evaluation
- financial and economic justification

Essential mechanisms

- integration
- coordination

Management issues

Traditional management issues

- predominate in undiversified economies typically dependent on natural resource-based activities
- associated with mix of activities typical of rural areas
- critical issues tend to be related to the rate of resource exploitation
- pollution issues usually of lesser importance

Management issue transition
- driven by economic diversification
- function of the mix of development activities

Modern management issues
- predominate in more diversified economies
- associated with mix of activities typical of urbanizing and urban areas
- critical issues tend to be related to pollution
- issues of over exploitation of natural resources usually of lesser importance

Dualism and synergism
- coexistence of traditional and modern management issues
- traditional issues exacerbated by modern issues

Opportunities for Management Intervention

Institutional and organizational arrangements
- clarification, monitoring and enforcement of rights and obligations needed for most interventions

Incentives and regulations to modify human behaviour
- work with the market when possible.

Direct public involvement and investment
- financial constraints limit coverage
- cost recovery should be pursued when possible

Source: Chua and Scura, 1992, p. 10.

Appendix 3.4
International guidelines for ICM

World Bank Guideline	*World Coast Conference Report*	*UNEP Guidelines*	*OECD Guidelines*	IUCN Guidelines
		1. Scope/purpose		
Guidelines are designed to ensure that development and management plans for coastal zones are integrated with (environmental including social) goals and are made with the participation of those affected. Included are sections on institutional roles and responsibilities and on triggering of the need for ICZM. A three-stage process of plan formulation, program implementation, and monitoring, enforcement, and evaluation is recommended	Guidelines stress the urgent need for coastal states to strengthen their capabilities for ICZM, and the need to develop strategies and programs by the year 2000; ICZM is described as the most appropriate process for anticipating and responding to long term concerns and needs while addressing present-day challenges. It is to be achieved through a planning process involving data collection and analysis, monitoring and evaluation, and an implementation process. Report states that the 'quest for a unique recipe for ICM was misguided' and that several strategies can be effective.	Guidelines state that integrated management of coastal areas is required to lay the foundation for sustainable development. ICZM guidelines are given in three main stages, initiation, planning (preparation of ICZM master plan), and plan implementation. Many of the challenges to sustainable development (population pressure, industry growth, coastal tourism) are illustrated in the context of the Mediterranean region.	Guidelines are the result of investigations using country information papers prepared by respondents in several countries and a survey instrument. The main stress is on ecologically sustainable development of the coastal zone. Recommendations are given for structure and process for ICM, including creation of the institutional body, generation of information, assessment of current policies, preparation of alternative plans, selection of a final plan, and monitoring and evaluation	Guidelines are provided for the development of a coastal area plan that can be applied at a national level, through a review of coastal problems and the need for integrated cross-sectoral management (ICSM). The process by which ICSM can be achieved (CICAP-Cross-sectoral integrated coastal area planning) is discussed; seven steps include problem definition, assessment and analysis, issues and options formulation, adoption, implementation, and monitoring and evaluation.

(contd.)

(Appendix 3.4 contd.)

2. Principles				
• Precautionary principle • Polluter pays principle • Use of proper resource accounting • Transboundary responsibility • Inter-generational equity	Follows the principles set out in the Rio Declaration-in particular, sustainable development and its long term focus and the precautionary principles.	Multidisciplinary approach; Problem solving, not problem transfer. Priority on prevention rather than cure; Precautionary approach.	Guidelines stress that integrated coastal zone management is well suited for ecologically sustainable development (ESD). Implies principles of long term sustainable growth, utilization of modern economic tools, etc.	Guidelines state that the starting point of ICSM is sustainable development. Therefore the guidelines endorse a long-term and intra-and inter generational focus. To be effective, the effort should be holistic, that is, interdisciplinary, combining social and natural sciences.
3. Definition of Management Area				
Ideally, the management zone should include all of the coastal resources of interest and all activities that are capable of affecting the resources and waters of the coastal zone (implies from the watershed.to the 200 mile limit).	Report does not recommend where nations should set boundaries. Case studies illustrate a wide diversity of strategies, from only the land side of the coastal zone to somewhat integrated coastal and ocean management.	Guidelines do not recommend specific boundaries. However, the first step of the planning stage is precise definition of coastal area boundaries,	Guidelines suggest an ecosystem approach that should cover part of the hinterland and include the 'associated aquatic ecosystems ' and seaward, potentially to the 200-nautical-mile limit.	Recognize that the significant variation in local natural and socioeconomic systems make setting up a management program for a specific scientific scale difficult. When the appropriate scale is selected, the CICAP must be consistent with that scale.

(contd.)

(Appendix 3.4 contd.)

4. ICM Function/Goals				
• Strengthen and harmonize sectoral management • Preserve and protect the productivity and biological diversity of coastal ecosystems • Promote rational development and sustainable utilization of coastal resource	• Anticipate and respond to long-term concerns while addressing present-day challenges and opportunities • Stimulate sustainable development of coastal areas • Promote increased economic development and benefits	• Provide guidelines for legal and institutional strategy in area management and planning • Form adhoc committees for dispute resolution • Combine land use controls and economic tools for pollution control and conservation	• Achieve ESD and Maintain critical stocks of resources • Maintain or enhance critical environmental quality • Preserve certain natural resources (usually public goods) • Maintain the amenity value of the coastal zone	• Set national development objectives for ICSM • Initiate the CICAP for long-term benefits and an evolutionary ICSM process
5. Legal Basis				
Agreed on goals and objectives by the agencies and subnational governments. Legislation for boundary setting and zoning of the coastal area but not necessarily a comprehensive coastal zone act.	There is no one measure for success. New institutional and legal framework must take into account social, economic, and political parameters of each specific situation.	Endorses use of the National Coastal Management Act or other legal means of ensuring enforcement of various sectoral laws. Guidelines utilize a 'top-down' approach.	Legislation is needed to create institutional bodies or the management council (lead agency) and to allow for coordination. Of importance is 'a consistent government policy at national or regional level that provides clear direction and support for integration'.	Within the CICAP steps, legal and administrative options are shown to be 'essential components' of a coastal or ocean planning programme. However, the guidelines provide no specific recommendations or suggestions for setting up those legal and institutional arrangements; they only emphasize the need for integration among the legal and administrative, socioeconomic, and biophysical components and among the public, scientists, managers, and users, including some form of dispute resolution

(contd.)

(Appendix 3.4 contd.)

		6. Horizontal Integratoin		
Alternatives include * Use of a national planning agency * Formal establishment of an interagency or interministerial council * Creation of a special coordinating commission or committee * Formal designation of a lead agency.	There is no one recipe for success. Case studies document successful ICZM efforts created from both top-down and bottom-up arrangements, allowing for the need for increased inter-sectoral and inter-governmental integration. Depends on specifics of the case.	Recommends designating a lead agency for coastal management at the national level and creating an interdepartmental committee for coastal management consisting of the major relevant ministries.	Stresses that effective ICM coordination is achieved through 'impr-oving the linkages' among sectors and development of regulatory and economic tools. A coor-dinating body should be created along with mana-gement councils and subgroups. No specific recipe is provided.	No specific recommendations are provided; guidelines state only that mechanisms for integration are needed.
		7. Vertical Integration		
There is little discussion of this dimension. Guidelines do suggest the following: * Define the primary level of implementation (not necessarily federal). * Have all government levels and stakeholders participate in the 'concept paper' for program formulation * Include local representation in the interagency coordi-nating mechanism.	There is no one recipe for success. Case studies document successful ICM efforts created from both top-–down and bottom-up arrangements, allowing for the need for increased intersectoral and intergovernmental integration. Depends on specifics of the case.	Suggests a degree of national planning to inform regional and local authorities of the intention of the national authorities on coastal development policies. Recommends implementing a process to establish consistency between local activities and regional and national activities.	Makes little or no mention of the intergovernmental aspects of ICM. There is some discussion of the benefits of regional level ICM planning, Regarding the coordinating body, the guidelines state that in many cases, local coordinating bodies that fit into the national system may be needed.	No specific recommendations are provided; guidelines state only that mechanisms for integration are needed.

(contd.)

(Appendix 3.4 contd.)

8. Financial Arrangements

Funding to put ICZM program in place can come from budgets of existing government agencies, new funding for research needs and new institutional arrangements should come from the national government, with assistance from international agencies.	Funding is to come from international and national funding institutions (including development banks) that take into account economic development, environmental and social considerations. Some of the burden is to be borne by coastal users ' groups and the general public.	* For administrative structure: National and regional government budgets. * For infrastructure and pollution control; use fees, taxes, economic incentives * For conservation: funds from interested environmental groups, park entry fees, etc.	Guidelines state that a major factor of successful ICM is how well the government implementing the program can raise its own funds, either independently or with assistance from the national government. This flow of financial resources must be dependable and ongoing.	Guidelines do not mention strategies or recommendations regarding financial arrangements or economic tools for funding ICSM.

(contd...)

(Appendix 3.4 contd.)

9. Prescriptions for Use of Science

Attention is given to the value of natural coastal resources and the fact that the coastal zone is a 'dynamic area with frequently changing biological, chemical and geological attributes'.	Given the strong tie between the IPCC and the World Coast Conference, natural science aspects are stressed, with emphasis on the role of vulnerability assessments in ICZM and the effects of sea-level rise.	There is a strong reliance on effective risk assessment studies. Emphasis is given to economic valuation techniques. A section of the planning stage is devoted to estimating: * current rates of resource use * waste being discharged into the system * effects of socio-economic activities on natural ecosystems. Additional emphasis is placed on water pollution issues.	It is emphasized that scientific analysis, natural resource monitoring, and impact assessment play a crucial role in successful ICM.	There is a strong prescription for using science in the assessment and analysis stage of the CICAP and for understanding the short and long term concerns fuelling the need for ICSM.

(contd...)

(Appendix 3.4 contd.)

10. Capacity Building

One aspect overseen by the interagency coordinating mechanism is human resources development. Guidelines also recognize the role of stakeholders and the general public in formulation and implementation of the programme . However, no mention is made of indigenous peoples and their role in ICM.	Use of funding for capacity building is stressed, as are education and training in the implementation process through: * Interdisciplinary curricula * Establishment of ICZM training centres * Coordination of existing training efforts * Networks to facilitate information exchange.	No mention is made of capacity building or attention to indigenous management.	No specific mention of capacity building is made in the main text, though there are references to it in the case studies.	Guidelines state that feedback and consensus building are needed among all interested parties in the coastal area. They state that communication and common linkages should be facilitated, though no formal measures for capacity building are outlined.

Source: Cicin-Sain and Knecht, 1998, pp.105-107.

Appendix 4.1
Mangrove areal extent (ha) in major areas of the world

Geographical location	*Mangrove Areal Extent*
Asia and the Orient	6,517,000
Africa	5,117,000
South America	4,105,000
North America	1,670,000
Oceania	1,515,000
Caribbean	962,000
Central America	888,000
Total	20,774,000

Source: Paw and Chua, 1991, p. 208.

Appendix 5.1
Block/panchayat-wise distribution of backwaters of Kerala

S.No.	District	S.No.	Name of the backwater	Area (ha)	Local/regional names	Location	
						Block	Panchayat
1.	Thiruvananthapuram	1.	Poovar Kayal	30.93	Poonthura Kayal	Parassala	Parassala
		2.	Poonthura Kayal	97.59			
		3.	Veli Kayal	22.48	Akkulam Kayal	Thiruvananthapuram Rural	Ulloor
		4.	Kadinamkulam Kayal	346.88	Kadinamkulam Kayal		
		5.	Anchuthengu Kayal	521.75	Anchuthengu Kayal	Chirayinkeezhu	Anchuthegu
		6.	Edava-Nadayara Kayal	157.65	Edava Kayal	Varkala	Edava
			Total	**1177.28**			
2.	Kollam	7.	Paravoor Kayal	662.46	Thanni Kayal	Mukhathala	Mayyanad
					Paravoor Reclamation Kayal	Mukhathala	Mayyanad
					Mala Kayal	Paravoor	Muncipality
					Paravoor Kayal	Paravoor	Muncipality

(contd.)

(Appendix 5.1 cont.)

S.No.	District	S.No.	Name of the backwater	Area (ha)	Local/regional name	Location	
						Block	Panchayat
		8.	Ashtamudi Kayal	6424.15	Akath Kayal	West Kallada	Sasthamkotta
					Chempu Kayal		
					Chempil Kayal	Chittumala	Kundara
					Kanjiramkodu Kayal	Chittumala	Perinadu
					Kanjirottu Kayal	Chittumala	Perinadu
					Kondachira Kayal	Chittumala	Perinadu
					Chambalarn Kayal	Chittumala	East Kallada
					Ashtamudi Kayal	Chittumala	Mundrothhuruth
					Ashtamudi Kayal	Chavara	Thekkumbhagaom
					Ashtamudi Kayal	Chavara	Thevalakkara
					Kannetty Kayal	Chavara	Panmana
					Ashtamudi Kayal	Chavara	Neendakara
					Ashamudi Kayal	Anchalumoodu	Kilikolloor
					Ashtamudi Kayal	Anchalumoodu	Thrikkaruva
					Vatta Kayal	Anchalumoodu	Sakthikulangara
					Katta Kayal	Anchalumoodu	Sakthikulangara
					Ashtamudi Kayal	Kollam	Municipality
		9.	Kayamkulam Kayal	140.58			
			Total	**7227.19**			

(contd.)

(Appendix 5.1 cont.)

S.No.	District	S.No.	Name of the backwater	Area (ha)	Local/regional names	Location	
						Block	Panchayat
		10.	Kayamukulam Kayal	1511.75	Kumlalangi Kayal		
3	Alappuzha				Puthenthodu		
					Manakattu padathodu		
		11.	Poomeen Kayal	3.37	Arookutty Kayal	Pattanakkad	Aroor
					Kaithapuzha Kayal		
		12.	Vadakkal Kayal	1.46	Chakarachal		
					Vembanattu Kayal		
		13.	Chethi Kayal	4.11	Konkerthodu		
					Panadithodu		
		14.	Arthungal Kayal	5.96	Vettuthullu Kayal	Pattanakkad	Ezhupunna
					Pillizathu Kayal		
		15.	Pozhichal Kayal	20.41	Vallyathodu	Pattanakkad	Kodamthuruthu
					Thayyilthodu		
					Kuthiathodu		
					Namanathuthodu		
		16.	Vettakkalchal Kayal	27.10	Pozhithodu		
					Karathodu		
		17	Vembanad Kayal	10661.23	Vellyappu Kayal	Pattanakkadu	Mannancherry
			Kayamkulam Kayal		Kurumbi Kayal		
			Total	**12235.39**			

(contd.)

(Appendix 5.1 cont.)

S.No.	District	S.No.	Name of the backwater	Area (ha)	Local regional nature	Location	
						Block	Panchayat
4.	Kottayam	18	Vembanad Kayal	2926.77	Vembanad Lake	Vaikkom	TV Puram
					Mundar Lake	Kaduthuruthy	Kallara
					Vembanad Lake	Ettumanoor	Aymanam
			Total	**2926.77**			
5.	Ernakulam	19.	Vembanad Kayal	2257.89			
		20.	Kochi Kayal	7503.80			
			Total	9761.69			
6.	Thrissur	21.	Azhikode Kayal	82.02		Chowannur	Venkidangu
		22.	Kadungalloor Kayal	613.81	Pulloot Kayal	Kodungalloor	Municipality
		23.	Chettuva Kayal	713.87			
		24.	Pattikkara Kayal				Choonlal
		25.	Manakkady Kayal			Anthikkad	Anthikkad
			Total	**1409.70**			
7.	Malappuram	26.	1. Puthupponnani	150.83			
		27.	2. Ponnani Kayal	757.19	Biyyem Kayal	Ponnani	Municipality
		28.	3. Poorappuzha	62.98	Ottumpuram Lake	Thanur	Thanur
		29.	4. Kadalundi Kayal	323.56	1. Ullanam Kaipuzha	Thirurangadi	Parappanangadi
					2. Kottachali	Thirurangadi	Valliukkunnu
					3. Velimmukku Chali	Thirurangadi	Moonniyoor
			Total	**1294.56**			

(contd.)

(Appendix 5.1 cont.)

S.No.	District	S.No.	Name of the backwater	Area (ha)	Local regional names	Location	
						Block	Panchayat
8.	Kozhikode	30.	Kadalundi Kayal	83.85			
		31.	Beypore Kayal	783.74			
		32.	Kallai Puzha	160.13			
		33.	Korapuzha	1038.08			
		34.	Payyoli Puzha	26.70			
		35.	Kottapuzha	584.12			
		36.	New Mahe Puzha	88.28			
			Total	**2764.90**			
9.	Kannur	37.	Mahe	91.89			
		38.	Dharmadam Kayal	359.06			
		39.	Valapattanam	3077.64			
		40.	Palakkode	598.25			
		41.	Cheruvathur	30.58			
			Total	**4157.42**			
10.	Kasaragod	42.	Cheruvathur	1123.12			
		43.	Nileswaram	824.69			
		44.	Chittari Kayal	89.33			
		45.	Bekal Kayal	43.37			
		46.	Kappil Pozhi	2.22			
		47.	Neembil Kayal	22.47			
		48.	Chandragiri	575.81		Kasaragod	Muliyar

(contd.)

(*Appendix 5.1 contd.*)

S.No.	*District*	*S.No.*	*Name of the backwater*	*Area (ha)*	*Local regional names*	*Location*	
						Block	*Panchayat*
		49.	Mogral Puthur	89.74		Kumbala	Manjeswar
		50.	Kumbala	221.54		Kumbala	Manjeswar
		51.	Suvarnagiri	6.22			
		52.	Manjeswaram	158.41		Manjeswaram	Manjeswar
		53.	Thalappady	17.12			
			Total	**3174.04**			
			Grand Total	**46128.94**			

Source: Department of Fisheries, 2002, pp. 126-129.

Appendix 5.2
Taluk-wise Distribution of Brackishwater Areas in Kerala

S.No.	Name of the district	S.No.	Name of the taluk	Area (ha)
1.	Thiruvananthapuram	1.	Neyyattinkara	99.28
		2.	Thiruvananthapuram	493.55
		3.	Chirayinkeezhu	831.15
	Total			**1423.98**
2.	Kollam	4.	Kollam	5402.38
			Kunnathoor	484.75
		6.	Karunagappally	2716.49
	Total			**8603.62**
3.	Alappuzha	7.	Karthikappally	2051.65
		8.	Kuttanadu	1192.26
		9.	Ambalapuzha	4515.19
		10.	Cherthala	7463.82
	Total			**15222.92**
4.	Kottayam	11.	Kottayam	691.54
		12.	Vaikom	3635.20
	Total			4326.74
5.	Ernakulam	13.	Kochi	6876.68
		14.	Kunnathunadu	25.52
		15.	Kanayannur	6707.88
		16.	Parur	2602.63
	Total			**16212.71**
6.	Thrissur	17.	Mukundapuram	1274.45
		18.	Kodungallur	1485.16
		19.	Thrissur	186.50
		20.	Chavakkad	1325.33
	Total			**4271.94**
7.	Malappuram	21.	Ponnani	556.02
		22.	Tirur	1240.24
	Total			**1796.26**
8.	Kozhikode	23.	Kozhikode	1495.85
		24.	Koyilandi	1802.25
		25.	Vadakara	864.54
	Total			4162.44

(contd.)

(Appendix 5.2 cont.)

S.No.	*Name of the district*	*S.No.*	*Name of the taluk*	*Area (ha)*
9.	Kannur	26.	Thalassery	737.35
		27.	Kannur	3304.21
		28.	Thaliparamba	1902.54
	Total			**5944.10**
10.	Kasaragod	29.	Hosdurg	2088.84
		30.	Kasaragod	1159.41
	Total			**3248.25**
	Grand Total			**65212.96**

Source: Department of Fisheries, 2002, p.125.

Appendix 5.3
Block/panchayat-wise distribution of mangroves in Kerala

S.No.	District	Location: Block	Location: Panchayat	Name of the area	Extent of mangrove area (ha)	Mangrove species
1.	Thiruvananthapuram	Thiruvananthapuram	Thiruvanathapuram Rural	Veli-Akkulam Area	120	*Avicennia officinalis Bruguiera gymnorrhiza, Acanthus ilicifolius* *Acorostichum acereurm, Cerbera odollam* *Callophyllum innophyllum*
				Panathura Kayal Area (Kovalam)	75	*Avicennia officinalis,* *Bruguiera gymnorrhiza, Acanthus ilicifolius* *Callophyllum innophyllum.* Sonneratia caseolaris *Avicennia officinalis* *Acrostichum aureund*

(contd.)

(Appendix 5.3 contd.)

S.No.	District	Location: Block	Location: Panchayat	Name of the area	Extent of mangrove area (ha)	Mangrove species
						Acanthus ilicifolins
						Barringtonia racemosa
						Ardisia littoralis
						Clerodendrum inerme
						Cerebra odollam
						Callophyllum innophyllum
						Phoenix–humilis(pedunculata)
						Ixova coccinea
						Justicia Spp
						Twinera Subulata
						Calotropis gigantea
						Rhizophova apicuieta
						Bruguiera gymnorrhiza
Total					**195**	
2.	Kollam	Ochira	Ochira	Karoorkadavu	8	*Avicennia officinalis*
		Kulasekharapuram	Clappana	Ayiramthengu		*Bruguiera gymnorrhiza*
			Mynagappally	Govt fish farm,	35	*Sonneratia cascolar*

(contd.)

(Appendix 5.3 contd.)

S.No.	District	Location: Block	Location: Panchayat	Name of the area	Extent of mangrove area (ha)	Mangrove species
				Mukkumpuzha temple		Marshy and Mangroveassociates
						Acanthus illcifolum Adenosma capitation
				Azheekkal Fisheries Station		Caesalpinia racemosa
						Cerebra spp.
						Avicennia officinalis Acanthus illicifallus
		Neendakara			12	Acrostichum
						Bruguiera gymnorrhiza
		Karunagapally	Thodiyoor		18	Sonneratia caseloris
		Chittumala	Perinad		17	Avicennia marina
		Chittumala	Kundara		11	Cerbera odollam
		Chittumala	East Kallada	Ayyamkinavupoika	12	Barringtonia racemosa
		Chittumala	Perayam	Peringalam	22	Camophythum inophyllum
		Chavara	Manrothuruthu		14	Dolichandrone Sapthacca
		Chavara	Thekkumbhagam		8	Lumnitzera racemosa
		Chavara	Chavara		12	Caesalpinia rugu

(contd.)

(Appendix 5.3 contd.)

S.No.	District	Location		Name of the area	Extent of mangrove area (ha)	Mangrove species
		Block	Panchayat			
		Chavara	Thevalakkara		7	*Calamus rotang*
		Chavara	Panmana	Arinelloor.S	14	*Callophyllum innophyllum Canavalia*
		Achalumoodu				*obtusifolia*
						Cerebera odollum
						Cissus trilobata
						Derris trilobata
						Derris scandens
						Dolichandrone spathaceae
						Drosera burmanii
						Excoecaria agallocha
						Glochideon Zeylanicum
						Hibiscus filiaceus
						Illysanthus hyssopiodes
						Illysanthes reptans
		Chavara	Panmana	Arinelloor. N	20	*Illysanthes rotundifolia*
		Chavara	Neendakara	Koivila	22	*Illysanthes serrata*

(contd.)

(Appendix 5.3 contd.)

S.No.	District	Location: Block	Location: Panchayat	Name of the area	Extent of mangrove area (ha)	Mangrove species
			Sakthi Kuangara Mayyanad	Kollaka area	19	*Impatiens diversifolia*
				Pannakkal thuruthu	26	*Lagenadndra ovata*
						Ipomea pes-capre
						Leca sambucina
				Velithuruthu	18	*Limnophila gratilodes*
		Anchalumoodu		Mangad area	19	*Lipa nodflorapill*
				Kandachira	17	*Malestoma Malabathricum*
						Moneira cunifolac
		Mukhathala		Vattakayal area	15	*Pandanus tectorus*
				Sasthamthodi	12	*Pandanus tectorus*
			Kollam Corpration Area	South Mukkam		*Parsonsia spiralis*
				Mukkam Kadavu		*Paspalum vaginattum*
				Eravipuram		*Premna latifolia*
				Poothakkulam		
				Chathannur	3	*Pongamia glaora*
				Adichanallur	7	*Sterisprmum tetragonum*

(contd.)

(Appendix 5.3 contd.)

S.No.	*District*	*Location*		*Name of the area*	*Extent of mangrove area (ha)*	*Mangrove species*
		Block	*Panchayat*			
				Asramam	8	*Stictocardia filiaefolia*
	Total				**376**	
3.	Alappuzha	Thykkattussery	Arookkutty	Arookutty Jetty	4	*Rhizophora manonata*
		Pattanakkad	Panavally	Anchuthuruthu	1	*Rhizophora apicutala*
			Aroor	Aroor	2	*Avicennia offcinalis*
				Chethipozhi	2	*Acanthus ilicifoluis*
				Thaneermukkam	5	
			Thaneermukkam	Muhamma	5	
		Muthukulam	Kandalloor	Kandalloor Pattoli	10	
				Velanchira		
		Muthukulam	Arattupuzha			
				Arattupuzha	10	
		Muthukulam	Devikulangara	Kahikkad		
				Valiyazheekkal		
				Devikulangara	40	
				Estuary		
	Total				**79.00**	
4.	Kottayam			Kumarakam	340	*Rhizophora apiculata*
						Biruguiera gymnorrhiza

(contd.)

(Appendix 5.3 contd.)

S.No.	District	Location: Block	Location: Panchayat	Name of the area	Extent of mangrove area (ha)	Mangrove species
						Sonneratia Caseolaris
						Aridisia littoralis
						Cesebera odollam
						Hibiscus litiasons
						Thespesia populrea
						Terminalia catapa
						Excoecaria agallocha
						Heritiera litteralis
	Total				**340**	
5.	Ernakulam	Palluruthy	Chellanam	Kandakadavu	20	*Avicennia acanthus*
				Thekke	12	*Avicennia acanthus*
				Chellanam	18	*Rhizophora illibflora*
			Kumbalangi	Kannamali	40	*Avicennia acanthus*
				Kattikonattu	15	*Avicennia officinalis*
				Kannacherry	25	*Rhizophora apiculata*
				Vadakkekumbalangi	12	*Rhizophora micronatax*
		Vypin	Edavanakkadu			*Rhizophora apiculata*
						Avicennia officinalis
				Pazhangad	20	*Candalia caudal*

(contd.)

(Appendix 5.3 contd.)

S.No.	District	Location		Name of the area	Extent of mangrove area (ha)	Mangrove species
		Block	Panchayat			
				Edavanakkad	15	*Acanthus ilicifolius*
						Acanthus ilicifolius
						Rhizophora micronatax
				Chathanangad		*Rhizophora apiculata*
				Puthuvypu pozhy	20	*Avicennia officinalis*
			Elamkunnapuzha			*Candalia Caudal*
				Puthuvypu west coast	10	*Acanthus ilicifolius*
						Rhizophora apiculata
			Perumbil			*Avicennia officinalis*
			Njarakkal	Chappa thodu	10	*Candalia caudal*
						Acanthus ilicifolius
		Vypin	Nayarambalam		15	*Rizophora micronatax*
						Rhizophora apiculata
						Avicennia officinalis
		Vypin	Mulavukad		20	*Candalia caudal*
				Puthuvypu pozhi	76	
			Pal ippuram	Puthuvypu west coast	15	*Rhizophora apiculata*
				Chappa thodu	17	*Avicennia Officinalis*

(contd.)

(Appendix 5.3 contd.)

S.No.	District	Location: Block	Location: Panchayat	Name of the area	Extent of mangrove area (ha)	Mangrove species
				Puthuvypu pozhi	12	*Candalia caudal*
		Vyttila		Puthuvypu west coast	8	*Acanthus ilicifolius (Mullan chutte)*
			Kumbalam			*Rhiziphora micronatax*
						Rhizophora apiculata
						Avicennia officinalis
				Panagad Kayal bank	3	*Acanthus ilicifolius*
				Kumbalam	4	*Avicennia officinalis*
			Maradu	Mundampilly	6	*Avicennia officinalis*
				Kundannoor river bank	3	*Rhizophora apiculata*
				Nettoor river Bank	5	*Acanthus ilicifolius*
					5	*Avicennia officinalis*
				Chambakara river Bank	16	*Avicennia officinaliis*
				Mangala Vanam	18	*Rhizophora apiculata*
		Kochi Corporation		Vimala Vanam	8	*Avicennia officinaliis*
				Vathuruthy area	10	*Candalia caudal*
		Kannamali				*Acanthus iilicifolius*
		Edappalli				*Rhizophora microsata*

(contd.)

(Appendix 5.3 contd.)

S.No.	District	Location		Name of the area	Extent of mangrove area (ha)	Mangrove species
		Block	Panchayat			
		Cochin				*Avicennia officinaliis*
						Rhizophora apiculata
						Bruguiera gymnorrhis
						Sonneratia caseolaris
	Total				**453**	
6	Thrissur	Thalikulam	Engandiyoor	Chettuvacheplimadu	10	*Avicennia officinalis*
		Chetuvai			16	*Acanthus ilieifolims*
						Bruguiera pasviflora
						Avicennie officinalis
						Exoecasia agallocha
						Avicennia marina
						Acrostichum aureum
	Total				**26**	
7	Kozhikode	Kozhikode	Ramanattukara	Near Neelithodu	2	*Avicennia officinalis*
			C-Nallalam	Madhura Bazar River side	10	*Acanthus ilicifolins*
						Dolichandroze Spathacea
			Olavanna	Mampuzha river side	2	*Lagerstromia Speciosa*

(contd.)

(Appendix 5.3 contd.)

S.No.	District	Location: Block	Location: Panchayat	Name of the area	Extent of mangrove area (ha)	Mangrove species
		Vadakara	Municipality			*Pongania Pinnata*
		Koyilandy	Municipality	Near Raiiway Station	2	*Derris frifoliata*
				Nelliadi kadavu		*Acrostichum auseum*
				Kakkulam		
				Amala and		
				Kanayamkode		
		Kozhikode		Kallayi	5	
		Corporation		Beypore		
	Total				**24**	
8.	Kannur	Payyannur	Cheruthazham	Chemballikundu	5	*Avicennia spp.*
				Perumba river	4	*Avicennia spp*
		Thaliparamba	Ezhome	Payangadi river side	2	*Avicennia spp*
				Kohila river side	2	*Avicennia spp*
			Kunhimangalam	Perumba river bank	10	*Avicennia spp*
				Chemballikundu	5	*Avicennia spp*
			Madai		5	*Avicennia spp*

(contd.)

(Appendix 5.3 contd.)

S.No.	District	Location: Block	Location: Panchayat	Name of the area	Extent of mangrove area (ha)	Mangrove species
				Palancode river bank	10	*Avicennia spp*
			Ramanthali		5	
			Pattuvam	Pattuvam Muthuka	40	
		Thaliparamba		Thavam Payangadi	48	
			Cherukkunnu		24	
			Kannapuram	Ayiramthengu, Ayyoth and Keezhara kaipad	15 30	*Avicennia officinalis* *Avicenia maverina*
			Kurumathoor	Kurumathoorpuzha side	34 10	*Binguiera parviflora* *Excoecaria agallocha*
				Kuppam river side	15	*Acanthus ilicifolius* *Aerostichum aureum*
			Pariyaram	Kambil Kadavu	12	*Kandelia candle* *Scirpus littoralis*
			Anthoor	Chakka soopy Kadavu	13	*Rhizophore apiculata*
		Kannur	Chtrakkal	Andallor area	16 13	*Avicennia* *Excore caria*
		Thalassery	Dharmadam Municipality	Mallor Area	13	*Acrostichum*

(contd.)

(Appendix 5.3 contd.)

S.No.	District	Location: Block	Location: Panchayat	Name of the area	Extent of mangrove area (ha)	Mangrove species
		Thaliparamba Municipality			25	*Avicennia officianalis* *Avicennia marina* *Excoecaria agalloda*
		Payyannur Municipality		Kuruvadu pathaya chira, Perumba, Keloth	5	*Kandelia Candle* *Bruguiera gymbossiliza* *Bruguiera partiflora* *Rhizophora apiculata* *Rhizophora immerorata*
				Karuvassery, Koduvally Venus Corner	15	
		Thailassery		Koyali	12	
		Total			**375**	
9.	Kasaragod	Nileswar	Thrikaripur		20	*Rhizophora apiculata* *Bruguiera Parvifilora*
		Padne	Kokkal island Padne		16	*Kandela Candel* *Avicennia officianalis*
		Valiyaparamba	Edayilakkad		20	Cerbara Odallom
		Total			**56**	

Source: Department of Fisheries, 2002, pp. 136-142.

Appendix 5.4
Details of areas suitable for aquaculture along Kerala coast

S.No.	*District*	*Coastal stretch*	*Mud/tidal flat including filtration ponds (ha)*	*Brackish water (ha)*
1.	Kasargode	Manjeswaram-Kasargode	138	286
		ChandragiriNileswaram	126	795
2.	Kannur	Payyannur-Ezhimala	133	2783
		Taliparamba	535	1095
		Mambaram	97	54
		Valapattanam-Dharmadom	789	2066
		Thalassery-Payyoli	281	1016
3.	Kozhikode	Quilandy	210	978
		Pudiyangadi	197	689
		Kozhikode-Parappanangadi	137	1598
4.	Malappuram	Tanur-Ponnani	153	1268
5.	Thrissur	Veliyankode-Edakkazhiyur	-	265
		Chavakkad	88	1008
		Thriprayar	854	1142
6.	Ernakulam	Kodungallur-Njarakkal	4248	3019
		Mala-Edappally	1679	1157
		Kochi-Chellanam	5540	10609
7.	Alappuzha	Cherthala-Punnamada	442	3508
		Alappuzha-Harippad	186	-
		Arattupuzha-Clappana	653	1562
		Kayamkularn-Karunagappally	519	543
8.	Kollam	Chavara-Edava	690	6732
9.	Thiruvananthapuram	Varkala	32	62
		Anjengo-Veli	18	1177
		Sangumughom-Vizhinjam	-	125
		Pulluvila-Poovar	-	188

Source: Baba, *et al.*, 1995, p.21.

Appendix 5.5
Details of brackishfish water fish/prawn farms owned by the Department of Fisheries, Kerala

S.No.	Name of farm	Area (ha)	District	Taluk
1.	Ayiramthengu estuarine fish farm	38.89	Kollam	Karunagappally
2.	Palaikari fish farm	48.00	Kottayam	Vaikom
3.	Edakochi fish farm	10.93	Ernakulam	Kochi
4.	Malippuram fish farm	21.14	Ernakulam	Kochi
5.	Njarakkal fish farm	22.40	Ernakulam	Kochi
6.	Poyyar barackish water fish farm	49.09	Thrissur	Kodungallur
7.	Kadappuram fish farm	6.33	Thrissur	Chavakkad
8.	Eranholi estuarine fish farm	10.96	Kannur	Thalassery
	Total	**207.74**		

Source: Department of Fisheries, 1993, p.28.

Appendix 5.6

District-wise and village-wise distribution of marine fishermen population of Kerala in 1998-99

S.No.	*Village*	*Fishermen population*	*S.No.*	*Village*	*Fishermen population*
Thiruvananthapuram District					
1.	Kollengode	4761	22.	Kannanthura	1570
2.	Paruthiyoor	5397	23.	Vettukadu	3254
3.	Poovar	5346	24.	Kochuveli	2646
4.	Karumkulam	2448	25.	Valiaveli	3606
5.	Kochuthura	3467	26.	Pallithura	547
6.	Puthiyathura	6372	27.	Vettuthura	3083
7.	Pallom	1434	28.	Puthenthope	2319
8.	Pulluvila	8688	29.	Valliyathura	1954
9.	Adimalathura	1792	30.	Mariyanadu	1448
10.	Chowara	5914	31.	Puthukurichi	6318
11.	Vizhinjam South	11529	32.	Porumathura	3417
12.	Vizhinjam North	8990	33.	Thazhampally	2351
13.	Kovalam	1459	34.	Poonthura	2420
14.	Panathura	2606	35.	Anjengo	5510
15.	Poonthura	11800	36.	Mampally	7282
16.	Beemapally	5238	37.	Kaikkara	1315
17.	Cheriyathura	1885	38.	Arivalam	1528
18.	Valiathura	5659	39.	Vettoor	6002
19.	Kochuthope	3699	40.	Chilakkur	3767
20.	Valiathope	1706	41.	Odayam	4019
21.	Sangumugham	1448	42.	Edava	1740
	Total				**1,67,734**
Kollam District					
43.	Paravavur South	1880	51.	Vady	3268
44.	Paravur North	3727	52.	Thankassery	3984
45.	Mayyanadu	2179	53.	Kunnummel	1656
46.	Eravipuram South	4243	54.	Sakthikulangara	5890
47.	Eravipuram North	1490	55.	Neendakara	3739
48.	Pallithottam	4149	56.	Puthenthura	3974
49.	Port	5437	57.	Karithura	3915
50.	Moodakkara	2779	58.	Kovilthottam	3568

(contd.)

(Appendix 5.6 cont.)

S.No.	Village	Fishermen population	S.No.	Village	Fishermen population
59.	Panmana	868	65.	Parayakkadavu	1974
60.	Pandarathura	3326	66.	Azheekal	7068
61.	Cheriazheekal	6498	67.	Srayikkad	2720
62.	Vellanathuruth	2703	68.	Maruthukulangara	4933
63.	Alappad	2600	69.	Kulasekharapuram	3325
64.	Kuzhithura	1403			
	Total				**94,401**
Alappuzha District					
70.	Valiazheekkal	3078	85.	Vadakkel North	5895
71.	Thurayilkadavu	4343	86.	Kanjiramthira	2745
72.	Kallikkadu	4009	87.	Thumboli South	3241
73.	Arattupuzha	3055	88.	Thumboli North	1574
74.	Pathiyankara	3007	89.	Chettikkad	5050
75.	Thrikunnapuzha	2288	90.	Kattoor	5899
76.	Pallana	2091	91.	Pollathai	4294
77.	Thottapally	3445	92.	Chethy	2688
78.	Punthala	3384	93.	Chennaveli	3443
79.	Purakkad	2801	94.	Arthunkal	5967
80.	Ambalapuzha	4019	95.	Thaikkal	3826
81.	Neerkunnam	3398	96.	Ottamassery	5249
82.	Punnapra South	3466	97.	Azheekal	4653
83.	Punnapra North	4687	98.	Pallithodu South	3694
84.	Vadakkel South	3935	99.	Pallithodu North	2821
	Total				**1,12,043**
Ernakulam District					
100.	Chellanam	5415	111.	Njarakkal	6374
101.	Maruvakkad	1359	112.	Nayarambalam	6434
102.	Kandakkadavku	3883	113.	Edvanakkadu	1276
103.	Kannamali	3790	114.	Pazhangad	2307
104.	Cheriyakadavu	2280	115.	Ayyamppilli	2250
105.	Manassery	4052	116.	Kuzhippilli	2975
106.	Fort Cochin	2468	117.	Pallipuram	4236
107.	Azheekal	2974	118.	Cherai	983
108.	Ochanthuruthu	2800	119.	Munambam	7069
109.	Malipuram	4855	120.	Saudi	1962
110.	Elankunnapuzha	3195	121.	Fishing Harbour (Cochin)	NA
	Total				72,937

(contd.)

(Appendix 5.6 cont.)

S.No.	Village	Fishermen population	S.No.	Village	Fishermen population
Thrissur District					
122.	Azheekode	6628	131.	Nattika	4301
123.	Eriyad	3554	132.	Thaikulam	4550
124.	Edavilangad	2823	133.	Vadanappally	2425
125.	Veemballoor	2178	134.	Engandiyoor	2678
126.	Kuimuttom	1671	135.	Blangad	4698
127.	Perinjanam	2198	136.	Manathala	5685
128.	Kaipamangalam	4826	137.	Kadappuram	5191
129.	Chandrappini	1603	138.	Edakkizhiyoor	5555
130.	Chappallipuram	4507	139.	Manthalamkunnu	5108
	Total				**70,179**
	Malappuram District				
140.	Palapetty	5252	152.	Puthiyakadappuram	2455
141.	Veliyankode	4972	153.	Cherankadappuram	2183
142.	Puduponnani	5397	154.	Osankadapuram	1662
143.	Thekkekadappuram	2318	155.	Pandarakadappuram	2564
144.	Mukkadi	5704	156.	Edakadappuram	1912
145.	Marakkadavu	2298	157.	Koramanakadappuram	3924
146.	Meentheruvu	3815	158.	Elavanakadappuram	1594
147.	Pallivalappu	2057	159.	Parappanangadi	2933
148.	Purathor	3424	160.	Ariyankadappuram	3447
149.	Kottayi	5518	161.	Ariyallur beach	4359
150.	Paravanna	4509	162.	Kadalundi beach	3649
151.	Thevarkadappuram	4543			
	Total				**80,489**
Kozhikode District					
163.	Chaliyam	5737	174.	Puthiyappa South	2636
164.	Beypore	2615	175.	Puthiyappa North	3929
165.	Kappakal	1779	176.	Elathur	5019
166.	Thaikadappuram	3659	177.	Kannakadavu	1819
167.	Marad	2046	178.	Edakadavu	2077
168.	Vellayil	4414	179.	Ezhukudikkal	2152
169.	Puthiya Kadavu	5669	180.	Valiyamangadu	1342
170.	Thoppayil	4679	181.	Cheriyamangadu	1880
171.	Kampuram	2003	182.	Virunnukandy	1704
172.	Puthiyangadi	2639	183.	Quilandy	3220
173.	Pallikkandy	1464	184.	Kollammudody	3163

(contd..)

(Appendix 5.6 cont.)

S.No.	Village	Fishermen population	S.No.	Village	Fishermen population
185.	Vanmughom	1708	191.	Kuriyadi	2344
186.	Thekkodi	2449	192.	Muttungal	2903
187.	Melady	4423	193.	Madappally	3592
188.	Iringal	1976	194.	Madakkara	1829
189.	Badagara South	3347	195.	Chombala	2339
190.	Badagara North	4614	196.	Azhiyoor	2162
	Total				**99,332**
Kannur District					
197.	Kurichiyil	5285	203.	Azhikodekadappuram	3967
198.	Chalilgopalapetta	7675	204.	Mattool	6840
199.	Palissery	3225	205.	Puthiyangadi	10000
200.	Edakkad	5182	206.	Palacode	4977
201.	Thayyil	4862	207.	Kavvai	1357
202	Kannur city	2766			
	Total				**56,106**
Kasargode District					
208.	Thrikkarippur	1990	216.	Pallikara	2366
209.	Valiyaparambu	2071	217.	Kottikulam	2390
210.	Padannakadappuram	3534	218.	Kizhoor	2380
211.	Thaikadappuram	4310	219.	Kasaba	5990
212.	Kadangode	2609	220.	Kavungoli	1538
213.	Poonjavikadappuram	2214	221.	Koyippady	3264
214.	Hosdurg	1459	222.	Siriya	1688
215.	Ajanoor	2744	223.	Bengramanjeswar	3459
	Total				**44,006**
	Grand Total				**7,97,227**

Source: Department of Fisheries, 2000, (b), pp. 13-25.

Appendix 5.7
District-wise and Village-wise distribution of inland fisherman population of Kerala in 1998-99

S.No.	Village	Fishermen population	S.No.	Village	Fishermen population
Thiruvananthapuram District					
1.	Atkupuram	159	3.	Chirayinkil	640
2.	Hariharapuram	128	4.	Vellayani	424
	Total				**1351**
Kollam District					
5.	Prayar	1078	18.	Chavara North	1207
6.	Sasthamkotta	893	19.	Koduvila	746
7.	Pudukkadu	1108	20.	Kumbalam	2870
8.	Mangadu	527	21.	Muttom	984
9.	Koyivila	1171	22.	Cherumakkodu	1034
10.	Kadavoor	2196	23.	Kanjirakkodu	1690
11.	Aravila	1076	24.	Manalikkadu	1157
12.	Neendakara	2105	25.	Kuripuzha	2346
13.	Prakulam	924	26.	Mukkad	1596
14.	Perumon	466	27.	Kottiyam	746
15.	Mundakkal	775	28.	Padappakkara	1962
16.	Sinkarapally	1548	29.	Ayramthengu	726
17.	Chavara South	884	30.	Arinallur	2508
	Total				**34,323**
Pathanamthitta District					
31.	Parumala	686	33.	Maramon	322
32.	Thiruvalla	442			
	Total				**1450**
Kottayam District					
34.	Changanacherry	4625	38.	Thalayazhom	1725
35.	Kumarakom	3570	39.	Chempu	2064
36.	Thiruvarpu	1647	40.	Kaduthuruthy	3295
37.	Vaikom (Town)	6367	41.	Kottayam	1692
	Total				**24,985**

(contd.)

(Appendix 5.7 cont.)

S.No.	Village	Fishermen population	S.No.	Village	Fishermen population
Alappuzha District					
42.	Kayamkulam	2325	54.	Thuravoor North	3060
43.	Kochiyard Jetty	3016	55.	Thuravoor South	2613
44.	Chodatheruvu	2831	56.	Vayalar East	2808
45.	Payippadu	2300	57.	Mannar Sanghom	3258
46.	Karuvata	2293	58.	Thalavady	2752
47.	Chenkole	1894	59.	Noornadu	2415
48.	Muhamma	2384	60.	Eraviperoor	2104
49.	Thirunellur	2516	61.	Marakattu Ward	2808
50.	Panavally	2510	62.	Ramankari	3268
51.	Arookutty	2782	63.	Kavalam	2395
52.	Perumpalam	2246	64.	Thevarvattom	2702
53.	Aroor	2522	65.	Thanneermukkom	2586
	Total				**62,388**
Idukki District					
66.	Idukki	52			
	Total				**52**
Ernakukam District					
67.	Kadamakudi	1052	75.	Poonithura	3732
68.	Ezhikkara	10219	76.	Nedamagramam	2656
69.	Mulavukadu	4014	77.	Eranakulam East	2514
70.	Cheranelloor	1596	78.	Kumbalangi	2375
71.	Maradu	1575	79.	Palluruthy	5609
72.	Kumbalam	4959	80.	Vadakkekara	7676
73.	Udayamperoor	9457	81.	Puthenvelikara	5853
74.	Earnkulam West	1195			
	Total				**64,482**
Thrissur District					
82.	Kadavanadukad	2781	86.	Nedupuzha	2821
83.	Pullute	2408	87.	Venkidongu	2279
84.	Poyya	2324	88.	Karalam	2114
85.	Puthenchira	2822	89.	Vellur	2398
	Total				**19,947**
Palakkad District					
90.	Muthalamada	370	91.	Palakkad	671
	Total				1041

(contd.)

(Appendix 5.7 cont.)

S.No.	Village	Fishermen population	S.No.	Village	Fishermen population
Malappuram District					
92.	Kadavanadu	639	95.	Kuttanapuzha	999
93.	Gomughom	703	96.	Palathungal	749
94.	Purathoor	582	97.	Kadalundipuzha	715
	Total				**4387**
Kozhikode District					
98.	Karuvanthuruthy	1816	102.	Vellur	1007
99.	Cheruvannoor	719	103.	Teragi	1807
100.	Eranjikkal	1599	104.	Ullookadavu	1860
101.	Vengalam	1877	105.	Akalapuzha	1339
	Total				**12,024**
Wayanad District					
106.	Wayanad District	1039			
	Total				**1039**
Kannur District					
107.	Kurinjimanagalam	223	110.	Mundalloor	281
108.	Ezhom	294	111.	Eranholi	241
109.	Kattampally	499			
	Total				**1548**
Kasargode District					
112.	Peelikode	584	113.	Thrikaripur	369
	Total				953
	Grand Total				2,30,070

Source: Department of Fisheries, 2000, (b), pp. 13-18.

Appendix 6.1

A general description of the land use parameters followed by Centre for Earth Science Studies in its 1998 study (Baba, et al. 1998).

In the present study, various land use pattern that are widely practised in the coastal areas and their adjoining land parts that fall under the coastal regulation zone are elaborated. The nature of the built-up areas and the land utilization pattern are also taken into account. Various land use categories that are outlined in the report are as follows:

Forest

An extensive and inaccessible area of land covered mainly with large trees. It includes wide variety of flora and fauna. Under this, reserve forest and social forest are also included.

1. *Reserve Forest:* Similar to the forest, but with a restricted area as notified by the Forest Department for administrative purposes. It is an area subjected to strict forest laws.
2. *Social Forestry:* Barren areas that are subjected to afforestation by the Forest Department, more commonly with casuarena plantations.

Agricultural land

The agricultural lands referred to in this report are of coconut palms, paddy, mixed garden crops, etc., widely seen in the coastal areas. The cashew plantations and the waste lands are also included in this category.

1. *Paddy:* In the coastal plain, paddy fields are mostly parallelling the coast, occupied within the swales and sandwiched between the elevated sand ridges. Most of the paddy fields were or are being converted to coconut palms groves. Linked to the availability of water, seasonal inter-cropping of vegetables are also carried out. In the mid-land area, paddy fields are occupied within the low-lying valley portions, mostly skirting a channel or stream.
2. *Coconut palms:* In this category, coconut palms and household coconut palm gardens are included. This land use category contain upto 25 per cent settlements. However, in the coastal barrier strip, where the personal land-holdings are limited to a few cents, the settlement is denser, compared to the landward part.
3. *Mixed vegetation:* Areas that are covered by coconut palms, mango, jackfruit, cashew, arecanut, casuarena, etc., in a group

come under this category. At many locations coconut palms are found to be the most single dominant cultivation, but not exceeding half of the total numbers. In the lowlands, mixed crops are also found in the settlement areas.

4. *Waste land:* Areas like lateritic mesa crest, rock outcrops, etc., where no cultivation is possible fall under this category. These areas are mostly barren and without any soil cover. However, at some selected locations, scrub vegetation are seen. Some of these areas are being brought under cashew cultivation also.
5. *Others:* Vegetation/crops that cannot be readily distinguished from air photos/satellite imagery and those not covered under the above are included.

Water bodies

The areas that are permanently underwater like lagoons, creeks, estuaries, backwaters and lakes are included under this category.

1. *Estuary:* It is the lower part of the river course that is affected by the mixing of freshwater and salt water. It is defined as a semi-enclosed body of water which has a free connection with the open sea and within which the seawater is measurably diluted with freshwater derived from land drainage. Kerala has many estuaries locally known as 'Kayals' all along it's coast.
2. *River/Stream:* Several rivers or streams flow perpendicular to the coast and debauch into the sea. Some of the smaller streams though reach the coast,do not join the sea directly, but drain into the backwater system. Other rivers form estuaries before joining the sea. Some of the smaller rivers open to the sea only during the monsoon season when they are flooded.
3. *Freshwater body:* The water bodies that have no free access to the brackish water bodies and that remain detached, and non-saline are categorized as freshwater bodies. There are a very few freshwater bodies along the Kerala coast.

Wetlands

These are the transitional lands between the terrestrial and aquatic systems, where the water table is usually at or near the surface. Here, the land areas are periodically exposed and flooded by salt water through tides and have mangroves swamps and/or marshes.

1. *Beach:* A beach is defined as a shore consisting at least partly of unconsolidated material, extending landward upto where a

definite alteration of material or physiographic features exist. Most often the material is composed of quartz sand and at some locations, it is black sands.

2. *Tidal flat with mangroves:* These are the wide expanses of fine grained soft mud along the shore, influenced by tidal waters and mangroves vegetation. Mangroves grow only in those areas which are constantly in contact with the seawater or brackish water.
3. *Tidal flat without mangroves:* These are the wide expanses of fine grained soft mud along the shore, influenced by tidal waters and are without mangroves vegetation.
4. *Filtration ponds:* These are the mud flat areas, where the rise and fall of tidal water is used by fishermen for fish culture by filtration processes. Such areas gives a regular pattern of well-defined boundaries of the bunds, and can be easily identified in the satellite images and air photos. In these areas, during the monsoon, paddy is cultivated.
5. *Marsh/Swamp (non-tidal):* These are the wide expanses of water saturated, poorly drained areas with fine grained soft mud, seen along the shore, frequented by tidal waters, which may or may not have mangroves. Marshy lands are very sparsely located.

Built-up land

Because of the thick vegetative cover of the coastal zone of Kerala, it is fairly difficult to map the settlements and other establishments with satellite data and air photos. However, an attempt is made to demarcate the built-up areas on a qualitative basis. Based on this, an area which can be clearly identified as built-up area and that has more than 75 per cent of area covered by settlements are demarcated as clustered settlements. When the settlements and vegetated area are almost in equal proportion, it is demarcated as settlement with vegetation. For all purpose, a square centimetre area in the 1:15000 air photos is taken as a unit.

1. *Clustered settlement:* Under this category, thick built-up areas with settlement clusters are included in a square centimetre of the air photo of 1:15000 scale, if the built-up area is more than 75 per cent then that part is included in this category. Rest of the 25 per cent area may come under either vegetation or under any other category.
2. *Settlement with vegetation:* In one square centimetre coverage, when 50 per cent of the area is built-up or 50 per cent falls under vegetative cover, it is included under this category.

3. *Industrial area:* There are a few industries in the coastal zone of Kerala. The industries that are located are related to fish processing, coir, cashew, chemical, boat building, etc.
4. *Other major establishments:* These include religious, educational, cultural, scientific and other establishments. Only those establishments which cover more than one square centimetre area in the aerial, photo are included under this category.

Transportation

These include National Highways, State Highways, arterial and panchayat roads, railways, waterways and canals. Coastal stretches of Kerala has a moderately well connected coastal transportation network, excepting the northern Kerala.

1. *Road (Highway):* National Highways 47 and 17 pass through several stretches very close to the coast.
2. *Other roads:* Some parts of the State Highway, several arterial and panchayat roads criss-cross the coastal zone of Kerala.
3. *Railway:* Most part of the railway network of Kerala passes through the coastal zone.

Coastal structures

Coastal structures are constructed for the protection of the coast and to facilitate location of harbours, ports, etc. These can alter the entire configuration of the coast for good or bad. Hence they require careful, planning before construction.

1. *Harbour/Port:* Harbour is constructed for the safe anchorage of ships or other vessels. A port has harbour and other facilities for the handling and storage of cargo.
2. *Fish landing centres:* All along the Kerala coast numerous fish landing centres have been established for smooth landing of small fishing crafts. The facilities include small jetties, gaps in the sea wall, fish storage sheds, etc.
3. *Seawall/Groin:* Sea wall is an artificial structure in the back shore, constructed to protect the hinterland from erosion during the high tide. A groin is constructed perpendicular and extends from the back shore into the littoral zone. The basic purpose of a groin is to facilitate the accumulation of sand or to retard sand loss.

Other features

These include the natural exposures like cliffs and sand dunes/ beach ridges which provide natural protection to the coast.

1. *Rocky cliff:* Rocky cliff is any high, very steep to perpendicular overhanging face of rock, above the shore face. At many places, the shoreline is interrupted by rocky promontories. They are made up of mainly khondolites and charnockites.
2. *Lateritic cliff:* Areas similar to the above but constitute laterite, which are highly friable and are subjected to cliff erosion to a great extent.
3. *Sand dune areas with vegetation:* Coastal sand dunes are the beach ridges, which are small topographical features of marine origin, composed of sand, deposited possibly of a period when the sea level was higher and the shoreline was occupying a portion much inward than that at present.
4. *Sand dune areas without vegetation:* Same as above and are without vegetation. Some of the sand dunes are utilized for coconut palms, whereas others for cashew plantations.
5. *Reclaimed area:* Mud flats and marshes are reclaimed for various purposes. Reclamation is mostly done for agricultural, port, construction or for real estate purposes.
6. *Mining area:* Heavy minerals (black sands), glass sands and beach/river sands are mined from several parts of the Kerala coast for multifarious purposes. Such mining may have adverse effects on the coast.
7. *Waste dumping, drains, and effluents discharge sites:* These sites normally cannot be identified with satellite imageries and air photos. Wherever possible, attempts have been made to derive these details from the field and other secondary data.
8. *Vacant/Open land:* Play grounds, temple/church/mosque, stadia, etc. are included. Vacant land associated with religious centres or educational institutions are not included as they are included under other major establishments.
9. *Areas of outstanding natural beauty:* These are areas categorized under CRZ 1, where no new construction shall be permitted. The demarcation of these areas are highly subjective, the methodology for which is given in *Baba et. al.*, 1996.
10. *Historical areas:* Forts, churches, temples and other important places of archaeological importance fall under this category. According to the CRZ notification, the historical areas fall under CRZ 1.
11. *Heritage area:* A few religious and other areas that fall under this category are marked. They also fall under CRZ 1.

Appendix 6.2
Land-use pattern of the CRZ at the district level in Kerala

(In hectarer)

Panchayat/Municipality /Corporation		Thiruvananthapuram		Kollam		Alapuzha		Kottayam		Ernakulam	
Map no.		1 to 13		13to19		19 to 32		30A.B.31A,B		33 to 38	
Coastal Regulation zone		500 m	100 m	500 m	100 m	500 m	100 m	500 m	100 m	500 m	100 m
Land use	code	(Area under different landuse categories)									
Forest	1										
Reserved forest	1.1										
Social forest	1.2	0.007		0.015		0.005				0.548	
Agricultural land	2										
Paddy	2.1	0.292	0.199	0.681	0 457	0.769	0.316		0.439		1.186
Coconut	2.2	6.489	2.633	6.429	7.54	28.362	12.347		2.289	1.367	4.629
Mixed crop	2.3	13.075	3.99	5.284	10 917	1.953	4.009		1.89	12.751	15.915
Wasteland	2.4	0.2	01	0.073	0.026		0.005				
Others	2.5	0.09		0.009	0139						
Water body	3	2.048		3.422	0.003	2.448					
Wetland	4										
Beach	4.1	4.03		0.919		3.07				1.33	
Tidal flat + Mangroves	4.2					1.586	0.527				
Tidal flat-Mangroves	4.3				0.056		0.019				
Filtration pond	4.4					1.424				0.652	1.925

(Cont.)

(Appendix. 6.2 cont.)

Panchayat/Municipality /Corporation		*Thiruvananthapuram*		*Kollam*		*Alapuzha*		*Kottayam*		*Ernakulam*	
Map no.		*1 to 13*		*13to19*		*19 to 32*		*30A.B.31A,B*		*33 to 38*	
Coastal Regularion zone		*500 m*	*100 m*	*500 m*	*100 m*	*500 m*	*100 m*	*500 m*	*100 m*	*500 m*	*100 m*
Land use	*code*	*(Area under different landuse categories)*									
Marsh (non tidal)	SS	0.112	0.076	0.126	1.541	0295	0.978			0.078	
Builtup area	5										
Clustered settlement	5.1	2.169		1.04		0.401	0.308				0.012
Settlement+ Vegetation	5.2	6.5	0.149	4.301	1.92	5.161	5.724			0.424	2.767
Industrial area	5.3	0.181	0.01	0.151	0.092						0.024
Others (major)	5.4	1.973	0.094	0.287	0.168	0.121	0.061			0.062	0.037
Other features	8										
Sand dunes+ Vegetation	8.3	0.272	0.025			0.092					
Sanddunes- Vegetation	8.4	0.716	0.096	0.055		0.204				0.038	
Reclaimed area	8.5	0.151	1.358	0.007	0.499		0.401				
Mining area	8.6		0.197	0.371	0.052						
Waste/effluent discharge	8.7	0.016	0.025								
Vacant/open land	8.8	0.509		0.082	0.014	0.329					
Total CRZ area		**38.83**	**8.952**	**23.252**	**23.424**	**46.220**	**24.685**		**4.618**	**17.250**	**26.495**

(Cont.)

(Appendix. 6.2 cont.)

Panchayat/Municipality /Corporation		Thrissur		Malappuram		Kozhikkode		Kannur		Kasargod	
Map no.		38 to 46		46 to 54		54 to 62 A		62A to 69		69 to 81	
Coastal Regularion zone		500 m	100 m	500 m	100 m	500 m	100 m	500 m	100 m	500 m	100 m
Land use	code	(Area under different landuse categories)									
Forest	1										
Reserved forest	1.1										
Social forest	1.2			0.191				0.279			
Agricultural land	2										
Paddy	2.1	0.09	1.53	0.868	1.327	0.392	1.104	3.064	6.64	6.093	4.301
Coconut	2.2	7.584	8.876	4.258	1.839	6.228	5.999	2.683	7.082	12.949	2.763
Mixed crop	2.3	18.34	10.97	13.028	5.578	17.194	13.039	18.932	7.469	7.495	3.285
Wasteland	2.4	0.131	0.442	0.167	0.016	0.28	0.3	0.237	0.213	1.25	0.079
Others	2.5		0.003								
Water body	3	2.643		0.766		1.706		0.667		0.482	
Wetland	4									5.476	
Beach	4.1	1.979		2.141		2.316		2.347		0.039	
Tidal flat + Mangroves	4.2		0.037	0.029	0.11		0.006			6.061	0.017
Tidal flat- Mangroves	4.3		0.06	0.06	0.011		0.002		0.04	0.558	
Filtration pond	4.4		13.591				0.005	0.143			

(Cont.)

(Appendix. 6.2 cont.)

Panchayat/Municipality /Corporation		*Thrissur*		*Malappuram*		*Kozhikkode*		*Kannur*		*Kasargod*	
Map no.		*38 to 46*		*46 to 54*		54 to 62 A		62A to 69		69 to 81	
Coastal Regularion zone		*500 m*	*100 m*	*500 m*	*100 m*	*500 m*	*100 m*	*500 m*	*100 m*	*500 m*	*100 m*
Land use	*code*	*(Area under different landuse categories)*									
Marsh (non tidal)	SS					0.096	0.128	0.109	1.208		
Builtup area	5										
Clustered settlement	5.1			0.465		3.843	0.047	0.875	0	0.035	
Settlement+ Vegetation	5.2	0.118	0.296	1.39		1.638	0.295	1.555	0.167	0.049	
Industrial area	5.3		0.031	0.008		0.062	0.317	0.019	0.032		
Others (major)	5.4			0.258	0.007	0.209	0.235	0.564	0.049		
Other features	8										
Sand dunes+ Vegetation	8.3	0.418		1.021	0.079	0.384		0.122		2.053	0.369
Sanddunes- Vegetation	8.4	0.548		0.429	0.049	0.582		0.945		1.821	0.055
Reclaimed area	8.5		0.166				0.313	0.038	0.177		
Mining area	8.6					0.007					
Waste/effluent discharge	8.7										
Vacant/open land	8.8	0.114	1.731	0.961		0.141	1.843	0.735		0.052	
Total CRZ area		**31.965**	**37.733**	**26.040**	**9.051**	**35.078**	**23.633**	**33.314**	**23.077**	**44.413**	**10.869**

Source: Baba et al., 1998, pp. 146-147.

Appendix 6.3
Trend in the production of major and minor varieties of inland fishes in Kerala from 1994-95 to 1999-2000

(in Tonnes)

S.No.	*Name of Species*	*1994-95*	*1995-96*	*1996-97*	*1997-98*	*1998-99*	*1999-2000*
1.	Prawn	12265	11984	12531	13010	14346	16459
2.	Etroplus	4468	4640	4883	4964	4756	4860
3.	Murrels	4179	4386	4616	4568	4369	4956
4.	Catfish	4546	4682	4928	5239	4420	4816
5.	Mullets	3943	4075	4289	4634	4532	4607
6.	Jew fish	2566	2652	2791	3181	3012	3054
7.	Tilapia	6836	7347	7732	8532	7219	8510
8.	Labeo Fimbriatus	598	642	676	986	2718	3055
9.	Barbus	507	465	489	509	498	518
10.	Singala	546	598	629	1400	3205	3605
11.	Crabs	638	686	722	712	697	719
12.	Common Carps	981	1056	1111	2082	4686	5620
13.	Catla	612	734	773	1583	3824	4250
14.	Carpio	–	–	–	–	–	–
15.	Gourami	–	–	–	–	–	–
16.	Chanus	364	385	405	447	434	445
17.	Eels	45	47	50	54	53	55
18.	Labeo Rohita	572	710	747	1508	3656	4167
19.	Other miscellaneous	4526	4497	4733	4806	3427	4794
Total		**48192**	**49586**	**52105**	**58215**	**65855**	**74130**

Source: Directorate of Economic and Statistics, 2002, p.163.

Appendix 6.4
Details of brackish water shrimp farming in India

Year	Area under culture (ha)	Production (Tonnes)
1990-91	65,100	35,500
1991-92	68,227	40,000
1992-93	70,700	47,000
1993-94	82,540	62,000
1994-95	1,40,700	82,850
1995-96	1,18,983	70,573
1996-97	1,35,582	70,686
1997-98	1,41,591	66,868
1998-99	1,35,077	82,634
1999-00	1,44,625	78,860
2000-01	1,45,906	97,096
2001-02	1,57,400	1,02,940

Source: MPEDA Records, 2002.

Appendix 6.5
Details of rural, urban and total coastal area, population and density of population in Kerala in 1991

S.No.	Particulars	Area (Km^2)	House holds	Population	Density (persons/ Km^2)
1.	Urban coastal area	669.95	498926	2755997	4114
2.	Urban Kerala	3662.21	1411033	7680294	2097
3.	Rural coastal area	2923.47	914677	5014611	1715
4.	Rural Kerala	35500.79	4102167	21418224	603
5.	Panchayats and Urban areas with seafront	1997.57	942346	5357895	2682
6.	Kerala's coastal area (total)	3593.42	1412973	7770608	2164
7.	Kerala's total area	38863.00	5513200	29098518	749

Source: Baba, et al., 1995, p. 4.

Appendix 7.1
Hotspots of industries/enterprises causing water pollution in the coastal areas of Kerala

S.No.	*Panchayat/ Block/Area*	*Polluting industry/ enterprise*	*Nature of pollutant /effluent*	*Area/water polluted*
Thiruvanathapuram District				
1.	Parvathy-Puthanar	–	Sewage	Canal
2.	Poonthura estuary	–	Sewage	estuary
3.	Veli estuary	–	Sewage	estuary
4.	Sea-shore-Veli, Shankumugham	Travancore Titanium Products Ltd.	titanium effluent	beach
5.	Kadinamkulam Kayal	–	coconut husk retting	backwater
6.	Amayiznjan thodu	–	Sewage	canal
Kollam District				
1.	Alappad	Coir	coconut husk retting	estuary
2.	Kundara	Ceramics	industrial effluents	backwater
3.	Parayam	KEL	industrial effluent	backwater
4.	Munrothuruth	Coir	coconut husk retting	backwater
5.	Munrothuruth	Limeshell	decayed organic matter	backwater
6.	Chavara-Thekkumbhagom	Coir	coconut husk retting	backwater
7.	Thevalakara/Chavara	Coir	coconut husk retting	backwater
8	Panmana/Chavara	K. M. M. L, Bharat Petroleum storage	petroleum waste	backwater
9.	Neendakara	Fish processing fishing boats	processing plant waste, kerosene from outboard engines	backwater backwater
10.	Kilikolloor	Coir	coconut husk retting	backwater
11.	Thrikkadavoor	Coir	coconut husk retting	backwater
12.	Thrikkaruva	Coir	coconut husk retting	backwater
13.	Sakthikulangara	Fish processing	processing plant waste diesel, kerosene and petrol	backwater backwater

(Contd.)

(Appendix. 7.1 contd.)

S.No.	Panchayat/Block/ Area	Polluting industry/ enterprise	Nature of pollutant/ effluent	Area/water polluted
14.	Eravipuram	Coir	coconut husk retting	backwater
15	Poothakulam	Coir	coconut husk retting	backwater
16.	Kollam Municipality	Fish processing	processing plant waste	backwater
		Sewage/Cotton mill	sewage, chemicals	backwater
17.	Paravoor Municipality	Coir	coconut husk retting	backwater
Alappuzha District				
1.	Panavally	Rekha Coir Mill	coconut husk retting	canal
		Purushan's Coir mill	-do-	-do-
		Papachan's Coir Mill	-do-	-do-
		Panartical Coir Society Mill	-do-	-do-
		Anjilithod Society Mill	-do-	-do-
		Lakeside toilets	faecal	-do-
		Peeling sheds	effcuents	backwater
2.	Kanjikuzhi	Coir	coconut husk retting	backwater
3.	Thanneermukkam	Thanneermukkam barrier	stagnant waste water	estuary
		McDowell Distillery	toxic wastes	estuary
		Matathil Coir Mills	coconut husk retting	estuary
		Laksmikant Coir Mill	coconut husk retting	estuary
		Chalil Coconut Mills	coconut husk retting	estuary
4.	Purakkad	Peeling sheds	shrimp waste	backwater and sea
5.	Thalavadi	Paddy field (Patasekharam)	agricultural waste	estuary
6.	Edathua	-do-	-do-	-do-
7.	Thakazhy	-do-	-do-	-do-
8.	Muttar	-do-	-do-	-do-
9.	Devikulangara	Peeling Sheds	shrimp waste	backwater
10.	Cherthala	Coir	coconut husk retting	-do-
11.	Alappuzha	Coir	-do-	-do-
		Weed	decayed weed	-do-

(Cont.)

(Appendix. 7.1 contd.)

S.No.	*Panchayat/Block/ Area*	*Polluting industry/ enterprise*	*Nature of pollutant/ effluent*	*Area/water polluted*
Kottyam District				
1.	Chempu	HNL	–	–
2.	Velloor	HPC Velloor	paper, pulp rayon wastes	canal, estuary
3.	Kumaranelloor	Premier Tyres, Natassery;	rubber waste	-do-
		Popular Automobiles,	oil and rubber waste	-do-
		Water hyacinth	decayed algae	estuary
		Domestic sewage	domestic sewage	-do-
4.	Nattakom	Electro-chemicals, Chingavanam;	chemicals	-do-
		Travancore Cements, Nattakom;	chemicals	-do-
		Creep Mills	rubber waste	-do-
5.	Vijayapuram	MRF Tyres,	–	–
		Bone Meal Factory	–	–
Ernakulam District				
1.	Karumaloor	Leather processing unit, Karumaloor	organic chemicals	Periyar river
2.	Varapuzha	FACT, Eloor Division	heavy, metals, ammonia,	-do-
		Edayar industrial units	organic chemicals	-do-
		Leather processing units	kerosene, hydrogen sulphide	-do-
3.	Kanjoor	Soft drink making units	chemicals	Pulayampilly canal
4.	Cheranalloor	FACT, TCC, Binani Zinc, HIL, Periyar Chemicals and 250 other small and medium units	ammoniacal tar, acids, ammonia, sulphur, mercury, radiation	periyar
5.	Kadamakudy	-do-	-do-	-do-
6.	Thrikkakara	FACT, TCC, etc.	-do-	Chirapuzha,
7.	Chellanam	Fish processing plants	shrimp waste	backwater canals
		Cochin Refinery tank	heavy metals, organic chemicals	-do-
8.	Kumbalangi	Peeling sheds	shrimp waste	-do-

(contd.)

(Appendix. 7.1 contd.)

S.No.	Panchayat/Block/ Area	Polluting industry/ enterprise	Nature of pollutant/ effluent	Area/water polluted
9.	Chittattukara	Coir industry	coconut husk retting	backwater
10.	Ezhikara	Industrial units of Eloor	chemical effluents	-do-
11.	Vadakkekara	Maliankara coconut husk retting	chemical effluents, coconut husk retting	-do-
		Chettikkadu coconut husk retting mill	-do-	-do-
		Vavakkadu coconut husk retting mill	-do-	-do-
		Kuriapilly coconut husk retting mill	-do-	-do-
12.	Vadavukodu, Puthencruz	FACT, HOC, CRL	chemicals	Chitrapuzha canal
13.	Kumbalam	Peeling sheds of Aroor	shrimp waste	estuary
14.	Tripunithura Municipality	HOC, CRL, FACT	heavy metals, ammonia and poisonous organic compound	-do-
15.	Cochin Corporation	FACT, Cochin Division	effluents	Champakara river
Trichur District				
1.	Pariyaram	Sakthi Paper Mill	paper waste, chemical	
2.	Varantharapilly	Harison Malayalam Rubber Factory Cochin Malabar Bulb Factory	chemicals	Kurumalipuzha
3.	Orumanyur	Guruvayoor, Azhikode, Thekkumkandam	municipal waste	Katamana Kayal
Malappuram District				
1.	Vazhakkad	Gwalior Rayons Ltd. Mavoor*	mercury	Chaliyar
Kozhikode District				
1.	Panangad	Kinaloor Rubber Estate	ammonia and polluted water	–
2.	Cheruvannoor	Gwalior Rayons Ltd., Mavoor	mercury	Chaliyar

(contd.)

(Appendix. 7.1 contd.)

S. No.	Panchayat/Block/ Area	Polluting industry/ enterprise	Nature of pollutant/ effluent	Area/water polluted
Kannur District				
1.	Cherukunnu	Annapoorneswari Wood Industries, Thavam	dyes, chemicals	–
		A. K. Saw Mill, Punnacheri	-do-	–
		Premier Plywoods, Thavam	-do-	–
		T. K. Plywoods, Thavam	-do-	–
2.	Kannapuram	K. R. Plywood Factory, Kannapuram	wooden waste	–
		Pappinissery Tile Factory Pappinissery	factory waste	–
Kasargode District				
1.	Thrikkaripur	Urban sewage	butchery	canal
2.	Padne	-do-	-do-	river

* Closed since 1991.

Source: Department of Fisheries, 2001, Pan Fish Books, 1, 2, 4, 5, 7, 8, 10, 11, 13, and 14.

Appendix 8.1

Extent of area under different categories of regulation zones in the coastal districts of Kerala

Thiruvananthapuram district

Place	Length of the coast (km)	Area of the beach (sq.km)	0–200 m zone Land (sq. km)	0–200 m zone Water (sq.km)	200-500 m zone Land (sq. km)	200-500 m zone Water (sq.km)	50 m zone* (sq.km)
Area under category CRZ-III							
Pozhiyoor—Pulinkudi	13.300	0.3470	1.0310	0.1870	1.7170	0.1410	0.2930
Pozhiyoor–Pulinkudi	–	0.4290	1.4650	0.0317	2.0100	0.0202	0.0580
Vizhinjam– Beemapalli	9.5800	0.0586	1.6680	0.1300	1.7750	–	–
Vizhinjam– Beemapalli	5.8000	–	–	–	0.3860	–	0.1120
Valiathura–Veli	8.1600	0.4520	–	–	–	–	0.1400
Thumba–Puthenthura	5.5000	0.2480	0.3820	–	0.4820	–	0.5240
Thumba–Puthenthura	5.0000	0.3110	0.9480	–	1.5190	–	0.3020
Channankara–Perumathura	6.8000	0.3200	1.3430	0.0320	1.7910	0.2860	1.3930
Mudalapozhi–Anjengo	6.3000	0.3210	0.8460	0.4410	1.6420	0.2890	1.7120
Kadakkavur–Chilakkoor	5.2000	0.2990	0.9850	0.7300	0.8240	0.1060	1.0570
Vettur–Edava	8.8000	0.3080	0.6450	0.1260	0.6760	0.1370	0.1380
Total	**74.4400**	**3.0936**	**9.3130**	**1.6777**	**12.8220**	**0.9792**	**5.7290**
Area under category CRZ-II							
Trivandrum corporation	–	–	1.0400	0.2340	0.2260	0.1089	0.3250
Trivandrum corporation	–	–	1.5220	0.0330	2.3050	0.0649	0.1460
Trivandrum corporation	–	–	0.7810	–	1.1550	–	–
Varkala muncipality	–	–	0.6890	0.1260	0.4240	–	0.4270
Total	**–**	**–**	**4.0320**	**0.3930**	**4.1100**	**0.1738**	**0.8980**
Area under category CRZ-I							
Anjengo Fort	–	–	–	–	0.0380	–	–
Papanasam	–	–	0.2050	–	–	–	–
Total	**–**	**–**	**0.2050**	**–**	**0.0380**	**–**	**–**

(Cont.)

(Appendix. 8.1 contd.)

Kollam district

Place*	Length of the coast (km)	Area of the beach (sq.km)	0–200 m zone Land (sq. km)	0–200 m zone Water (sq.km)	200-500 m zone Land (sq. km)	200-500 m zone Water (sq.km)	50 m zone* (sq.km)
Area under category CRZ-III							
Kappil-Mayyanad	4.0000	0.0960	0.0960	0.1912	0.3020	0.3528	1.0060
Kappil-Mayyanad	4.7500	0.1230	0.2960	0.2330	0.0810	0.5570	0.6370
Thanni-Asramam	7.5000	0.3280	1.0440	0.1170	1.3040	0.2950	–
Nedungolam-Pilakkad	–	–	–	–	–	–	7.2100
Thangasseri-Neendakara	9.0000	0.3803	0.8480	–	1.2010	–	1.0890
Kuppanabhagom-Uliyakovil	–	–	–	–	–	–	1.0140
Neendakara-Kovilthottam	7.0000	0.2940	1.4710	0.4400	2.1800	–	2.4940
Kanjaveli-Munrothuruttu	–	–	–	–	–	–	4.1290
Perinad-Kumbalam	–	–	–	–	–	–	2.1210
Panmana-Alumkadavu	7.4810	0.2560	1.2630	0.2510	1.6440	0.5650	1.1680
Mullikkala-Kallribhagom	–	–	–	–	–	–	1.5080
Thekkekara-Pazhayur	–	–	–	–	–	–	1.5250
Total	**39.7310**	**1.4775**	**5.0183**	**1.2318**	**6.7124**	**1.7696**	**23.9000**
Area under category CRZ-II							
Paravur Municipality	–	–	0.5090	–	1.0500	–	0.2620
Paravur Municipality	–	–	0.3570	–	0.9130	–	0.3770
Kollam Municipality	–	–	0.6690	–	1.0140	–	0.1940
Kollam Municipality	–	–	0.9300	–	2.0590	–	0.1870
Kollam Municipality	–	–	–	–	–	–	0.2560
Total	**–**	**–**	**2.4650**	**–**	**5.0360**	**–**	**1.2760**

* *No entry under CRZ-1 is found in the source.*

(Contd.)

(Appendix. 8.1 contd.)

Alappuzha district

Place	Length of the coast (km)	Area of the beach (sq.km)	200 m zone Land (sq.km)	200 m zone Water (sq.km)	200-500 m zone Land (sq.km)	200-500 m zone Water (sq.km)	50 m zone* (sq.km)
Area under category CRZ-III							
Alappad-Tarayilkadavu	5.780	0.298	1.103	0.045	1.006	0.712	0.133
Alappad-Tarayilkadavu	6.250	0.458	0.945	0.287	0.759	1.108	1.159
Perumpally-Arattupuzha	2.920	0.213	0.542	0.033	0.556	0.290	0.598
Perumpally-Arattupuzha	5.387	0.289	1.070	–	1.263	0.316	0.495
Mangalamthura-Thottappally	5.344	0.299	1.077	–	1.507	0.140	0.718
Mangalamthura-Thottappally	6.955	0.497	1.350	0.064	2.012	0.123	–
Kuruttur-Vandanam	4.998	0.406	1.014	–	1.431	–	–
Kuruttur-Vandanam	7.489	0.981	1.521	0.019	2.150	0.011	–
Punnapra-Omanapuzha	6.850	0.454	0.744	0.009	1.183	0.009	–
Punnapra-Omanapuzha	7.147	0.250	0.682	0.019	1.010	0.018	0.030
Mararikulam-Ayiramtal	7.101	0.483	1.410	0.029	2.021	0.041	–
Mararikulam-Ayiramtal	7.044	0.078	1.340	0.053	2.036	0.043	–
Thaikkal-Kadapuram	7.060	0.393	1.364	0.058	1.247	0.218	0.120
Thanneerukkom-Pallipuram	–	–	–	–	–	–	1.570
Vechur-Thottakam*	–	–	–	–	–	–	0.353
Pallipuram-Puchakkal	–	–	1.2320	0.0677	1.8500	0.087	0.880
Pallipuram-Vadutala	–	–	–	–	–	–	1.740
Pallipuram-Vadutala	–	–	–	–	–	–	1.622
Kulasekharamangalam-Puttodu*	–	–	–	–	–	–	0.886
Total	**80.325**	**5.098**	**15.392**	**0.684**	**20.032**	**3.117**	**10.303**

Includes portions of Kottayam district.

(Contd.)

(Appendix. 8.1 contd.)

Place	Length of the coast (km)	Area of the beach (sq.km)	200 m zone		200-500 m zone		50 m zone* (sq.km)
			Land (sq.km)	Water (sq.km)	Land (sq.km)	Water (sq.km)	
Area under category CRZ-II							
Kayamkulam Municipality	–	–	–	–	–	–	0.243
Alappuzha-Municipality	–	–	0.606	0.009	0.854	0.010	–
Alappuzha-Municipality	–	–	0.703	0.016	1.124	0.012	–
Cherthala Municipality	–	–	–	–	–	–	0.398
Total	**–**	**–**	**1.309**	**0.025**	**1.978**	**0.023**	**0.641**
Area under category CRZ-I							
Thayikkal-Kadapuram	–	–	–	–	0.182	0.428	1.104
Anthakaranazhi-Chellanam	–	–	–	–	0.267	0.414	1.766
Pallipuram-Puchakkal	–	–	–	–	–	–	2.091
Panavalli-Vadutala	–	–	–	–	–	–	1.221
Kulasekharamangalam-Puttodu*	–	–	–	–	–	–	2.085
Total	**–**	**–**	**–**	**–**	**0.449**	**0.842**	**8.267**

* Includes portions of Kottayam district.

(Contd.)

(Appendix. 8.1 contd.)

Ernakulam district

Place	Length of the coast (km)	Area of the beach (sq.km)	200 m zone Land (sq.km)	200 m zone Water (sq.km)	200-500 m zone Land (sq.km)	200-500 m zone Water (sq.km)	50 m zone* (sq.km)
Area under categrory CRZ-IIII							
Chellanam-Kumbalangi	7.134	0.160	1.348	0.083	0.268	1.377	0.000
Kannamali-Palluruthi	7.173	0.134	1.113	–	1.648	–	0.955
Arur-Nettur	–	–	–	–	–	–	1.396
Perramballi-Kandanadu	–	–	–	–	–	–	0.128
Thoppinpadi-Murukkumpadam	4.870	0.458	0.568	–	0.579	–	0.269
Elankunnapuzha-Njarakkal	7.120	0.337	1.054	–	0.589	–	0.350
Pachalam-Pizhala	–	–	–	–	–	–	0.746
Nayarambalam-Kuzhipilli	7.086	0.193	1.005	–	–	0.052	–
Varappuzha-Kottuvalli	–	–	–	–	–	–	1.684
Iyyampilli-Pallipuram	7.237	0.223	1.095	–	0.137	–	1.199
Chennamangala–Kaitaram	–	–	–	–	–	–	2.815
Total	**40.620**	**1.505**	**6.183**	**0.083**	**3.222**	**1.429**	**9.542**
Area under category CRZ-II							
Cochin Corporation	–	–	0.078	–	0.245	–	2.756
Cochin Corporation	–	–	0.850	–	1.368	–	1.295
Cochin Corporation	–	–	–	–	–	–	2.147
Cochin Corporation	–	–	–	–	–	–	0.873
Thripunithura Municipality	–	–	–	–	–	–	0.071
Parur Municipality	–	–	–	–	–	–	0.022
Parur Municipality	–	–	–	–	–	–	0.062
Total	–	–	**0.928**	–	**1.613**	–	**7.071**

(Contd.)

(Appendix. 8.1 contd.)

Place	Length of the coast (km)	Area of the beach (sq.km)	200 m zone		200-500 m zone		50 m zone* (sq.km)
			Land (sq.km)	Water (sq.km)	Land (sq.km)	Water (sq.km)	
Area under category CRZ-I							
Chellanam-Kumbalangi	–	–	–	–	0.470	–	2.798
Kannamali-Palluruthi	–	–	0.094	–	0.282	–	3.366
Arur-Nettur	–	–	–	–	–	–	1.094
Thoppinapadi-Murukkumpadam	–	–	0.050	0.057	0.146	0.342	0.334
Kundannur-Ernakulam	–	–	–	–	–	–	0.107
Elankunnapuzha-Njarakkal	–	–	0.218	0.203	0.614	1.160	2.062
Pachalam-Pizhala	–	–	–	–	–	–	2.734
Nayarambalam-Kuzhipilli	–	–	–	–	0.122		3.792
Varappuzha-Kottuvalli	–	–	–	–	–		1.361
Iyyampillii-Pallipuram	–	–	0.324	–	0.135		1.826
Chennamangalam-Kaitaram	–	–	–	–	–		0.086
Total	**–**	**–**	**0.686**	**0.260**	**1.769**	**1.502**	**19.560**

(Contd.)

(Appendix. 8.1 contd.)

Thrissur district

Place	Length of the coast (km)	Area of the beach (sq.km)	200 m zone		200-500 m zone		50 m zone (sq.km)
			Land (sq.km)	Water (sq.km)	Land (sq.km)	Water (sq.km)	
Area under category CRZ-III							
Munambam-Vakadappuram	7.7809	0.3740	1.4030	0.0620	1.9350	0.2630	1.0110
Vadakkupuram-Chapra	–	–	–	–	–	–	1.8960
Pattayakadu-Perinjom	7.2400	0.3200	1.4326	0.0147	2.0844	0.0073	0.6821
Chervu-Arippalam	–	–	–	–	–	–	0.9680
Panaparambu-Chandrapinni	6.8660	0.2390	1.3620	0.0020	1.9910	0.0170	0.5690
Edamuttom-Nattika	7.5500	0.4460	1.5310	–	3.8240	–	0.5760
Edatturutti-Kizhupillikara	–	–	–	–	–	–	0.4900
Talikulam-Vadanapalli	7.7400	0.4330	1.6430	–	3.8150	0.1270	0.7720
Engandiyur-Aditirutti	7.8900	0.3370	1.5890	0.0730	3.3830	0.5870	2.0590
Manalur-Mullasseri	–	–	–	–	–	–	0.7050
Mada-Tiruvatta	7.5800	0.3310	0.6150	–	1.6620	–	0.7280
Edakkazhiyur-Edakkara	7.7200	0.5580	1.6030	–	3.9250	–	0.6040
Veliyangod-Kappirikkad	7.7900	0.6480	1.4130	0.0260	3.4430	0.5020	0.3850
Total	**68.157**	**3.686**	**12.592**	**0.358**	**26.062**	**1.503**	**11.445**
Area under category CRZ-II							
Kodungallur Municipality	–	–	–	–	–	–	0.0426
Kodungallur Municipality	–	–	–	–	–	–	0.2760
Kodungallur Municipality	–	–	–	–	–	–	0.3130
Chavakkad Municipality	–	–	1.0040	–	2.2050	–	0.3080
Total	**–**	**–**	**1.004**	**–**	**2.205**	**–**	**0.940**

(Contd.)

(Appendix. 8.1 contd.)

Place	Length of the coast (km)	Area of the beach (sq.km)	200 m zone		200-500 m zone		50 m zone* (sq.km)
			Land (sq.km)	Water (sq.km)	Land (sq.km)	Water (sq.km)	
Area under category CRZ-I							
Munambam-Vakadappuram	–	–	–	–	–	–	0.0550
Vakadappuram-Chapra	–	–	–	–	–	–	0.9640
Pattayakadu-Perinjom	–	–	–	–	–	–	0.3420
Chervu-Arippalam	–	–	–	–	–	–	1.8120
Manalur-Mullasseri	–	–	–	–	–	–	0.0580
Total	**–**	**–**	**2.008**	**–**	**4.410**	**–**	**5.068**

(Contd.)

(Appendix. 8.1 contd.)

Malappuram district

Place	Length of the coast (km)	Area of the beach (sq.km)	200 m zone		200-500 m zone		50 m zone* (sq.km)
			Land (sq.km)	Water (sq.km)	Land (sq.km)	Water (sq.km)	
Area under category CRZ-III							
Puthiya Ponnani-Kottattara	6.7300	0.5730	0.4130	0.3720	0.6780	0.9210	1.3470
Purathur-Padiyam	7.1650	0.5130	1.4920	–	1.8810	0.1240	1.1530
Parasseri-Niramaruttur	7.3500	0.3460	1.4220	0.0200	3.5390	0.0230	0.4980
Kalatkadappuram-Ullanam	3.7400	0.0816	0.8020	–	1.9480	–	–
Kalatkadappuram-Ullanam	7.2200	0.4660	1.4350	0.0350	3.1990	0.3710	0.3120
Pottingal-Ariyalllur							
Total	**32.205**	**1.9800**	**5.5640**	**0.4270**	**11.2450**	**1.4390**	**3.3100**
Area under category CRZ-II							
Ponnani Municipality	–	–	0.9200	–	2.1770		0.3730
Tirur Muncipality	–	–	–	–	–	–	0.6910
Total	**–**	**–**	**0.9200**	**–**	**2.1770**	**–**	**1.0640**
Area under category CRZ-I							
Parasseri-Niramaruttur	–	–	–	–	–		0.3430
Total	**–**	**–**	**–**	**–**	**–**	**–**	**0.3430**

(Contd.)

(Appendix. 8.1 contd.)

Kozhokode district

Place	Length of the coast (km)	Area of the beach (sq.km)	200 m zone		200-500 m zone		50 m zone* (sq.km)
			Land (sq.km)	Water (sq.km)	Land (sq.km)	Wate (sq.km)	
Area under category CRZ-III							
Vattikkunnu-Chaliyam	8.1300	0.1510	1.5930	0.0960	3.5690	0.3230	1.1480
Velimuk-Tuzhipalam	—			—		—	0.3690
Karuvanthiruthi-Panniankara	7.4200	0.2720	1.1330		2.5730		1.5780
Ramanattukara-Kadal	—	—					0.8628
Kallayi-Kacheri	8.3520	0.5080	—	—	—	—	0.1480
Olavanna-Iringallur	—		—		—		0.5620
Mannankadavu-Perumana	—	—					0.6756
West Hill-Elattur	8.5700	0.4810	1.0840	—	1.3900		1.9810
Talakulattur-Kadalur	7.9300	0.4260	1.4090	0.1740	2.0230	0.4360	1.1550
Ichchanur-Annasseril	—	—					0.4640
Mannamangalam-Kadalur	8.2300	0.2580	1.5640	—	1.8660	—	
Mangad-Kollam	5.8067	0.2238	1.1918	—	1.9175	—	1.2126
Tuvakkad-Mannankavu	—	—	—	—	—		0.9500
Vanmugom-Ayinikad	7.6600	0.3610	1.5600	—	2.3740	—	0.7150
Kodakkad-Turayur	—	—	—	—	—	—	0.9570
Iringal-Badagara	7.4200	0.3820	0.5170	—	—	—	1.1720
Mattungal-Mahe	5.0200	0.2210	0.8580	—	1.2110'	—	—
Mattungal-Mahe	8.0700	0.3190	1.2520	—	1.8280	—	0.5630
Total	**82.609**	**3.603**	**12.162**	**0.270**	**18.752**	**0.759**	**14.513**

(Contd.)

(Appendix. 8.1 contd.)

Place	*Length of the coast (km)*	*Area of the beach (sq.km)*	*200 m zone*		*200-500 m zone*		*50 m zone* (sq.km)*
			Land (sq.km)	*Water (sq.km)*	*Land (sq.km)*	*Water (sq.km)*	
Area under category CRZ-II							
Kozhikode Corporation	–	–	0.3100	–	0.4250	–	–
Kozhikode Corporation	–	–	1.5040	0.0194	2.0680	0.2380	1.3860
Kozhikode Corporation	–	–	–	–	–	–	0.0320
Kozhikode Corporation	–	–	0.6850	–	1.6850	–	0.5020
Badagara Muncipality	–	–	0.9080	0.1160	0.6630	0.8790	0.1490
Badagara Muncipality	–	–	0.1450	–	0.0650	–	–
Total	–	–	**3.552**	**0.135**	**4.906**	**1.117**	**2.069**
Area under category CRZ-I							
Mangad-kollam	–	–	–	–	–	–	0.3570

(Contd.)

(Appendix. 8.1 contd.)

Kannur district

Place	Length of the coast (km)	Area of the beach (sq.km)	200 m zone Land (sq.km)	200 m zone Water (sq.km)	200-500 m zone Land (sq.km)	200-500 m zone Water (sq.km)	50 m zone* (sq.km)
Area under category CRZ-III							
Onchiyam-Puliyanabram	–	–	–	–	–	–	0.7780
Edannur-Eranjholi	10.1800	0.2680	0.5500	–	0.7780	–	0.3100
Iringannur-Menapram.	–	–	–	–	–	–	0.5180
Dharmadam-Edakkad	10.6500	0.4110	1.9020	0.0600	2.5620	0.0600	1.2010
Kavumbhagom-Vada-Kumpad	–	–	–	–	–	–	1.0540
Adikadalayi-Chalad	10.5500	0.3320	0.6860	–	0.9300	–	0.0400
Kizhunna -Kizhattalli	2.2930	0.1330	0.4910	–	0.8220	–	0.0580
Palliyamoola-Azhikkal	9. 9710	0.7720	1.9240	–	2.4230	–	0.5200
Valapatnam-Narath	–	–	–	–	–	–	0.8110
Puthiyangadi-Ettikulam	6.8670	0.4060	1.2280	–	1.0270	–	–
Mattul South-Mattul North	6.5230	0.5260	1.3810	–	2.1380	–	3.5940
Kalyasseri-Kuttikol	–	–	–	–	–	–	0.9590
Pattayam-Kodallur	–	–	–	–	–	–	1.4190
Chuttad-Vadakumpad	9.1900	0.8800	1.4120	0.4000	1.7530	1.0550	–
Pazhayangadi-The-kkumpad	1.9940	0.2360	0.4350	0.0420	0.6530	0.0545	–
Pattuvam- Kuppam	–	–	–	–	–	–	1.4060
Total	**68.218**	**3.964**	**10.009**	**0.502**	**13.086**	**1.170**	**12.668**
Area under category CRZ-II							
Thalasserry Municipality	–	–	1.3380	–	2.1220	–	0.5800
Thalasserry Municipality	–	–	–	–	–	–	0.1750
Kannur Municipality	–	–	1.2 660	0.0490	1.7610	0.0130	0.1320
Payyannur Municipality	–	–	–	–	–	–	0.2180
Payyannur Municipality	–	–	–	–	–	–	0.9320
Total	–	–	**2.604**	**0.049**	**3.883**	**0.013**	**2.037**

(Contd.)

(Appendix. 8.1 contd.)

Place	Length of the coast (km)	Area of the beach (sq.km)	200 m zone Land (sq.km)	200 m zone Water (sq.km)	200-500 m zone Land (sq.km)	200-500 m zone Water (sq.km)	50 m zone* (sq.km)
Area under category CRZ-I							
Edannur-Eranjholi	–	–	–	–	–	–	0.3030
Dharmadam-Edakkad	–	–	–	–	–	–	0.3130
Kavumbhagam-Vada-kkumpad	–	–	–	–	–	–	2.5920
Palliyamoola-Azhikkal	–	–	–	–	–	–	0.1260
Velapatnam-Naratt	–	–	–	–	–	–	0.9290
Pazhayangadi-Thekkumpad	–	–	–	–	–	–	2.7778
Paltuvam-Kuppam	–	–	–	–	–	–	4.3010
Total	**–**	**–**	**–**	**–**	**–**	**–**	**11.342**

(Contd.)

(Appendix. 8.1 contd.)

Kasargode district

Place	Length of the coast (km)	Area of the beach (sq.km)	200 m zone Land (sq.km)	200 m zone Water (sq.km)	200-500 m zone Land (sq.km)	200-500 m zone Water (sq.km)	50 m zone* (sq.km)
Area under category CRZ-III							
Kavayi-Yedelekkad	7.5100	0.6700	1.0100	0.4020	0.1870	1.9780	1.5900
Ayitti-Orimukku	7.4000	0.8440	1.4630	0.3100	1.8390	0.4510	1.9020
Thaikadapuram-Ozhinjavalappu	7.5300	0.7070	0.9420	0.0740	0.9510	0.5330	2.1080
Cheruvattur-Ramanchira	--	--	—	—	—	—	0.2470
Punchavi-Kanhangad	7.6400	0.4400	0.0960	—	0.1250	—	0.3180
Kalavayal-Agasarahole	4.53o0	0.2110	0.6820	0.2530	1.0060	0.3160	0.2410
Kalavayal-Agasarahole	6.3500	0.2990	1.1450	0.0352	1.7470	0.1238	0.3020
Trikannad-Chimmanad	4.5500	0.2260	0.8620	0.0148	1.1929	0.6532	0.2250
Trikannad-Chimmanad	7.7800	0.6140	0.7580	0.6450	1.1160	0.9350	0.3600
Nellikkunnu-Kumbala	4.5600	0.3030	0.2180	0.0780	0.4180	—	—
Nellikkunnu-Kumbala	7.6700	0.6350	0.9640	0.5160	1.5280	0.4660	0.2790
Arkadi-Uppala gate	4.2900	0.2450	0.5240	0.3630	1.1170	0.1960	2.1250
Arkadi-Uppala gate	7.6060	0.5910	0.5990	—	2.1300	0.1200	0.1930
Manjeswar-Karnataka border	7.2900	0.5960	1.3140	0.1870	1.8460	0.3260	0.2040
Total	**84.706**	**6.381**	**10.577**	**2.878**	**15.203**	**6.098**	**10.094**
Area under category CRZ-II							
Payyannur Municipality	–	–	0.5440	–	0.8270	–	0.0680
Kanhangad Municipality	–	–	1.4850	–	2.1400	–	0.7800
Payyannur Municipality	–	–	0.2690	–	0.1360	–	0.3340
Payyannur Municipality	–	–	0.5930	–	0.9260	–	–
Total	**–**	**–**		**–**	**4.029**	**–**	**1.182**
Area under category CRZ-I	–	–	0.0920	–	0.0220	–	–

* Area extend upto 100m as per CRZ Notification of 1991 and Supreme Court ruling of 1996.

Source. Adapted from Baba et al. (1995), pp. 43-71.

Appendix 9.1
The ICZM planning process as specified by Chua. T.E.

Sl. No.	*Steps*
1.	Triggers of process by one or combination of factors: (a)resource depletion, (b) pollution, (c) environment incident, (d) concern for sustainable development, (e) other factors.
2.	Preliminary action: awareness of coastal issues and initiation of formal process.
3.	Feasibility study: Preliminary assessment of coastal issues, management needs.
4.	Setting up of project framework: project formulation, determining coordinating institution, project document, work plan.
5.	Setting up the analysis framework, coastal profile, goals/objectives, targets, time frame, boundaries, approaches/scenarios, criteria for evaluation/monitoring, legal/institutional framework.
6.	Carrying out analysis: issues, caused impacts, constraints.
7.	Estimating demands for products/services: types of products and services generated, demand level.
8.	Analysing production possibilities: output estimate strategies, attainments.
9.	Quantification and valuation of impacts: present and future economic activities, ecological risks, sensitive areas.
10.	Management options: conflict resolution, impacts.
11.	Policy formulation: general and specific policies based on management options selected.
12.	Action plans: finalising specific activity with budget, manpower, institution involved, implementation strategies.
13.	Evaluation and decision making bodies, acceptance or rejection of proposals.
14.	Pilot testing: Pilot site selection, plan, implementation, refinement.
15.	Implementation: implementing institution to carry out action.
16.	Monitoring/evaluation: assessing attainment of objectives and impacts; feedbacks and refinement; setting up feedback mechanism, refinements needed.
17.	Integration: integrating CAM into national/local government development plans.

Source: Chua, 1993'b,p.95.

Bibliography

Ajithkumar, M. (1993), 'Grains of Truth in Kuttanad's Discontent', *The Economic Times*, Bombay, 8.8.1993.

Alberto, G.L. (1995), 'Utilisation and Management of the Coastal Zone in Latin America and the Caribbean' in *Coastal Ocean Space Utilisation III*, (eds.) Croce, N.D., Connel,S. and Abel, R., Chapman and Hall, London, 1995, pp. 75-94.

Alcala, A.C. (1996), 'Coastal Resource Management as practised in the Philippines', paper presented at the International Workshop, *Integrated Coastal Management in Tropical Developing Countries; Lessons Learned from Successes and Failures* , May 24-28, Xiamen, Peoples Republic of China, 1996.

Alcala, A.C. (1998),'Community based Coastal Resource Management in the Philippines: A Case Study', *Ocean and Coastal Management*, 38, 1998, pp. 179-186.

Alder, J., N.Sloan and Uktolseya (1994), 'Advances in Marine Protected Area Management in Indonesia: 1988-1993', *Ocean and Coastal Management*, 25, 1994, pp.63-75.

Aby Mohammed, A.A.A. (1999), 'Coastal Zone Management in Egypt', *Ocean and Coastal Management*, 42, 1999, pp.835-848.

Amarasinghe, S.R. and H.J.M. Wickremeratne (1983), 'The Evolution and Implementation of Legislation for Coastal Zone Management in a Developing Country.The Sri Lankan Experience'. In *Coastal Zone '83, Vol.III.* American Society of Civil Engineers, New York, 1983, pp. 2822-2841.

Amarasinghe, S.R., H.J.M. Wickremeratne and G.K.Lowty, Jr. (1987), 'Coastal Zone Management in Sri Lanka, 1973-1986', in *Coastal Zone '87*, American Society of Civil Engineers, 1987, pp.2822-2841.

Anonymous (2000), 'Wetlands in Thalassery Vanishing', *Indian Express,* 7.6.2000.

Anonymous (2001 a), 'Noisy Scenes at Seminar: Pathiramanal', *The New Indian Express,* Cochin, 19.11.2001.

Anonymous (2001 b), 'HC Sets Aside Notification on Tourism Project', *The New Indian Express,* 12.12.2001.

Anonymous (2002 a), 'Pathiramanal Development: HC Admits Plea Against Government Move', *The New Indian Express,* Cochin, 14.3.2002.

Anonymous (2002 b), 'Proposed Oil Terminal May Pose Threat to Tourism: Minister', *The New Indian Express,* Cochin, 30.5.2002.

Anonymous (2002 c), 'CPT to Explore Ways to end SBM Row Amicably', *The New Indian Express,* Cochin, 27.6.2002.

Anonymous (2002 d), 'Move to Set Up Oil Cargo Terminal May Mar Tourism Projects', *The New Indian Express,* Cochin, 20.7.2002.

Anutha, K. and D.Johnson (1996), 'Aquaculture Planning and Coastal Management in Tasmani', *Ocean and Coastal Management,* 33(1-3), 1996, Special Issue: *Ocean and Coastal Management Issues in Australia and New Zealand,* pp.167-192.

Anutha, K. and L.K.Kriwoken (1996), Introduction to the 'Special Issue on Ocean and Coastal Management Issues in Australia and New Zealand', *Ocean and Coastal Management,* 33(1-3), 1996, pp.1-4.

Archer, J.H. (1988), *Coastal Management in the United States: A Selective Review and Summary,* University of Rhode Island, Centre for Ocean Management Studies, Kingston, 1988.

Archer, J.H., D.Connors, K.Lawrence, S.C.Columbia and R,Brown (1994) *The Public Trust Doctrine and the Management of America's Coasts*, University of Massachusetts Press, Massachusetts, 1994.

Arico, S. and Rakotoary, J.C. (1997), 'Beginning Integrated Coastal Management Efforts in Madagaskar', *Ocean and Coastal Management,* 37(3) 1997. *Special issue: Integrated Coastal Management in Africa,* pp.359-384.

ASEAN/US Coastal Resources Management Project (1992), *The Integrated Management Plan for Seqare Anakon-Cilacap*

Central Java, Indonesia. Directorate General of Fisheries, Indonesia, ICLARM Technical Report 34, 1992.

Australian Bureau of Agricultural and Resource Economics (ABARE) (1993), *Use of Economic Instruments in Integrated Coastal Zone Management,* Canberra, ABARE, 1993.

Baba, M., Shamsuddin, M. and Thomas, K.V. (1993), 'Coastal Erosion and Sustainable Management', in Swaminathan, M.S., Ramesh, H. (eds.), *Sustainable Management of Coastal Ecosystems,* Anna University, Madras, 1993, pp.63-70.

Baba, M., Shamsuddin, M. and Thomas, K.V. (1995), *Coastal Zone Management Plan of Kerala,* Centre for Earth Science Studies, Trivandrum, 1995.

Baba, M., Shamsuddin, M. and Thomas, K.V. (1996), *Coastal Zone Management Plan Map of Kerala,* A Revised Report, submitted to the STEC, Govt. of Kerala by CESS, August 1996.

Baba, M., Shamsuddin, M., Thomas, K.V., John Mathai and John Paul (1998), *Coastal Zone management Plan of Kerala: Final Report; Vol.1, Coastal Land Use and Resources; Vol. II,* CZM of Iravipuram Panchayat; Vol.III, *Coastal Land Use Map of Kerala,* Centre for Earth Science Studies, Thiruvananthapuram, December, 1998.

Balchand, A.N., Rasheed, K. and Joseph, K.A. (1995), 'Training, Education and Information Services in Developing Countries on Coastal Zone Management', in *Proceedings of the International Conference on Coastal Change '95,* Bordeaux: Bordomer, 1995, pp.715-724.

Ballinger, R.C.,Smith, H.D. and Warren, L.M. (1994), 'The Management of the Coastal Zone of Europe', *Ocean and Coastal Management,* 22(1), 1994, pp.45-85.

Ballinger, R.C. (1999), 'The Evolving Organisational Framework for Integrated Coastal Zone Management in England and Wales', *Marine Policy,* 1999, 23.(4-5).

Ballinger, R.C. and Lalwani, C.S. (2000), 'The Role of Internships in Marine Policy and Integrated Coastal Management Higher Education'. *Ocean and Coastal Management'* , 43,2000, GENOA Special Issue on Education and Training in Integrated Coastal Management, pp.409-426.

Barbosa, Duarte (1970-Reprint), *A Description of the Coasts of East Africa and Malabar in the Beginning of the Sixteenth Century,* translated by H.E.J. Stanley, London, Hakluyt Society.

Barbier, E. (1989), *The Economic Value of Ecosystems: Tropical Wetlands,* LEEC Gate-keeper 89-02, London Environmental Economic Centre, London 1989.

Barcena, A. (1992), 'UNICED and Ocean and Coastal Management', *Ocean and Coastal Management,* 18(1), 1992, pp.15-53.

Barston, R.P. (1994), 'International Dimensions of Coastal Zone Management', *Ocean and Coastal Management,* 23(1), 1994, pp.93-116.

Bascom, W. (1974), 'The Disposal of Waste in the Ocean', *Scientific American,* Vol.231, August, 1974.

Basiron, M.N. (1998), 'The Implementation of Chapter 17 of Agenda 21 in Malaysia: Challenges and Opportunities'. *Ocean and Coastal Management,* 41, 1998, pp.1-17.

Bateman, S. (1996), 'Environmental Issues with Australian Ports', *Ocean and Coastal Management,* 33(1-3), 1996; *Special Issue: Ocean and Coastal Management Issues in Australia and New Zealand,* pp.229-247.

Beatly, T., Brower, D.J. and Schowob, A.K. (1994), *An Introduction to Coastal Zone Management,* Island Press, Washington, 1994.

Beck, R.E. (1994), 'The Movement in the United States to Restoration and Creation of Wetlands', *Natural Resources Journal,* Vol. 34, 1994, pp.781-822.

Bergin, A. (1996), 'The Royal Australian Navy and the Marine Environment', *Ocean and Coastal Management,* 33(1-3) 1996, *Special Issue, Ocean and Coastal Management Issues in Australia and New Zealand,* pp.213-227.

Black K. and Baba, M., Developing a District Coastal Management Plan and Training for Environmental Improvement, Ashtamudi Estuary, Kollam, India, ASR Ltd. and CESS, Thiruvananthapuram, 2000.

Boelaert-Suominen, S. and C. Cullinan (1994), *Legal and Institutional Aspects of Integrated Coastal Area Management in National Legislation,* Food and Agriculture Organisation, Department of Law Service, Rome, 1994.

Borgese, E.M. (1994), 'Training and Education in Ocean Management for the 2lst Century: Regional and Global Aspects', Paper presented at *The Second International Conference on Oceanography; Towards Sustainable Use of Ocean and Coastal Zones,* November 14-29, Lisbon, 1994.

Bose, A.N. (ed.) (1989), *Coastal Zone Management of West Bengal,* Sea Explorers Institute, Calcutta, 1989.

Boulding, Kenneth, E. (1966), 'The Economics of the Spaceship Earth', in Henry Jerret (ed.), *Environmental Quality in a Growing Economy,* John Hopkins, Baltimore.

Bower, B.P. (1992), *Producing Information for Integrated Coastal Management Decisions: An Annotated Seminar Outline.* National Oceanic and Atmospheric Administration, Silverspring, Maryland, 1992.

Bower, B.T., Ehler, C. and Basta, D.A. (1994), *A Framework for Planning for Integrated Coastal Zone Management,* Office of Ocean Resources Conservation and Assessment, National Ocean Service, National Oceanic and Atmospheric Administration, Silverspring, Maryland, 1994.

Bower, B.T. and Turner, R.K. (1995), 'Characterising and Analysing Benefits from Integrated Coastal Management (ICM)', *Ocean and Coastal Management,* 38, 1998, pp.41-66.

Brahtz, J.F.P. (ed.) (1972), *Coastal Zone Management -Multiple Use With Conservation.* John Wiley and Sons, Inc. New York, 1972.

Brown, K.R. (1996), 'Coastal Resource Management: Interdisciplinary, Multi-disciplinary and Trans-disciplinary - The Role of Universities in Capacity Building', paper presented at the *International Workshop, Integrated, Coastal Management in Tropical Developing Countries: lessons Learned From Successes and Failures.* May 24-28, Xiamen, Peoples Republic of China, 1996.

Burbridge, P.R. and Koesoabione (1981), 'Coastal Zone Management in South East Asia', in *South East Asia Seas. Frontiers for Development,* McGraw Hill, pp.110-135.

Burbridge, P.R. (1987), 'Economic Considerations in Management of Coastal Resources', *CAMP Network Newsletter.* May 1987, pp.2-3.

Burbridge, P.R., N.Dankers, and J.R. Clark (1989), 'Multiple Use Assessment for Coastal Management', in *Coastal Zone '89,* Vol.I, American Society of Civil Engineers, New York, 1989, pp.33-45.

Burbridge, P.R. and Burbridge, V. (1993), *Experiences of IWCN. WWF* and UNEP with Integrated Coastal Management, FAO, Rome, 1993.

Burbridge, P.R. (1997), 'A Generic Framework for Measuring Success in Integrated Coastal Management', *Ocean and Coastal Management,* 37(2), 1997, *Special Issue, Lessons Learned in Integrated Coastal Management,* pp.175-190.

Byju Aryad (2001), 'Thanneermukkam Bund - No End in Sight to the Controversy', *The New Indian Express,* Cochin, 31.10.2001.

Byju Aryad (2002), 'Crisis Grips Kuttanad Farmers' *The New Indian Express,* Cochin, 23.1.2002.

Caddy, J.F. and Griffiths, R.C. (1995), *Living Marine Resources and Their Sustenable Development. Some Environmental and Institutional Perspectives,* FAO, Fisheries Technical Paper No.353, FAO, Rome, 1995.

California Coastal Zone Conservation Commission (1975), *California Coastal Plan,* California Coastal Conservation Commission, Sacremento, 1975.

Cambers, G. (1985), *An Over View of Coastal Zone Management in Six East Caribbean Islands.* U.N.Educational Scientific and Cultural Organisation Office for Science and Technology, Montevedio, 1985, 69 pp.

Cambers, G. (1987), 'Coastal Zone Management Programmes in Barbados and Grenada', in *Coastal Zone '87, Proceedings of the Fifth Symposium on Coastal and Ocean Management,* Vol.1, pp.1384-1394, New York, American Society of Civil Engineers.

Carter, R.W.G. (1989), *Coastal Environments : An Introduction to the Physical, Ecological, and Cultural systems of Coastlines,* Academic Press, London, 1989.

CESS, (2001) 'CESS Develops Integrated Coastal Zone Management Plan' *CESS News,* Vol.11, No.2. Centre for Earth Science Studies, Thiruvananthapuram, June 2001.

Chalapan, K.(1996), 'Coastal Area Management in the Pacific Island Nations', Paper presented to the *Commission on Sustainable Development.* United Nations, New York, 1996.

Chancharaswat, K. (1991), 'The Role of Environmental Protection and Coastal Resources Management in National Development Planning in Thailand', in Chua, T.E. and L.F.Scura, (eds.), *Managing Asean's Coastal Resources for Sustainable Development: Role of Policy Makers, Scientists, Donors. Media and Communities.* ICLARM Conference Proceedings, 30, Manila, 1991, pp.49-58.

Chape, S.P. (1990), 'Coastal Tourism and Environmental Management in Fiji', in *Proceedings of the 1990 Congress on Coastal and Marine Tourism,* Vol.I, M.Miller and J.Auyong (eds.), National Coastal Resources Research and Development Institute, Newport, Origon, 1990, pp.66-67.

Chaverri, R. (1989), 'Coastal Management: The Costa Rica Experience', in *Coastal Zone '87.* Vol.V, American Society of Civil Engineers, New York, pp. 5723-5785.

Chiau, W.Y. (1998), 'Coastal Zone Management in Taiwan: A Review', *Ocean and Coastal Management,* 38, 1998, pp. 119-132.

Ching, L.K. (1987), 'Coastal Zone Management Plan Development in Malaysia: Issues and Possible Solutions', in *Coastal Zone '87,* O.T.Magoon, H.Converse, D.MInor and I.T.Tobln (eds.) pp. 4601-4615, American Society of Civil Engineers, New York, 1987.

Chou, L.M., T.E.Chua, H.W.Khoo, P.E.Lim, J.N.Paw, G.T.Silvestre, M.J.Valencia, A.T.White and P.K.Wang, (eds.), (1991), *Towards an Integrated Management of Tropical Coastal Resources,* ICLARM Conference Proceedings, 22, National University of Singapore, National Science and Technology Board, Singapore and International Centre for Living Aquatic Resource Management, Manila, 1991.

Chua, T.E. (1986), 'Managing ASEAN Coastal Resources', *Tropical Coastal Area Management,* Vol.1, No.1, International Centre for Living Aquatic Resource Management, Manila, pp.8-10.

Chua, T.E. (1989), 'Developing Coastal Area Management Plans in the South East Asian Region', in *Symposium on Coastal and*

Ocean Management 1989. Charleston, South Carolina, *Coastal Zone '89.* Vol.3, New York, 1989,

Chua, T.E. (ed.) (1991 a), 'Coastal Area Management Education in the ASEAN Region', *ICLARM Conference Proceedings* 29, ICLARM, Manila, 1991.

Chua, T.E. (1991 b), 'Managing Coastal Resources for Sustainable Development: The Asean's Initiative', in Chua, T.E. and Scura, L.F. (eds.), *Managing Asean's Coastal Resources for Sustainable Development: Role of Policy Makers. Scientists, Donors. Media and Communities,* ICLARM Conference Proceedings 30, ICLARM, Manila, 1991, pp.23-36.

Chua, T.E. (1992), 'The ASEAN/US Coastal Resources Management Project: Initiation, Implementation and Management', *in Inteqrative Framework and Methods for Coastal Area Management.* T.E.Chua and L.F.Scura (eds.), ICLARM and US Coastal Research Management Project, Manila, 1992, pp.71-92.

Chua, T.E. (1993 a), 'Regional Efforts in the Management of the Coastal, and Marine Environments in the ASEAN Region', in *Ocean and Coastal Management,* 19(2), 1993, pp.190-195.

Chua, T.E. (1993 b), 'Essential Elements of Integrated Coastal Zone Management', *Ocean and Coastal Management,* 21, 1993, *Special Issue: Integrated Coastal Management,* pp. 81-108.

Chua, T.E. (1996), 'Integrated Coastal Management in Tropical Developing Countries: Lessons Learned from Successes and Failures', *MPP-EAS Technical Report* No.4, Coastal Management Centre, Quezon City, Philippines, 1996.

Chua, T.E. (1997 a), 'Application of Integrated Coastal Management System for Sustainable Coastal Fishery Development', in *Environmental Aspects of Responsible Fisheries. Proceedings of the APFIC Symposium.* Seoul, 15-18, October, 1996. Asia Pacific Fishery Commission, FAO, Bangkok, 1997.

Chua, T.E. (1997 b), 'Introduction to the Special Issue on Lessons Learned in Integrated Coastal Management', *Ocean and Coastal Management. 37(2), 1997, Special Issue, Lessons Learned in Integrated Coastal Management,* pp. 153-154.

Chua, T.E. (1998), 'Lessons From Practicing Integrated Coastal Management in South East Asia' Ambio, 1998, 27, pp.590-610.

Chua, T.E. and D. Pauly (eds.) (1989), 'Coastal Area Management in Southeast Asia: Policies, Management Strategies and Case Studies', *ICLARM Conf. Proceedings.* 19, ICLARM, Manila, 1989.

Chua, T.E. and L.F. Scura (eds.)(1991), *Managing Asean's Coastal Resources for Sustainable Development': Role of Policy Makers, Scientists, Donors, Media and Communities,* ICLARM, Conference Proceedings, 30, 1991.

Chua, T.E. and I.F.Scura (eds.) (1992), 'Integrative Framework and Methods for Coastal Area Management', *ICLARM Conference Proceedings.* No.37, International Centre for Living Aguatic Resources Management, Manila, 1992.

Chua, T.E. and Paw, J.N. (1996), 'A Dichotomy of the Planning Process Used in the ASEAN-US Project on Coastal Resources Management', paper presented at the *International Workshop on Integrated Coastal Management in Tropical Developing Countries: Lessons Learned from Successes and Failures.* May 24-28, 1996, Xiamen, Peoples Republic of China.

Chua, T.E. and Yu, H., (1996), 'From Sectoral to Integrated Coastal Management: A Case Study in Xiamen, China', Paper presented at *International Workshop on Integrated Coastal Management in Tropical Developing Countries*: Lessons Learned from Successes and Failures. May 24-28, 1996, Xiamen, Peoples Republic of China.

Chua, T.E., Huming Yu and Chen Gouqiang (1997), 'From Sectoral to Integrated Coastal Management: A Case in Xiamen, China', *Ocean and Coastal Management.* 37(2), 1997, Special Issue, *Lessons Learned in Integrated Coastal Management*, pp. 233-252.

Cicin-Sain, B. (1982), 'Managing the Ocean Commons: US Marine Programmes in the 70s and 80s.' *Marine Technology Society Journal,* 6(18), 1982.

Cicin-Sain, B. (1992), 'Multiple Use Conflicts and Their Resolution: Towards a Comparative Research Agenda', in *Ocean Management in Global Change*, P. Fabbri (ed.), Elsevier Applied Science, London, 1992, pp.280-307.

Cicin-Sain, B. (1993 a), Introduction to the Special Issue on' Integrated Coastal Management: Concepts, Issues and

Methods'. *Ocean and Coastal Management,* 21, 1993, *Special Issue: Integrated Coastal Management:* pp.1-9.

Cicin-Sain, B. (1993 b), 'Sustainable Development and Integrated Coastal Management', *Ocean and Coastal Management.* 21, 1993, *Special Issue: Integrated Coastal Management,* pp.11-43.

Cicin-Sain, B. (1993 c), 'Education and Training in Ocean and Coastal Management: Activities of the Marine Affairs and Policy Associations, (MAPA), *Ocean and Coastal, Management,* 2(1-3) 1993, pp.375-377.

Cicin-Sain, B. and R.W.Knecht (ed.) (1993 a), 'Integrated Coastal Management' *in Ocean and Coastal Management,* Special Issue, *Integrated Coastal Management,* 21(1-3),1993, pp.1-377.

Cicin-Sain, B. and Knecht, R.W. (1993 b), 'Implications of the Earth Summit for Ocean and Coastal Governance'. *Ocean Development and International Law,* 24, 1993, pp.121-153.

Cicin-Sain, B. and Knecht, R.W. (eds.) (1995 a), 'Earth Summit Implementation: Progress Achieved on Ocean and Coasts', *Ocean and Coastal Management, Special Issue.* 29(1-3), 1995.

Cicin-Sain, B. and Knecht, R.W. (1995 b), 'Measuring Progress on UNCED Implementation', *Ocean and coastal Management: Special Issue: Earth Summit Implementation: Progress Achieved on Ocean and Coasts.* 29(1-3). 1995, pp.1-11.

Cicin-Sain, B., R.W. Knecht and G.W.Fisk (1995 c) 'Growth in Capacity for Integrated Coastal Management Since UNCED: An International Perspective'. *Ocean and Coastal Management,* 29(1-3): *Special* Issue, *Earth Summit Implementation: Progress Achieved on Ocean and Coasts,* 1995, pp.93-123.

Cicin-Sain, B., Knecht, R.W. and Fisk, G.W.(1996) 'Growth in Capacity for Integrated Coastal Management Since UNCED; An International Perspective', *Ocean and Coastal Management,* 1996, 29(1-3), pp.93-123.

Cicin-Sain, B., C.N.Ehler, R. W. Knecht, S. South and R.Weiher, (1997) , 'Guidelines for Integrating Coastal Management Programmes and National Climate Change Action Plans', *International Workshop on Planning for Climate Change Through Integrated Coastal Management,* February 24-28, 1997, Taipei, Taiwan.

Cicin-Sain, B. and R.W. Knecht (1998), *Integrated Coastal and Ocean Management, Concepts and Practices*. Island Press, Washington, D.C. 1998.

Cicin-Sain, B., Knecht, R.W., Vallega, A. and Harakunarak, A. (2000), 'Education and Training in Integrated Coastal Management: Lessons from the International Arena', *Ocean and Coastal Management,* 43, 2000, *GENOA Special Issue on Education and Training in Integrated Coastal Management*, pp.291-330.

City Express, (2003), 'Local Fishermen Lay Seige to Cochin Fishing Harbour', City Express. Cochin, 4.10.2003.

Clark, J.R. (1977), *Coastal Ecosystem Management; A Technical Manual for the Conservation of Coastal Zone Resources, John Wiley and Sons, New York, 1977.*

Clark, J.R. (1980), *Coastal Environmental Management Guide.lines for Conservation of Resources and Protection Against Storm Hazards*, Federal Emergency Management Agency, Washington, D.C., 1980, 161 pp.

Clark, J.R. (1983), *Coastal Ecosystem Management: A Technical Manual for the Conservation of Coastal Zone Resources,* Robert E. Krieger Publishing Co., Melbourne (First edition by John Wiley - Inter Science, New York, 1977), 928 pp.

Clark, J.R. (ed.) (1985), *Coastal Resource Management: Development Case Studies, Coastal Management Publications No.3.* NPS/AID Series, Research Planning Institute, Columbia, S.C. 1985, 749 pp.

Clark, J.R. (1991), *The Status of Integrated Coastal Management. A Global Assessment*, Coastal Area Management and Planning Network (CAMPNET), Rosentiel School of Marine and Atmospheric Science, University of Miami, Miami.

Clark, J.R. (1992), *Integrated Management of Coastal Zones.* FAO Fisheries Technical Paper No.327, Rome, Food and Agriculture Organisation of the United Nations, Rome.

Clark, J.R. (1996), *Coastal Zone Management Handbook*, Lewis Publishers, New York.

Clark, J.R. (1997),'Coastal Zone Management for the New Century', *Ocean and Coastal Management* 37(2), 1977, *Special Issue, Lessons Learned in Integrated Coastal Management*, pp.191-216.

Clark, M.J. (1977), 'The Relationship Between Coastal Zone Management and Off-shore Economic Development', *Maritime Policy and Management*, 4(6), 1977, pp.431-449.

Coetzee, M.D. (1991), 'The Importance of Public Participation in Coastal Management', in *The Status of Integrated Coastal Zone Management. A Global Assessment*, Clark, J.R. (ed.) CAMPNET/University of Miami/RSMAS, Miami, Fla. pp.29-30.

CAMPNET (1989), *The Status of Integrated Coastal Zone Management; A Global Assessment.* Coastal Area Management and Planning Network, University of Miami, 1989.

Cordell, J. (1993), 'Indigenous People's Coastal-Marine Domains: Some Matters of Cultural Documentation', in *Turning the Tide*: Papers presented at the *Conference on Indigenous Peoples and Sea Rights.* Faculty of Law. Northern Territory University, Darwin, 1993.

Coast Conservation Department (1990), *Coastal Zone Management Plan.* Sri Lanka Coast Conservation Department, Colombo, Sri Lanka, 110 pp.

Cobb, J.S. (1995), 'Building Capacity for Coastal Management at Universities', in Crawford B.R., Cobb, J.S. Ming, C.L. (eds.), *Educating Coastal Managers: Proceedings of the Rhode Island Workshop*, W. Alton Jones Campus, University of Rhode Island, March 4-10, 1995, pp.102-109.

Coombs, H.C. (1994), *Aboriginal Autonomy: Issues and Strategies.* Cambridge University Press, U.K. 1994.

Coughanow, C. and Kullenberg, (1993), 'On the Need for Scientific Input on an International Scale: The Inter-governmental Oceanographic Commission's Perspective on Integrated Coastal Management', *Ocean and Coastal Management*, 21(1-3), 1993, pp.339-352.

Crawford, B.R., J.S.Cobb, and A.Friedman (1993), Building Capacity for Integrated Coastal Management in Developing Countries'. *Ocean and Coastal Management.* 21(1-3), pp.311-337.

Crawford, B.R.,Cobb, J.S., Ming, C.L. (eds.) (1995), 'Educating Coastal Managers', Proceedings of the Rhode Island Workshop. W.Alton Jones Campus, University of Rhode Island, March 4-10, 1995.

Cullen, P. (1982), 'Coastal Zone Management in Australia', *Coastal Zone Management Journal*, 10(3), pp.183-212.

Dahl, C. (1997), 'Integrated Coastal Resource Management and Community Participation in a Small Island Setting', *Ocean and Coastal Management*, 36, 1997, *Special Issue: Community Based Coastal Management*, pp.23-46.

Dahuri, R. (1991), 'The Need for Integrated Coastal Resource Management', in *The Status of Integrated Coastal Zone Management; A Global Assessment*. Clark, J.R. (ed.), CAMPNET/ University of Miami/RSMAS, Miami, Fla. pp.108-111.

Dahuri, R. (1996), 'Coastal Zone Management and Trans-Migration in Indonesia', Paper presented at International Workshop on *Integrated Coastal Management in Tropical Developing Countries: Lessons Learned from Successes and Failures.* May 24-28 Xiaman, Peoples Republic of China.

Davis, B.W. (1996), 'Contemporary Ocean and Coastal Management Issues in Australia and New Zealand-An Overview', *Ocean and Coastal Management.* 33(1-3), 1996, *Special Issue. Ocean and Coastal Management Issues in Australia and New Zealand*, pp.5-18.

Deb, A.K. (1996), 'Fake Blue Revolution: Environmental and Socio-economic Impacts of Shrimp Culture in the Coastal Areas of Bangladesh. *Ocean and Coastal Management*, 41,1996, pp.63-88.

Das, M.K. (1999), 'CRZ Notification May be scrapped', *The New Indian Express,* Cochin, 20.11.1999.

Das, M.K. (2002), 'Navy Trains its Guns on CPT Crane', The New Indian Express. Cochin, 16.9.2002.

Degong, C. (1989), 'Coastal Zone Development, Utilisation, Legislation and Management in China', *Coastal Management*, 17(1), pp.55-62.

Department of Animal Husbandry and Dairying (2001), *Handbook on Fisheries Statistics* 2000. Government of India, New Delhi, 2001.

Directorate of Fisheries (1969), *Master Plan for Fisheries Development. Kerala State.* Government of Kerala, Trivandrum.

Department of Fisheries (1991), *Kerala Fisheries —Facts and Figures 1990*. Department of Fisheries, Kerala, Thiruvananthapuram, 1991.

Department of Fisheries (1992), The Integrated Management Plan for the Coastal Zone of Brunei Darussalam, Department of Fisheries, Ministry of Industry and Primary Resources, Brunei, Darussalam, ICLARM Technical Report 29, 1992.

Department of Fisheries (1993), *Kerala Fisheries - An Overview 1992,* Government of Kerala, Thiruvananthapuram, 1993.

Department of Fisheries (2000 a), *Marine Fisheries of Kerala at a Glance 1998*, Government of Kerala, Thiruvananthapuram, 2000.

Department of Fisheries (2000 b), *Inland Fisheries of Kerala at a Glance 1998*, Government of Kerala, Thiruvananthapuram, 2000.

Department of Fisheries (2000 c), *Inland Fisheries of Kerala at a Glance, 1999*, Government of Kerala, Thiruvananthapurara, 2000.

Department of Fisheries (2001), *Pan Fish Books Series*, Government of Kerala, Thiruvananthapuram.

Department of Fisheries (2002), *Master Pan Fish Book 1.* (Data on the Water Resources for the Development of Inland Fisheries in Kerala), Government of Kerala, Thiruvananthapuram.

Department of Fisheries and Oceans, Canada (1996), *Integrated Coastal Area Management: A Canadian Retrospective and Update, Presentation to the United Nations Commissions on Sustainable Development*, United Nations, New York, April 1996.

Department of Tourism (2001), *Tourist Statistics 1999 and 2000*, Government of Kerala, Thiruvananthapuram.

Department of the Environment and Welsh Office (1993), *Develpment Below Low Water Mark. A Review of Regulations in England and Wales*. HMSO. London, 1993.

Desai, P.N. (1997), Coastal Marine Environment of Gujarat - *A Bench Mark Survey*. vol.I-IV, Gujarat Ecological Society, Vadodara, 1997.

Devaraj, M. , Menon, N.G. , Pillai, V.K. and Balachandran, K. (1999), 'Coastal Zone Governance: Kerala, in Relation to National and International Situations', *Marine Fisheries Information Service*, No.162, Cochin, Oct.-Dec. 1999, pp.1-22.

Directorate of Census Operations (1961), *Village Survey Monographs of Trivandrum District*, Government of Kerala, Trivandrum.

Directorate of Economics and Statistics (2002), *Statistics for Planning 2001*, Government of Kerala, Thiruvananthapuram.

Diegues, A. (1992), 'Managing Brazil's Coastal Wetlands: The Contribution of Research Amid the Realities of Politics', in Malby, E., Dugan, P. and Lefeuvre, J. , (eds.), Conservation and *Development: The Sustainable Use of Wetland Resources. Proceedings of the Third International Wetlands Conference. IUCN, Switzerland, 1992* .

Dixit, R. B. (2003), 'Changing Chemistry Opens a Pandora's Box in Eloor', *City Express*. Cochin, 12.9.2003.

Dobias, R.J. (1989), 'Beaches and Tourism in Thailand', in *Coastal Area Management in Southeast Asia: Policies, Management Strategies and Case Studies*. Chua, .E.and D.Pauly (eds.), pp.43-55: *ASEAN-USAID Coastal Resources Management Project*, ICLARM *Proceedings, No.2*. Manila, International Centre for Living Aquatic Resources Management.

Donalson, C. (1994), 'An Unholy Alliance: Working With Coastal Community - A Practitioners Perspective', in *Coastal Zone Canada 94*, R.G.Wells and P.J.Ricketts (eds.), pp.696-705. Halifax, Nova Scotia, Coastal Zone Canada Association.

Du Bois, R. and E.L. Towle (1985), 'Coral Harvesting and Sand Mining Management Practices', in *Coastal Resources Management - Development Case Studies*, J.R.Clark (ed.), pp.443-508. Washington, DC., U.S. Department of the Interior, National Park Service, and U.S. Agency for International Development.

Ducrotoy, J.P. and Pullen, S. (1999), 'Integrated Coastal Zone Management: Commitments and Developments from an International, National and U.K.Perspective', *Ocean and Coastal Management*, 42, 1999, pp.1-18.

Ducrotoy, J.P., S.Shastri and P.Williams (2000), 'Coastal Sciences and Management: The Need for Net-Working in Higher Education', *Ocean and Coastal Management*, 43, 2000, *GENOA Special Issue on Education and Training in Integrated Coastal Management,* pp.427-444.

Edmund, C.P. , Penning-Roswell, Colin, H. Green, Paul, M. Thompson, Annabel, M. Coker, Sylvi, M.Tunstall, Cethy Richards and

Dennis, J. Parker (1992), *The Economics of Coastal Management: A Manual of Benefit Assessment Techniques*, Belhaven Press, London, 1992.

Edwards, S.D., P.J.S., Jones and D.E.Nowell (1997), Participation in Coastal Zone Management Initiatives: A Review and Analysis of Examples from the U.K.', *Ocean and Coastal Management*, 36, 1997, *Special Issue Community Based Coastal Management* pp. 143-166.

Edwards, S.F. (1987), *An Introduction to Coastal Zone Economics: Concepts, Methods and Case Studies.* Taylor and Francis, New York, 1987.

Ehler, C.N., 'Coastal Ocean Space Management: Challenges for the Next Decade', in *Coastal Ocean Space Utilisation III*, Croce, N.D., Connel, S. and Abel, R. (eds.), Chapman and Hall, London, 1995, pp.175-188.

Eichenberg, T. and J.Archer (1987), The Federal Consistency Doctrine: Coastal Zone Management and the New Federalism', *Ecology Law Quarterly*, 14(1), pp.9-68.

Eid, E.M. and Hulbergen, C.H. (1992), 'Sea Level Rise and Coastal Zone Management', *Proceedings of the Second World Climate Conference*, Geneva, Switzerland, 29 October-7 November 1990, pp.301-309. Also Published as Delft Hydraulics publications, No. 471, 1992.

Ekins, P. (2000), *Economic Growth and Environmental Sustainability.* Routledge, London.

Ellsworth, J.P., L.P.Hildebrand and E.A.Glover (1997), 'Canada's Atlantic Coastal Action Programme: A Community-based Approach to Collective Governance', *Ocean and Coastal Management* 36(1-3): *Special Issue; Community-Based Coastal Management*, pp.12-142.

El-Sabh, M.I., de Mora,S, Walsh, G., Demers, S. and Hill, P. (eds.),(1996) Integrated Management and Sustainable Development in Coastal Zone', *Coastal Zone Canada. 1996* International Conference, Abstract Volume, University of Qubec, 1996.

El-Sabh, M., Demers, S. and Lafontaine,D. (1998), 'Coastal Management and Sustainable Development: From Stockholm to Rimouski', *Ocean and Coastal Management*, 39, 1998, pp.1-24.

Englander, E., Feldman, J. and Hershman, M. (1977), 'Coastal Zone Problems: A Basis for Evaluation', *Coastal Zone Management*, 3(3), 1977, pp.217-236.

Expert Committee (1985), *Report of the Expert Committee on Marine Fisheries in Kerala*, Central Institute of Fisheries Education, Bombay.

Fabbri, P. (ed.), (1992), *Ocean Management in Global Change*, New York, Elsevier Applied Science.

Fabbri, P. (1998), 'A Methodology for Supporting Decision Making in Integrated Coastal Zone Management', *Ocean and Coastal Management*, 39, 1998, pp.51-62.

Factoran, Jr. F.S. (1991), 'The Need for an Integrated Coastal Zone Management in the Philippines', in Chua, T.E. and Scura, L.F. (eds.), *Managing Asean's Coastal Resources for Sustainable Development: Role of Policy Makers, Scientists, Donors, Media and Communities*, ICLARM Conference Proceedings 30, ICLARM Manila, 1991, pp.43-48.

Faizi, S. (2002), 'J'o'burg: A Step Forward or Back?' *The New Indian Express*, Cochin, 23.8.2002.

Fisk, G.W. (1996), *Integrated Coastal Management in Developed Countries: The Case of Australia*, Master's Thesis, Graduate College of Marine Studies, University of Delaware.

Fishing Chimes (1997), 'Coastal Aquaculture, Writ Petition, S.C.Judgement; dt. 11.12.1996, S.Jagannathan Vs Union of India and Others. Extract of Operative Part', *Fishing Chimes*, January 1997.

FAO (1991), *Development of Coastal Areas and Enclosed Seas*, UN Conference on Environment and Development,Research Paper No.4, Food and Agriculture Organisation of the United Nations, Rome,

FAO (1994), *Mangrove Forest Management Guidelines*, FAO Forestry Paper No.117, FAO, Rome, 1994.

FAO (1996 a), *Integration of Fisheries in to Coastal Area Management*. FAO Technical Guidelines for Responsible Fisheries, No.3, FAO, Rome, 1996.

FAO (1996 b), *Report of the Task Force on Integrated Coastal Management*, FAO, Rome, 1996.

Frihy, O.E. (1996), 'Some Proposals for Coastal Management of the Nile Delta Coast'. *Ocean and Coastal Management*, 30(1), 1996, pp.43-59.

Fuavo, V., 'Coastal Management in Small Island Developing States', in *Small Islands, Big Issues: Critical Issues in the Sustainable Development of Small Developing Islands,* World Development Studies 1, World Institute for Development Economics Research, The United Nations University, Helsinki, 1995, pp.84-111.

Gagliano, S.T. (1995), 'The Role of Public-Private Partnership in the Governance of Coastline', in *Coastal Ocean Space Utilisation III*, Croce N.D., Connel, S. and Abal, R. (eds.), Chapman and Hall, London, 1995, pp.105-112.

Ganter, E. (1996), 'Indigenous Participation in Coastal Management in the Northern Territory, Australia: Issues and Options', *Ocean and Coastal Management*, 33(1-3). 1996, *Special Issue. Ocean and Coastal Management Issues in Australia and New Zealand*, pp.193-212.

Garcia, S.M. (1994), *The Precautionary Approach to Fisheries with Reference to Straddling Fish Stocks and Highly Migratory Fish Stocks*, FAO, Fisheries Circular No.871, FAO, Rome, 1994.

Gazetteers Department (1989) , Kerala State Gazetteer, Vol.III Economic Affairs, Government of Kerala, Teivandrum, 1989.

Geoghegan, T. (1983), *Guidelines for Integrated Marine Resources Management in the Eastern Caribbean.* Caribbean Conservation Association, Caribbean Environment Technical, Report No.2, 56 pp.

Gilbert, C. (1995), *Action on the Coast.* Local Government Management Board, Luton, U.K., 1995.

Godschalk, D.R. (1992), Implementing Coastal Zone Management: 1972-1990', *Coastal Management*, 20, 1992, pp.93-116.

Gosh, S. , Dasgupta, D.D. and Srinivas, M.N.K. (1999), 'Port Development and Coastal Zone Management (Indian Scenario): A Few Case Studies', *Proceedings of the Fifth International Conference on Coastal and Port Engineering in Developing Countries.* Cape Town, 1999, pp.720-732.

Grigalunas, T.A. and Congar,R. (eds.),(1995), *Environmental Economics for Integrated Coastal Area Management: Valuation*

Methods and Policy Instruments, UNEP Regional Seas Report Studies, Nairobi, No.164.

Griffith, M.K. and Asha, J. (1993), 'Sustainable Development of Coastal and Marine Areas in Small Island Developing States: A Basis for Integrated Coastal Management', *Ocean and Coastal Management.* 21(1-3), 1993. *Special Issue, Integrated Coastal Management*, pp.269-284.

Group of Experts on the Scientific Aspects of Marine Environmental Protection (GESAMP),(1996), *The Contribution of Sciences to Integrated Coastal Management*, GESAMP Reports and Studies, No.61, GESAMP.

Gubbay, S. (1990), *A Future for the Coast: Proposals for a U.K. Coastal Zone Management Plan.* Report prepared for the World Wide Fund for Nature and the Marine Conservation Society, London, World Wide Fund for Nature.

Gubboy, S. (1995), *Integrated Coastal Zone Management, Opportunities for Scotland: Briefing for the World Wide Fund for Nature*, Scotland.

Guochen, Z. (1993), 'Coastal Zone Management in China', in *World Coast Conference 1993.* Proceedings Vols. 1 and 2, CZM Centre Publication No.4, Coastal Zone Management Centre, The Hague, 1993.

Haq, B.U., Haq, S.M., Kullenberg, G. and Stel, J.H. (1997), Coastal Zone *Management, Imperative for Maritime Developing Nations*, Kluwer Academic Publishers, Dordrecht, 1997.

Harish, CM., (1973), *Impact of Sea Level Rise due to Green-house Effect - Statistical Analysis of Tide Gauge Data Along the Entire West Coast of India*, Final Report submitted to Department of Environment and Forests, Government of India, 1973, 53 p.

Hatziolos, M.E. (1997), 'A World Bank Framework for ICZM With Special Emphasis on Africa', *Ocean and Coastal Management*, 37(3), 1997, pp.281-294.

Hatziolos, M.E. and I. Trumbic (1997), *Preliminary Results of an Assessment of Coastal Zone Management Initiatives in the Mediterranean,* Memorandum, World Bank, Washington, D.C., 1997.

Hawaii Office of State Planning (1990), *Hawaii Coastal Zone Management Programme*, Hololulu, Hawaii Office of State Planning.

Haward, M. and Vanderzwaag (1995), 'Implementation of UNCED Agenda 21, Chapter 17 in Australia and Canada: A Comparative Analysis', *Ocean and Coastal Management*, 29(1-3), 1995, *Special Issue: Earth Summit Implementation; Progress Achieved on Oceans and Coasts*, pp.279-296.

Haward, M. (1996), 'Institutional Framework for Australian Ocean and *Coastal management*', *Ocean and Coastal Management, 33(1-3), 1996, Special Issue: Ocean and Coastal Management in Australia and New Zealand*, pp.19-40.

Hegarty, A., 'Start With What the People Know: A Community Based Approach to Integrated Coastal Management', *Ocean and Coastal Management*. 36, 1997, *Special Issue, Community Based Coastal Management*, pp.167-204.

Heikoff, Joseph, M. (1976), *Politics of Shore Erosion: Westampton Beach*. Ann Arbor Science Publishers Inc., Ann Arbor, 1976.

Heikoff, Joseph, M. (1980), *Marine and Shoreland Resources Management*, Ann Arbor Science Publishers Inc., Ann Arbor, l980.

Hershman, M.J., Bernd Cohen, J.W. Good, B.Goodwin, M.Gordon, V. Lee and P. Pogue (1997), 'National CZM Effectiveness Study - Findings and Recommendations', Paper presented at the Conference, *Coastal Zone*, 97,July 22-24, Boston, Massachusetts.

Hershman, M.J., Good, J.W. Bernd Cohen, Goodwin, R.F. , Lee,V. and Pogue, P. (1999), 'The Effectiveness of Coastal Zone Management in the United States', *Coastal Management*, 27, 1999, pp.113-38.

Herz, R. (1989), 'Coastal Ocean Space Management in Brazil', in *Coastal Ocean Space Utilisation*, S.D. Holsey and R.B. Abel (eds.), New York, Elsevier Applied Science, 1989, pp.29-52.

Herz, R. and A. S.Mascarenhas, Jr. (1993), 'Political and Planning Action on the Brazilian Coastal Management Programme', in *Coastal Zone '93*. O.T.Magoon, W.S.Wilson and H.Converse (eds.), pp.1084-1091, New York, American Society of Civil Engineers.

Hewawasam, I. (2000), 'Advancing Knowledge: A Key Element of the World Bank's Integrated Coastal Management Strategic Agenda in Sub-Saharan Africa', *Ocean and Coastal*

Management. 43, 2000. *GENOA Special Issue on Education and Training in Integrated Coastal Management*, pp. 361-378.

Hildebrand, L.P. (1989), *Canada's Experience with Coastal Zone Management*, Ocean Institute of Canada, Halifax, Nova Scotia.

Hildebrand,L.P.,(1994), 'Cooperation in Coastal Zone', *Ocean and Coastal Management*, 25, 1994, pp.233-235.

Hildebrand, L.P. (1996), 'Canada: National Experience with Coastal Zone Management', in Coastal Zone Management Hand Book, J.R.Clark (ed.), pp. 506-508, New York, Lewie.

Hildebrand, L.P. (1997), 'Introduction to the Special Issue on Community-based Coastal Management', *Ocean and Coastal Management*. 36(1-3), Special Issue, Community-based Coastal Management, pp.1-10.

Hildreth, R. (1975), 'Coastal Land Use Control in Sweden', *Coastal Zone Management*, 2(1), 1975, pp.1-29.

Hite, J.C. and Stepp, J.M. (1971), *Coastal Zone Resource Management'* Praeger Publishers, New York, 1971.

Hodgson, G.P , and J.A. Dixon (1988), 'Measuring Economic Losses due to Sediment Pollution: Logging Versus Tourism and Fisheries', *Tropical Coastal Area Management*. (April 1988), pp.5-7.

Holland, G.L. (1998), 'The Role of Intergovernmental Organisations in Coastal Zone Management', *Ocean and Coastal Management*. 39, 1998, pp.25-31.

Hong, S.Y. (1991), 'Assessment of Coastal Zone Issues in the Republic of Korea', *Coastal Management*, 19, pp.391-415.

Hong, S.Y. and Huh, H.T. (1995), 'Coastal Zone Development in the Republic of Korea', in *Coastal Ocean Space Utilisation III*, Croce, N.D., Connel, S., and Abel, R. (eds.), Chapman and Hall, London, 1995, pp.409-424.

Hood, Donald,W. (ed.) (1971), *Impingement of Man on the Oceans*. Wiley-interscience, New York, 1971.

Hotta, K. and Dutton, I.M. (eds.) (1995), *Coastal Management in the Asia-Pacific Region: Issues and Approaches*, Japan International Marine Science and Technology Federation, Tokyo, 1995.

Huggett, D. (1998), 'The Role of Federal Government Interaction in Coastal ZonePlanning and Management', *Ocean and Coastal Management.* 39 1998, pp.33-50.

Huming, Y. and Chua,T. E (1998) 'ICM Training For Marine Pollution Prevention and Management', *Ocean and Coastal Management.* 38,998, pp.69-86.

Independent World Commission on the Oceans (1998) *The Oceans, Our Future,* Cambridge, 1998.

Institution of Civil Engineers (1989), *Coastal Management,* Proceedings of the Conference Organised by the Marine Engineering Board of the Institute of Civil Engineers, Bourne Mouth, 9-11 May, 1989, Thomas Telford, London, 1989.

Institution of Civil Engineers (1992), *Coastal Management 92., Integrating Coastal Zone Planning and Management in the Next Century,* Conference Organised by the Maritime Engineering Board of the Institution of Civil Engineers Blackpool, 11-13 May,1992, Blackpool, 1992.

Inter Coast Network (1992), *Inteqrated Coastal Area Management Programmes, Pilot Programmes and Feasibility Studies,* Coastal Resources Centre, The University of Rhode Island, Kingston, Rhode Island, USA, 1992.

Inter-Governmental Panel on Climate Change (IPCC) (1990), *Strategies for Adaption to Sea level Rise. Report of the Coastal Zone Management Sub-Groups,* The Netherlands, 1990, 121 p.

Inter-Governmental Panel on Climate Change (IPCC) (1993), *Preparing to Meet the Coastal Challenges of the 21st Century.* Conference Report, World Coast Conference 1993, Coastal Zone Management Centre, The Hague, 1994.

International Coral Reef Initiative (1995), *Final Report of the International Coral Reef Initiative Workshop,* May 29 - June 2, ICR Secretariat, Washington, DC.

Jacoby,C.,C.Manning, S.Fritz and L. Rose (1997), Three Recent Initiatives for Monitoring of Australian Coasts by the Community', *Ocean and Coastal Management.* 36, 1997, *Special Issue, Community-based Coastal Management,* pp.205-226.

Jaison, C. Cooper (2002), 'Sea Erosion Threatens Fort Kochi Beach', *The New Indian Express*, Cochin, 10.6.2002.

Jentoft, S. (2000), 'Comanaging the Coastal Zone: Is the Task Too Complex', *Ocean and Coastal Management, 43. 2000. GENOA Special Issue on Education and Training in Integrated Coastal Management*, pp.527-535.

Jeftic, L. (1996), 'Integrated Coastal and Marine Areas Management (ICAM)', in the *Mediterranean Action Plan of UNEP' Ocean and Coastal Management.* 30(2-3), Special Issue, *Coastal Zone Management in the Mediterranean*, (ed. E.Ozhan), 1996, 89-113.

Jhingran, A.G. and P.K.Chakrabarti (1990), *An Approach to Coastal Zone Management and Planning in West Bengal*, Inland Fisheries Society of India, Calcutta, India, 53 pp.

Johnson, D.E., Fletcher, S.,Shiloae, V.S.V., Shkit Sky, V.A., Upton, A.C. and Zogorodny, A.V. (2000), 'Integrated Coastal Management Education in the Russian Federation Through Academic Partnership', *Ocean and Coastal Management*'. 43, 2000, *GENOA Special Issue on Education and Training in Integrated Coastal Management*, pp.953-962.

Joliffe, I.P. and C.R.Patman (1985), 'The Coastal Zone: The Challenge', *Journal of Shoreline Management'*, 1985, 1(1), pp.3-36.

Jorge, M.A. (1997), 'Developing Capacity for Coastal Management in the Absence of the Public Sector: A Case Study in the Dominican Republic', *Ocean and Coastal Management.* 36(1-3), *Special Issue: Community-based Coastal Management*, pp.47-72.

Jull, P. (1993), *A Sea Change: Overseas-Indigenous Government Relations in the Coastal Zone.* Australian Government Publishing Service, Canberra, 1993.

Kahawita, B.S. (1993), 'Coastal Zone Management in Sri Lanka', in *World Coast Conference* 1993 *Proceedings*, pp. 669-675, CZM Centre Publication No.4, Coastal Zone Management Centre, The Hague, 1993.

Kaladharan, P., Pillai, V.K.,Said Koya, K.P.,Leela Bhai, K.S. and Palaniswamy, N. (1999), 'Oilslick in the Inshore Waters to the North of Cochin Port Channel', *Marine Fisheries Information Service*, Cochin, July-Sept. 1999, pp.16-17.

Kalaw, Jr., M.T. (1991), 'The Role and Involvement of Non-Governmental Organisations in the Sustainable Development of Coastal Resources', in, Chua, T.E. and L.F.Scura (eds.), *Managing Asean's Coastal Resources for Sustainable Development: Role of Policy Makers, Scientists. Donors, Media and Communities.* ICLARM Conference Proceedings, ICLARM, Manila, 1991, pp.103-106.

Kam, S.P., Paw, J.N. and Loo, M. (1992), 'The Use of Remote Sensing and Geographic Information Systems in Coastal Zone Management', in *Integratlve Framework and Methods for Coastal Area Management,* T.E.Chua and L.F.Scura (eds.), ICLARM and U.S. Coastal Resource Management Project, Manila, 1992, pp.107-131.

Karunakaran, B. (2001), 'Mangroves Fast Depleting in State Due to Urbanisation, Pollution', *The New Indian Express*, Cochin, 20.3.2001.

Kay, Robert and Alder, Jacqeline (1999), *Coasta' Planning and Management.* E. and FN Spon, London, 1999.

Kenchington, R. (1990), *Managing Marine Environments*, Taylor and Francis, New York.

Kenchington, R. and D.Crawford (1993), 'On the Meaning of Integration in Coastal Zone Management', *Ocean and Coastal Management*, 21(1-3), pp.109-128.

Kerala Gazetteers Department (1989), *Kerala State Gazetteer*, Vol.III, Government of Kerala, Trivandrum.

Ketchum, B.H. (1972), *The Water's Edge: Critical Problems of the Coastal* Zone, The MIT Press, Cambridge, MA, 1972.

Kinball, L.A. (1995), 'International Regime for Managing Land-based Activities that Degraded Marine and Coastal Environments', *Ocean and Coastal Management.* 29(1-3), *Speeial Issue: Earth Summit Implementation; Progress Achieved on Oceans and Coasts*, pp.187-206.

Knecht, R.W. (1979), 'Coastal Zone Management: The First Five Years and Beyond', *Coastal Zone Management Journal*, 6, pp.259-272.

Knecht, R.W., J.M. Broadus, M.E.Silva, R.E. Bowen, H.W.Markus, and S.B.Petersen, (1984), *The Management of Ocean and*

Coastal Resources in Columbia: An Assessment, Technical Report, Woods Hole Oceanographic Institution, Marine Policy and Ocean Management Centre.

Knecht, R.W. (1992), 'National Ocean Policy in the United States: Less Than the Sum of its Parts', in *Ocean Management in Global Change*. P.Fabbri (ed.), pp.184-208, Elsevier Applied Science New York.

Knecht, R.W., Cicin-Sain, B. and Nieto, P. (1992), *Summary of Workshop on Integrated Coastal Management and Sea Level Rise*, Caracas, January 28-29, 1992, UNCED, New York.

Knecht, R.W. (1993), A Perspective on the Relationship Between the Local and National Levels of Government in Coastal Zone Management', Paper presented at *MED COAST 1993*, the First International Conference on the Mediterranean Coastal Environment, November 2-5, Ankara, Turkey.

Knecht, R.W. and J. Archer (1993), 'Integration in the U.S.Coastal Zone Management Programme', *Ocean and Coastal Management*, 21, pp. 183-199.

Knecht, R.W., B.Cicin-Sain and G.W.Fisk (1996), 'Perceptions of the Performance of State Coastal Zone Management Programmes in the United States', *Coastal Management*, 24, pp. 141-164.

Koekebakker, P. and G. Peet (1987), 'Coastal Zone Planning and Management in the Netherlands', *Coastal Management*, 15, pp.121-134.

Korakandy, R. (1994), *Technological Change and the Development of Marine Fishing Industry in India*, Daya Publishing House, New Delhi, 1994.

Korakandy, R. (1996), *Economics of Fisheries Management - A Critique in Third World Perspectives* - Daya Publishing House, Delhi, 1996.

Korakandy, R. (1997), 'Coastal Zone Management - A Must for Kerala', *Southern Economist*, vol.35, No.18, Jan. 14, 1997.

Krishnakumar, P.K. (2002), IWAI's Rs 65 Crore Expansion Project in Troubled Waters', *The New Indian Express*, Cochin, 25.9.2002.

Kurien, N.P., Samsuddin, M., Ramachandran, K.K., Salim, M.D. and Nayak, S. (1993), *Coastal Land use Mapping of the Kerala*

Coast for Brackish Water Aquaculture Site Selection, Project Report submitted to Space Application Centre (SAC), Ahmedabad, 1993.

Kusuma-Atmadja, M. and T.H.Purwaka (1996), 'Legal and Institutional Aspects of Coastal Zone Management in Indonesia', *Marine Policy*. 20(1), pp.63-86.

Lee, J.H., Y. Lee, S.Y.Hong and M.Kwon (1993), Coastal Zone Utilisation of the Republic of Korea: Status and Prospects', in *International Perspectives on Coastal Ocean Space Utilisation*. P.M.Grifman and J,A.Faucet (eds.), pp.253-264. University of Southern California, Sea Grant Programme, Los Angeles.

Leekpai, C. (1991), 'The Value of Coastal Resources in National Economic Development', in Chua, T.E. and Scura, L.F. (eds.) (1991), *Managing Asian's Coastal Resources for Sustainable Development; Role of Policy Makers, Scientists, Donors, Media and Communities*. ICLARM Conference Proceedings, 30, ICLARM, Manila, pp.15-20.

Logan, William (1887), *Malabar Manual*, Kerala Gazetteers Department, Thiruvananthapuram, 2000 (Reprint).

Levy, J.P.,(1988), 'Towards Integrated Marine Policy in Developing Countries', *Marine Policy*, July, 1988, pp.326-342.

Lohani, B.N. (1991), 'The Asian Development Bank's Efforts in Sustainable Development of Coastal Resources' in Chua, T.E. and L.F. Scura (eds.), *Managing Asian's Coastal Resources for Sustainable Development: Role of Policy Makers, Scientists, Donors, Media and Communities*, ICLARM Conference Proceedings, 30, ICLARM, Manila, 1991, pp. 73-82.

Loi, H.K. (1993), 'Coastal Zone Management in Malaysia', in *World Coast Conference 1993 Proceedings. Vols. 1 and 2*, CZM Centre Publication No.4, Coastal Zone Management Centre, The Hague, 1993.

Lowry, K., Casey Jarman and Machida, S. (1993), 'Federal State Coordination in Coastal Management: An Assessment of the Federal Consistency Provision of the Coastal Zone Management Act', *Ocean and Coastal, Management*, 19, 1993, pp.97-120.

Lowry, K. (1993), 'Coastal Management in Sri Lanka', Coastal Management in Tropical Asia. No.1, Coastal Resources Centre, University of Rhode Island, pp.1-7.

Lowry, K. and H.J.M. Wickremeratne (1988), 'Coastal Area Management in Sri Lanka', in *Ocean Year Book* 7, E.M.Borggese, N.Ginsberg, and J.R. Morgan (eds.), pp.263-293, University of Chicago Press, Chicago.

Lowry, K., Olsen, S. and Tobey, J. (1999 a), 'Donor Evaluations of ICM Initiatives: What can be Learned from Them'. *Ocean and Coastal Management*, 42, 1999, pp.767-789.

Lowry, K., Pallewatte, N. and Dainis, A.P. (1999 b), 'Policy Relevant Assessment of Community Level Coastal Management Projects in Sri Lanka', *Ocean and Coastal Management*, 42, 1999, pp. 717-745.

Macaraig, C. (1991), 'Sustainable Development of Coastal Resources: A Challenge and Choice', in *Managing Asian's Coastal Resources for Sustainable Development: Role of Policy Makers,Scientists, Donors, Media and Communities*, Chua, T.E. and L.F.Scura (eds.), ICLARM Proceedings 30, ICLARM, Manila 1991, pp.9-14.

Malaysian Coastal Resource Study Team (1992), *The Coastal Resources Management Plan for South Johore.* Malaysia, ICLARM, Manila, 1992.

Makoloweka, S. and Schurcliff, K. (1997), '*Coastal Management in Tanga*, Tanzania: A Decentralised Community-based Approach', *Ocean and Coastal Management*, 37(3), *Special Issue, Integrated Coastal Management in Africa*, pp.349-358.

Mathews, P. (1991), 'The Role of Local Press in Creating Public Awareness of Coastal Resource Management', in Chua, T.E. and L.F.Scura (eds.), *Managing Asian's Coastal Resources for Sustainable Development, Role of Policy Makers, Scientists, Donors, Media and Communities* ICLARM Conference Proceedings, ICLARM, Manila, 1991, pp.91-96.

Mediterranean Environment Technical Assistance Programme (METAP) (1991), *Coastal Zone Management {CZM) in Turkey.* Consultant Report to the World Bank.

Micallof, A. (1995), 'Socio-economic Aspects of Insular Coastal Management', in *Proceedings of the Second International Conference on the Mediterranean Coastal Environment, Medcoast '95*, Ozhan, E. (ed.), Middle East Technical University, Ankara, Vol.1, 1995, pp. 551-562.

Ministry of Agriculture (1976), *Reports of the National Commission on Agriculture, Part VIII Fisheries* (Mimeo), Government of India, New Delhi.

Mitchell, B. (1990), 'The Evolution of Integrated Resource Management', in *Integrated Approaches to Resource Planning and Management*, R. Lang (ed.), Banff School of Management, Alberta, Canada, 1990, pp.13-24.

Mitchell, J.K. (1989), 'Coastal Zone Management: A Comparative Analysis of National Programmes', in Ocean Year Book 3, Borgesse, M., N. Ginsburg and J.R.Morgan (eds.), University of Chicago Press, Chicago, Illinois, USA, 1989, pp.265-272.

Msangi, J.P. (1991), 'The Integrated Utilisation of the Sea Coast off the Coast of Tanzania', in *The Development of Integrated Sea-Use Management*, H.D.Smith and A.Vallega (eds.), pp.230-237, London.

Nadia Scialabba (ed.) (1998), *Integrated Coastal Area Management and Agriculture, Forestry and Fisheries, FAO Guidelines*, Environment and Natural Resources Service, FAO, Rome, 256 p.

Naeve, H. and Garcia, S.M. (1995), 'The United Nations System Responds to Agenda 21.17: Oceans', *Ocean and Coastal Management*, 29, 1-3, pp.23-33.

Nair, Ramachandran Adoor, K.K. (1986), *Kerala State Gazetteer*, Vol.1, Government of Kerala, Trivandrum, 1986.

Nandakumar, D. and M. Muralikrishna, (1998), *Mapping the Extent of Coastal Regulation Zone Violations of the Indian Coast*, National Fish Workers Forum, Thiruvananthapuram, 1998.

National Economic Development Authority (1992), *The Lingayen Gulf Coastal Area Management Plan.* International Centre for Living Aquatic Resources Management, Technical Reports, No.32, Manila, 1992.

National Environment Board, Thailand (1992), The Integrated *Management Plan for Ban Don Bay and Phanganga Bay, Thailand*, Office of the National Environment Board, Ministry of Science, Technology and Environment, Thailand, 1992.

National Institute of Oceanography (1989), *National Conference on Coastal Zone Management*, 20-23 February 1989, Cochin, 1989.

National Oceanic and Atmospheric Administration (1993), *Biennial Report to Congress on the Administration of the U.S. Coastal Zone* Management Act, U.S. Department of Commerce, National Oceanic and Atmospheric Administration, Silver Spring, Maryland.

National Oceanic and Atmospheric Administration (1995), *Economic Valuation of Natural Resources: A Handbook for Coastal Resource Policy Makers*, NOAA Coastal Ocean Programme Decision Analysis Series No.5, U.S.Department of Commerce, National Oceanic and Atmospheric Administration, Coastal Ocean Programme Office, Silver Spring, Maryland.

Nayak, B.U., P.Chandramohan and B.N.Desai (1992), Planning and Management of the Coastal Zone in India; A Perspective', *Coastal Management*, 20, pp. 365-375.

Nayak, S. (1997), 'Intgrated Coastal Zone Management', in Nayak, S. (ed.), *Proceedings of Panel Discussions of Second Indian National Conference on Harbour and Ocean Engineering, Inchoe '97*, Trivandrum, 1997, pp.49-61.

Nazeer, M. (1997), 'Mangrove Destruction Despite Protests', *The Hindu*, Thiruvananthapuram, 1.1.1997.

Needham, B. (ed.) (1991), *Case Studies of Coastal Management Experience from the United States*, Coastal Resource Centre, University of Rhode Island, Naragansett, R.I.

Needham, B. (1998), 'An Innovative Approach to Training and Capacity Building for Integrated Coastal Management', *Ocean and Coastal Management*, 38, 1998, pp.279-283.

Neelakantan, K.S. (1994), *Management Plan for the Gulf of Mannar Marine Biosphere Reserve*. Forest Department, Tamil Nadu, India, 118 pp.

Ngoile, M.A.K. (1997), 'Coastal Zone Issues and ICM Initiatives in Sub-Saharan Africa', *Ocean and Coastal Management*, 37(3), 1997, *Special Issue, Integrated Coastal Management in Africa*, pp.269-280.

Ngoile, M.A.K. and Lindon, O. (1997), 'Lessos Learned from Eastern Africa: The Development of Policy on ICZM at National and Regional Levels', *Ocean and Coastal Management*, 37(3), 1997, *Special Issue, Integrated Coastal Management in Africa*, pp.295-318.

O'Brien, R.J. (1988), 'Western Australia's Non-statutory Approach to Coastal Zone Management: An Evaluation', *Coastal Zone Management*. 16(3), pp.201-214.

Ogden, J.C. and E.H.Gladfelter (eds.) (1983), *Coral Reefs, Seagrass Beds and Mangroves: Their interaction in the Coastal Zone of the Caribbean*. Reports in Marine Science No.23, UN Educational Scientific and Cultural Organisation, Paris, 133 pp.

Ohta, P. (1991), 'Development in Hawaii', in *Case Studies of Coastal Management: Experience from the United States*. B.Needham (ed.), Coastal Resources Centre: University of Rhode Island, Narragansett.

Olsen, S.B. (1993), 'Will Integrated Coastal Management Programmes be Sustainable? The Constituency Problem', *Ocean and Coastal Management*, 21(1-3), 201-225.

Olsen, S.B., (1995), 'The Skills, knowledge and Attitudes of an Ideal Coastal Manager', in Crawford, B.R., Cobb, J.S. and Ming, C.L. (eds.), *Educating Coastal Managers*, Proceedings of the Rhode Island Workshop, March 4-10, 1995, University of Rhode Island.

Olsen, S.B. (2000), 'Education for the Governance of Coastal Ecosystem: The Dimensions of the Challenge', *Ocean and Coastal Management*. 43, 2000, GENOA Special Issue on *Education and Training in Integrated Coastal Management*, pp.331-342.

Olsen, S.B., J.Tobey and M.Kerr (1997), 'A Common Framework for Learning from ICM Experience', *Ocean and Coastal Management*. 37(2), 1997, *Special Issue, Lessons Learned in Integrated Coastal Management*, pp.155-174.

Olsen, S. , Lowry, K. and Tobey, J. (1998), *Coastal Management Planning and Implementation: A Manual for Self-Assessment*, University of Rhode Island, Narragansett, R.I. Coastal Resource Centre, 1998.

Okemwa, E.N., Ruwa, R.K. and Mwandotto, B.A.J. (1997), 'Integrated Coastal Zone Management in Kenya: Initial Experiences and Progress', *Ocean and Coastal Management*, 37(3), 1997, *Special Issue, Integrated Coastal Management in Africa*, pp.319-348.

Organisation for Economic Cooperation and Development (OECD) (1991), *Report on CZM: Integrated Policies and Draft Recommendations of the Council on Integrated Coastal Zone* Management. Organisation for Economic Cooperation and Development, Paris.

OECD (1993 a), *Coastal Zone Management*, Integrated Policies, OECD, Paris.

OECD (1993 b), *Coastal Zone Management. Selected Case Studies.* OECD, Paris.

Ozhan, E. (1996 a), 'Coastal Zone Management in Turkey', *Ocean and Coastal Management*, 30(2-3), *Special Issue'. Coastal Zone Management in the Mediterranean*, E. Ozhan,1996 (ed.), pp.153-176.

Ozhan, E. (ed.) (1996 b), *Ocean and Coastal Zone Management*, 30(2-3), 1996, *Special Issue, Coastal Zone Management in the Mediterranean.*

Ozhan, E. (2000), 'An NGO Role in Enhancing Integrated Coastal Management in the Mediterranean and the Black Sea, The MEDCOAST Experience', *Ocean and Coastal Management, 43, 2000, GENOA Special Issue on Education and Training on Integrated Coastal Management*, pp.379-388.

Ozhan, E. and E.B.Culhaogie (1995), 'MEDCOAST Institute: A Training Programme on Coastal Zone Management in the Mediterranean and the Black Sea', in *Proceedings of the Workshop on Educating Coastal Managers*, B.R. Crawford, J.S. Cobb and L.M.Chou (eds.), 84-109 July 5-10, Kingston, University of Rhode Island, Coastal Resources Centre.

Parliament of the Common Wealth of Australia (1991), *The Injured Coastline Protection of the Coastal Environment*, Report of House of Representatives Standing Committee on Environment, Recreation and the Arts, Australian Government Publishing Service, Canberra, 1991.

Patterson, R.G., R.J.Burby and A.C.Nelson (1991), 'Sewering the Coast: Bane or Blessing to Marine Water Quality', *Coastal Management*, Vol.19, pp.239-252.

Paulraj, R.M., Rajagopalan, M., Vijayakumaran, E., Vivekanandan and R.Satyadas (1998), 'Environmental and Social Issues on

Coastal Aquaculture - A Case Study', Bay of Bengal News, Vol.11(11), 1998, pp.15-18.

Paw, J.N. and T.E.Chua (1991), *An Assessment of the Ecological and Economic Impact of Mangrove Conversion in Southeast Asia*, ICLARM Conference Proceedings, 22, International Centre for Living Aquatic Resources Management, Manila, pp. 201-212.

Pernetta, J.C. and Elder, D.L. (1992), 'Climate, Sea Level Rise and the Coastal Zone: Management and Planning for Global Changes', *Ocean and Coastal Management*, 18(1), 1992, 113-160.

Pernetta, J.C. and D.L. Elder (1993), *Cross-sectoral Integrated Coastal Area Planning* (CICAP): *Guidelines and Principles for Coastal Area Development*, Marine Conservation and Development Report, Gland, Switzerland, World Conservation Union.

Pido, M.D. and T.E.Chua (1992), 'A Framework for Rapid Appraisal of Coastal Environments', in *Integrative Framework and Methods for Coastal Area Management*, T.E.Chua and L.F.Scura (eds.), ICLARM: Conference Proceedings, No.37, Manila: International Centre for Living Aquatic Resources Management, Manila, 1992, pp.133-148.

Pintukanok, A. and S.Borothanarat (1993), 'National Coastal Resources Management in Thailand', in *World Coast Conference 1993. Proceedings. vol.1 and 2*, CZM Centre Publication No.4, Coastal Zone Management Centre, The Hague, 1993.

Plink, N.L. (1998), 'Training and Education in Integrated Coastal Zone Management', *Ocean and Coastal Management*. 41, 1998, pp. 273-279.

Pomeroy, R.S. (1992), 'Economic Valuation: Available Methods', in *Integrative Framework and Methods for Coastal Area Management*, T.E. Chua and L.F. Scura (eds.), International Centre for Living Aquatic Resource Management, Manila, 1992, pp.149-162.

Post, J.C. and C.G. Lundin (eds.) (1996), *Guidelines for Integrated Coastal Zone Management*, Environmentally Sustainable Development Studies and Monograph Series No.9, Washington, DC. World Bank.

Premaratne, A. (1991), 'Difficulties of Coastal Resources Management in Developing Countries: Sri Lanka Experience', in *Coastal Zone* '91, O.T.Magoon, H.Converse, V. Tippie, L.T. Tobin and D. Clark (eds.), pp. 3026-3041, New York, American Society of Civil Engineers.

Prescott, R.N. (1989), 'Current Concerns of Coastal Planning', *Planning, and Management of the Coastal Heritage*, Symposium Proceedings, Southport, 1989.

Public Works Department (1974), *Water Resources of Kerala*, Government of Kerala, Trivandrum, 1974.

Raghu, K.V. (2002), 'Impact of Coastal Aquaculture on Environment and its Management', *Proceedings of the National Seminar on Current Environmental Problems and Management*, Irinjalakuda, 1-3, Aug, 2002, pp. 216-218.

Rahman, S. (2003), 'Hotel Project at Pathiramanal may hit Ramsar Road block, *The New Indian Express*. 29.3.2003.

Rais, J. (1993), 'Marine Resource Evaluation and Planning Project for an Integrated Coastal Zone Planning and Management in Indonesia', in *World Coast Conference 1993. Proceedings*. Vol.1 and 2, CZM Centre Publication No. 4, The Hague, Coastal Zone Management Centre, The Hague, 1993.

Rajeev, P.I. (2000), As Heavy Weights Throw Rules to the Winds ... Wetlands Turn Hot Property', Indian Express, Cochin, 6.6.2000.

Ranjith, M.W. and Silva, N.D. (1998), 'The Coastal Resources Management Programme in Brunei Darussalam', *Ocean and Coastal* Management. 38, 1998, pp.147-160.

Renard, Y. (1986), 'Citizen Participation in Coastal Area Planning and Management, *CAMP Newsletter*. October 1986, National Park Service, Office of International Affairs, Washington, D.C., pp.1-3.

Resource Assessment Commission, Australia (1993), *Resource Assessment Commission: Coastal Zone Inquiry*, Final Report, Australian Government Publishing Service, 1993.

Rivera, R. and G.F. Nowkirk (1997), 'Power From the People: A Documentation of NGO Experience in Community-based Coastal Resource Management in the Philippines', *Ocean and Coastal Management*. 36(1-3), *Special Issue, Community-based Coastal Management*, pp. 73-95.

Rizvi, S.H.N. (1993), 'Coastal Zone Management Issues in Pakistan– An Overview', Paper presented at the *IPCC Eastern Hemisphere Workshop on Vulnerability of Sea-Level Rise and Coastal-Zone Management*, August 3-6, Tsukuba, Japan.

Robadue, D.D., Jr. (ed.) (1995), *Eight Years in Equador: The Road to Integrated Coastal Management*, Kingston, University of Rhode Island, Coastal Resources Centre.

Rosier, J. and W. Hastie, (1996), 'New Zealand Coastal Planning: An Issue-based Approach', *Ocean, and Coastal Management*, 33(1-3), 1996, *Special Issue, Ocean and Coastal Management Issues in Australia and New Zealand*, pp. 147-166.

Rowstow, W.W. (1960), '*The Stages of Economic Growth -A Non-Communist Manifesto*', Cambridge University Press, New York, 1960.

Rothwell, D.R. (1996), The Legal Framework for Ocean and Coastal Management in Australia', *Ocean and Coastal Management*, 33(1-3), 1996, *Special Issue, Ocean and Coastal Management Issues in Australia and New Zealand*, pp.41-62.

Ruddle, K. and R.E. Johannes (eds.) (1985), *The Traditional Knowledge and Management of Coastal Systems in Asia and the Pacific*. UNESCO Regional Office for Science and Technology for Southeast Asia, Jakarta, 313 pp.

Sahasranaman, P. B. (ed.) (1996), *The Law Relating to Protection of Coastal Areas*. Swamy Law Publishers, Cochin, India, 1996.

Salim, R.V. and J.R. Clark (1989), *Marine and Coastal Protected Areas: A Guide for Planners and Managers* (Second Edition), International Union for the Conservation of Nature, Gland, Switzerland, 302 pp.

Schroder, P.C. (1993), 'The Need for International Training in Coastal Management', *Ocean and Coastal Management*, 21(1-3), 1993, pp. 303-310.

Scura, L.F., T.E. Chua, M.D. Pido and J.N.Paw (1992), 'Lessons for Integrated Coastal Zone Management: The ASEAN Experience', in *Integrative Framework and Methods for Area Management*, T.E.Chua and L.F. Scura (eds.), ICLARM Conference Proceedings 37, International Centre for Living Aquatic Resource Management, Manila, 1992, pp.1-68.

Sharma, V. K. (2000), *Coastal Areas in India, Environmental Problems of Coastal Areas in India*, Book Well, New Delhi, 2000.

Siem, C.L. (1998), 'Coastal Management in Singapore: Institutional Arrangements and Implementation', *Ocean and Coastal*, Management, 38, 1998, pp. 111-118.

Sen Gupta, R. and Deshmukhe Geetanjali (2000), *Coastal and Marine Environments of Gujarat: Ecology and Economics*, Gujarat Ecological Society, Vadodara, 2000, Vadodara, Gujarat, India.

Shaji, R.A. (2001), 'Fisherfolk Agitated Over Lack of Civil Amenities', *The New Indian Express*, 12.7.2001.

Silas, E.G., Dharmaraja, S.K. and Rengarajan, K. (1976), *Exploited Marine Fishery Resources of India–A Synoptic Survey with Comments on Potential Resources*, Bulletin No. 27, CMFRI, Cochin.

Singh, H.S. (1997), 'Issues and Problems Involved in Managing Marine Protected Areas: A Case Study of Marine National Park, Jamnagar; in *Proceedings of the Workshop on Integrated Coastal Zone Management*, Ahmedabad, pp.105-122.

Smith, H.D. (2000), 'Education and Training for Integrated Coastal Area Management: The Role of the University System', *Ocean and Coastal Management*, 43, 2000, *GENOA Special Issue on Education and Training in Integrated Coastal Management*, pp. 361-378.

Snoussi, M. and Aoul, E.H.T. (2000), 'Integrated Coastal Zone Management Programme–North West African Region Case', *Ocean and Coastal Management*, 43, 2000, *GENOA. Special Issue on Education and Training in Integrated Coastal Management*, pp. 1033-1045.

Smith, R. (1992), Conflicting Trends of Beach Resort Development: A Malaysian Case', *Coastal Management*, 20, pp.167-187.

Soegiarto, A. (1991), 'Asean's Efforts in Managing Coastal Resources for Sustainable Development', in *Managing Asean's, Coastal Resources for Sustainable Development: Role of Policy Makers, Scientists, Donors, Media and Communities*, Chua, T.E. and L.F.Scura (eds.), ICLARM Conference Proceedings 30, ICLARM, Manila, 1991.

Soegiarto, A. (1996), 'Integrated Coastal Zone Management in Indonesia: Problems and Plans of Action', *Paper presented at*

International Workshop, Integrated Coastal Management in Tropical Developing Communities: Lessons Learned from Successes and Failures, May 24-28, Xiamen, People's Republic of China.

Sorensen, Jens (1978), *State-Local Collaborative Planning: A Growing Trend in Coastal Zone Management*. Office of Coastal Zone Management and Office of the Sea Grant, NOAA, U.S. Department of Commerce, 1978.

Sorensen, J. (1979), 'State Local Relations in Oastal Zone Management: Implications for Change', *Coastal Zone Management Journal*, Vol.6, No.4, 1979, pp. 295-302.

Sorensen, J. (1982), 'Towards an Overall Strategy in Designing Wetland Restoration', in *Wetland Restoration and Enhancement in California*, J. Zedler (ed.), California Sea Grant, University of California, La Jolla, pp.85-96.

Sorensen, J., McCreary, S.T., and Hershman, M.J. (1984), *Institutional Arrangements for Management of Coastal Resources*, Coastal Renewable Resources Information Series, Coastal Management Publication 1, *1984*.

Sorensen, J. and S.T.McGreary (1990), *Institutional Arrangements for Managing Coastal Resources and Environments* Coastal Management Publication No.I (Rev.) NPS/USAID Series, National Park Service, Office of International Affairs, Washington, D.C., 194 pp.

Sorensen, J. (1993 a), 'A Conceptual Framework for Integrated Coastal Zone Management', *OECD. World Coast Conference*.

Sorensen, J. (1993 b), 'The International Proliferation of Integrated Coastal Zone Management Efforts', *Ocean and Coastal Management*. 21(1-3), pp.45-80.

Sorensen, J. (1997), 'National and International Efforts at Integrated Coastal Management: Definitions, Achievements and Lessons', *Coastal Management*. 25, pp.3-41.

Southern Railway (1998), *Time Table*, Madras, August 15, 1998.

South, G.R. and Veitayaki, J. (1998), 'Capacity Building in the South Pacific and the Role of the Marine Studies Programme at the University of the South Pacific; *Ocean and Coastal Management*. 41, 1998, pp.103-113.

South Pacific Regional Environment Programme (1995), *Coastal Area Management in the Pacific Island Nations*, South Pacific Regional Environment Programme, Apia, Western Somoa.

Squirres, D. F. (1983), *The Ocean Dumping Quandary*, State University of New York, Abbany, 1983.

Sreedhara Menon, A. (1998), *A Survey of Kerala History* (reprint), S.Viswanathan (Printers and Publishers) Pvt. Ltd., Madras, 1998.

Sreedhara Menen, A. (1999), *Kerala History and its Makers* (3rd edition), S.Viswanathan (Printers and Publishers) Pvt. Ltd., Madras, 1999.

Sri Lanka Coast Conservation Department (1987), *Coastal Zone Management Plan*, Coast Conservation Department, Colombo, Sri Lanka.

State Planning Board (1973), *Fifth Five Year Plan*. 1974-79, Government of Kerala, Trivandrum

State Planning Board (1980), *Draft Sixth Five Year Plan 1980-85 and Annual Plan 1981-82*, Vol.1, Government of Kerala, Trivandrum, 1980.

State Planning Board (1997), *Ninth Five Year Plan 1997-2002 and Annual Plan 1997-98*, Government of Kerala, Thiruvananthapuram.

State Planning Board (1999), *Ninth Five Year Plan of Kerala 1997-2002 - Mid Term Appraisal*. Government of Kerala, Thiruvananthapuram.

State Planning Board (2001), *Economic Review. 2000*. State Planning Board, Thiruvananthapuram.

Steers, J. (1978), 'Saving the Coast: The British Experience', *Coastal Zone Management Journal*. 4(1-3), 1978.

Subash Babu, K. K., K. John Thomas and S.Sreekumar (2002), 'The Species Diversity of Fish Fauna of Muriyad Wetlands', *Proceedings of National Seminar on Current Environmental Problems and Management*, Irinjalakuda, 1-3 August, 2002, pp.59-63,

Sudara, S. (1999), 'Who and What is to be Involved in Successful Coastal Management: A Thailand Example', *Ocean and Coastal Management*, 42, 1999, 39-47.

Swanson, Tmmothy, M. (1995), *The Economics and Ecology of Biodiversity Decline; The Forces Driving Global Change*, Cambridge University Press, Cambridge.

Swedish Agency for Research Cooperation with Developing Countries (SAREC) (1994), *Technical Recommendations of the Workshop on Integrated Coastal Zone Management in Eastern Africa including the Island States*. April 21-22, Arusha, Tanzania, SAREC Marine Science Programme, Stockholm, 1994.

Talaue-McMamus, L. and T.E.Chua (1997), 'The Lingayaif Gulf (Philippines) Experience: If We Have to Do it Again', *Ocean and Coastal Management*, 37(2), 1997, *Special Issue, Lessons Learned in Integrated Coastal Management*, pp.217-232.

Tharakan, M. (1999), 'Development of Colonial Economy in Kerala (1500-1947)' in P.J.Cherian (ed.), *Kerala State Gazetteer, vol.II, Part II, Perspectives on Kerala History*, Government of Kerala, Thiruvananthapuram, 1999, pp.360-401.

The New Indian Express (2001 a), 'Lease Granted to IRE to Collect Uranium Rich *Karimanal* Challenged', *The New Indian Express*. Cochin, 20.7.2001.

The New Indian Express (2001 b), 'Privatisation of Mineral Mining: MP Flays CMRL', *The New Indian Express*, Cochin 11.12.2001.

The New Indian Express,(2002) 'Mineral Sand Mining Poses a Threat; Warns DCC Leader', *The New Indian Express*. Cochin 6.8.2002.

The New Indian Express (2003), 'Indo-US Naval Exercise a Threat to Country – Pinarayi' - *The New Indian Express*, Cochin. 8.10.2003.

Thomas, V.I. (2002), 'Stir Against Privatisation of Mineral Sand Mining', *The New Indian Express*, Cochin, 7.7.2002.

Thomas, V.I. (2002), 'Interlinking of Rivers Harmful–Says Experts', *The New Indian Express*. Cochin, 13.11.2002.

Thoraugh, A., 'Restoration of Mangrove and Seagrass: Economic Benefits for Fisheries and Mariculture', in *Environmental Restoration*. J.Berger (ed.), San Francisco, Island Press, 1990, pp.265-281.

Throsby, Davis (2001), *Economics and Culture*, Cambridge University Press, Cambridge.

Tobin, R.J. (1992), 'Legal and Organisational Considerations in the Management of Coastal Areas', in *Integrative Framework and Methods for Coastal Area Management*, T.E. Chua and L.F. Scura (eds.), International Centre for Living Aquatic Resources Management, Manila, pp.93-105.

Tol, R.S.J., Klein, R.J.T., Jansen, H.M.A. and Verbruygen, H. (1996), 'Some Economic Considerations on the Importance of Pro-active Integrated Coastal Zone Management', *Ocean and Coastal Management*, 32(1), 1996, pp.39-55.

Trivandrum District Fishermen's Union (1996), 'CRZ. Rules and Fishermen' (Malayalam), Alakal, Vol.112, November 15-31, November 1996.

Turner, R.K. (1988), 'Wetland Conversion; Economics and Ethics', in Collard, D. *et al.*, (eds.), *Economics, Growth and Sustainable Environments*, London: Macmillan, 1988.

Turner, R.K., Bower, B.T. (1995), 'The Benefits of Integrated Coastal Zone Management', *Coastal Zone '95, Spot Light on Solutions Conference*, Tampa, Florida, July 1995.

Turner, R.K. , Suloak, S. and Adger, N. (1996), 'Pressures, Trends and Impacts in Coastal Zones: Interactions Between Socio-Economic and Natural Systems', *Environmental Management*. 20, 1996, pp.159-173.

United Kingdom Department of Environment (1992), *Coastal Zone Protection, and Planning; The Government's Response to the Second Report from the House of Commons Select Committee on the Environment*, Department of the Environment, London.

United Kingdom Department of Environment (1993), *Managing the Coast: A Review of Coastal Management Plans in England and Wales and the Powers Supporting Them*. October 1993, Stationery Office, London.

United Nations (1982), *Coastal Area Management and Development*, Pergamon Press, Oxford, U.K. 1982.

United Nations Environment Programme (UNEP) (1995 a), *Global Programme of Action for the Protection of the Marine Environment from Land-based Activities*, United Nations Environmental Programme, UNEP (OCA)/L3A/192/75, December 1995.

United Nations Environmental Programme (1995 b), *Guidelines for Integrated Management of Coastal and Marine Areas with Special Reference to the Mediterranean Basin*, UNEP Regional Seas Reports and Studies No.161, Nairobi, Kenya: United Nations Environmental Programme.

United Nations Environmental Programme (1995 c), *Report of the Second Meeting of the Conference of Parties to the Convention on Biological Diversity*, November 6-17, Jakarta, Indonesia, UNEP, Nairobi, Kenya.

United Nations Environmental Programme (1996), *Guidelines for Integrated Planning and Management of Coastal and Marine Areas in the Wider Caribbean Region*, UNEP, Caribbean Environment Programme in Cooperation with Island Resource Foundation, Kingston, Jamaica, 141 p.

U.S.Army Coastal Engineering Research Centre (1975), *Shore Protection Manual*, Vol.II (2nd ed.). Port Beloir, Virginia, 1975.

U.S. Army Corps of Engineers (1971), *National Shoreline Study* Regional Inventory Report, North Atlantic Region, vol. I and II, U.S. Army Corps of Engineers, 1971.

U.S.Army Corps of Engineers (1984), *Shore Protection Manual 1984*, U.S. Army Corps of Engineers, U.S. Government Press, Washington, D.C., 1984.

U.S. Commission on Marine Science Engineering and Resources (Stratton Commission, 1969), *Our Nation and the Sea*, U.S. Government Printing Office, Washington, D.C. 1969, 305 pp.

University of Rhode Island Coastal Resources Centre (1996), *Data Base of Integrated Coastal Management Efforts World Wide*, internet: http: brook trout, gso. uri. edu.

Untawale, A.G. (1993), 'Significance of Mangroves for the Coastal Communities of India', in *Proceedings of the Seventh Pacific Science Inter-congress Mangrove Session*, July 1, Okinawa, Japan, Okinawa, Japan, International Society for Mangrove Ecosystems.

Valencia, M. (ed.) (1979), *Proceedings of the Workshop on Coastal Area Development and Management in the Pacific*, East West Centre and University of Hawaii, Hawaii Island, USA, 1979.

Vallega, A. (1992), *The Changing Water Front in Coastal Area Management*, Milano, Franco Angeli, 1992.

Vallega, A. (1993), '*A Conceptual Approach to Integrated Coastal Management*', Ocean and Coastal Management, 21, pp.149-162.

Vallega, A. (1995 a), 'The Coastal Use Framework as a Methodological Tool for Coastal Area Management', in *Coastal Ocean Space Utilisation, III*, N, Delia Croce, S. Connell R. Abel and F.N.Spon (eds.), London, 1995, pp.117-130.

Vallega, A. (1995 b), 'Regional Level Implementation of Chapter 17; The UNEP Approach to the Mediterranean', *Ocean and Coastal Management, Special Issue: Earth Summit Implementation: Progress Achieved on Oceans and Coasts*, 29(1-3), 1995, pp.251-278.

Vallega, A. (2000), 'Introduction: Coastal Education; A Multifaceted Challenge', *Ocean and Coastal Management*, 43, 2000, *GENOA Special Issue on Education and Training in Coastal Management* pp. 277-290.

Vallejo, S.M. (1987), Development and Management of Coastal and Marine Areas: An International Perspective', in *Ocean Year Book*, E. Borgesse, N, Ginsberg and J. Morgan (eds.), University of Chicago Press, 1987.

Vallejo, S.M. (1991), 'The Development and Management of Coastal, and Marine Areas: An international Perspective', in Smith H.D. and Vallega, A. (eds.), *The Development of Integrated Sea Use Management*, Routledge, London, 1991, pp.17-36.

Vallejo, S.M. (1993), 'The Integration of Coastal Zone Management into National Development Planning', *Ocean and Coastal Management*, 21, 1993, pp.163-181.

Vandermeulon, H. (1998), 'The Development of Marine Indicators for Coastal Zone Management', *Ocean and Coastal Management*, 39, 1998, pp. 63-71.

Vander Weide, J. (1993), 'A Systems View of Integrated Coastal Management', *Ocean and Coastal Management*, 21(1-3), 1993, pp.129-148.

Vellinga, P. and R.J.T. Klein (1993), 'Climate Change, Sea Level Rise and Integrated Coastal Zone Management', An IPCC Approach, *Ocean and Coastal Management*, 21(1-3), 1993, pp.245-268.

Velupillai, T.K. (1940), *Travancore State Manual*, Vol. III, Reprint 1996, Government of Kerala, Thiruvananthapuram.

Vijayachandran, K. (2003, 'Decentralisation on Wrong Track', *The New Indian Express*, Cochin, 2.9.2003.

Wafar, M. (1992), 'Management and Conservation Options for Indian Coral Reefs', in *Tropical Ecosystems: Ecology and Management*, K. Singh and J. Singh (eds.). Wiley Eastern Ltd., New Delhi, pp. 173-183.

Wang, Y. (1992), 'Coastal Management in China', in *Ocean Management in Global Change*, P. Fabbri (ed.), Elsevier Applied Science New York, pp. 460-469.

Warford, T.J. (1991), 'Evolution of World Bank's Environmental Policy', in Chua, T.E. and L.F.Scura (eds.), *Managing Asean's Coastal Resources for Sustainable Development, Role of Policy Makers, Scientists, Donors, Media and Communitiest,* ICLARM Conference Proceedings 30, ICLARM, Manila, 1991, pp.63-72.

Waterman, R.E. (1995), 'Integrated Coastal Policy via Building with Nature', in *Coastal Ocean Space Utilisation III*, Croce N.D., Connel, S. and Abel, R. (eds.), Chapman and Hall, London, 1995, pp.465-484.

White, A.T. (1988), *Marine Parks and Reserves. Management! Coastal Environments in Southeast Asia*, ICLARM, Education Series 2, International Centre for Living Aquatic Resource Management, Manila, 36 pp.

Williams, C. and Davis, B. (1993), 'Land-based Activities: What Remains to be Done', *Ocean and Coastal Management, Special Issue, Earth Summit Implementation: Progress Achieved on Oceans and Coasts*, 29(1-3), 1993, pp. 207-222.

Williams, C. (1996), 'Combating Marine Pollution from Land-based Activities: Australian Initiatives', *Ocean and Coastal Management*, 33(1-3), 1996, *Special Issue, Ocean and Coastal Management Issues in Australia and New Zealand*, pp. 87-112.

Winseraius, P. (1995), 'Community Integration of Policies--A Requirement for Coastal Zone Management', *Ocean and Coastal Management*, 26(2), 1995, pp.151-162.

Wong, P.P. (1998), 'Coastal Tourism Development in South-east Asia - Relevance and Lessons for Coastal Zone Management', *Ocean and Coastal Management*, 38, 1998, pp. 89-109.

World Bank (1993), *Noordwijk-Guidelines for Integrated Coastal Zone Management, Issued at the World Coast Conferenee*, Noordwijk, The Netherlands, 1-5 November 1993.

World Bank (1995), *Africa–A Framework for Integrated Coastal Zone Management*, World Bank, Washington DC, 1995.

World Bank (1996), *World Development Report 1996: From Plan to Market*, New York; Oxford University Press.

World Bank (1999), *Integrated Coastal Management in Sub-Saharan Africa: A Strategic Agenda*, World Bank, Washington, DC, USA, 1999.

World Coast Conference (1993), *Preparing to Meet the ·Coastal Challenge of the 21st Century*, the World Coast Conference Report, Noordwijk, The Netherlands, 1-5, November 1993.

World Commission on Environment and Development (WCED) (1987), *Our Common Future*. Oxford University Press, Oxford.

World Wide Fund for Nature (WWF) (1995), *Integrated Coastal Zone Management: U.K. and European Initiatives, Marine Update*, World Wide Fund for Nature, Surrey, England.

Worm, K. (1997), 'Coastal Zone Planning in Denmark', *Ocean and Coastal Management*, 37(2), 1997, *Special Issue, Lessons Learned in Integrated Coastal Management*, pp.253-268.

WU, R.S.S., Cheung, R.Y.H. and Shin, P.K.S. (1998), 'The Beneficial Uses Approach in Coastal Management in Hong Kong: A Compromise Between Rapid Urban Development and Sustainable Development', *Ocean and Coastal Management*, 41, 1998, pp. 89-102.

Yong, K.T. (1991), 'Reconciling Economic Development with Environmental Protection in Malaysia', in Chua, T.E. and L. F. Scura (eds.), *Managing Asian's Coastal Resources for Sustainable Development: Role of Policy Makers, Scientists, Donors, Media and Communities*, ICLARM Conference Proceedings 30, ICLAHM, Manila, 1991, pp.59-62.

Zann, L.P. (1996), 'The State of the Marine Environment Report for Australia (SOMER): Process, Findings and Perspectives', *Ocean and Coastal Management*, 33(1-3), 1996, *Special Issue, Ocean and Coastal Management Issues in Australia and New Zealand*, pp.63-86.

Zhijie, F. and R.P. Cote (1990), 'Coastal Zone of the People's Republic of China: Management Approaches and Institutions', *Marine Policy* 14(4), pp.305-314.

Zile, Z. (1974), 'The Legislative Political History of the Coastal Zone Management Act of 1972', *Coastal Zone Management Journal*, 1(3), 1974, pp. 235-274.

Zingde, M.D. (1997), 'Quality of Coastal Waters in India' in *Proceedings of the Workshop on Integrated Coastal Zone Management*, Ahmedabad, April 1997.

Zingde, M.D. and N.M. Anand (1994), 'Implications of Coastal Refineries to the Ecology of the Gulf of Kachchh', in Rao, S.R. (ed.), *Proceedings of the First Indian Conference on Marine Archaeology of Indian Ocean Countries*, National Institute of Oceanography, Goa, 1994.

Index

J

K

L

M

T

U

V

W